ALSO AVAILABLE FROM BLOOMSBURY:

Žižek: A Guide for the Perplexed, Seán Sheehan

The.Bloomsbury Handbook to Slavoj Žižek, edited by Dominik Finkelde

Žižek Country

Mapping Speculative Thought

Seán Sheehan

BLOOMSBURY ACADEMIC
LONDON • NEW YORK • OXFORD • NEW DELHI • SYDNEY

BLOOMSBURY ACADEMIC
Bloomsbury Publishing Plc, 50 Bedford Square, London, WC1B 3DP, UK
Bloomsbury Publishing Inc, 1359 Broadway, New York, NY 10018, USA
Bloomsbury Publishing Ireland, 29 Earlsfort Terrace, Dublin 2, D02 AY28, Ireland

BLOOMSBURY, BLOOMSBURY ACADEMIC and the Diana logo are trademarks of Bloomsbury Publishing Plc

First published in Great Britain 2026

A catalogue record for this book is available from the British Library.

A catalog record for this book is available from the Library of Congress.

ISBN: HB: 978-1-3504-6899-3
PB: 978-1-3504-6898-6
ePDF: 978-1-3504-6900-6
eBook: 978-1-3504-6901-3

Typeset by Newgen KnowledgeWorks Pvt. Ltd., Chennai, India
Printed and bound in Great Britain

For product safety related questions contact productsafety@bloomsbury.com.

To find out more about our authors and books visit www.bloomsbury.com
and sign up for our newsletters.

Contents

Abbreviations

A	*Antigone* (2016)
ADB	*Against the Double Blackmail* (2016)
AP	*Against Progress* (2025)
AR	*Absolute Recoil* (2014)
ARS	*The Art of the Ridiculous Sublime* (2000)
CA	*Christian Atheism* (2024)
CH	*The Courage of Hopelessness* (2017)
CZ	*Conversations with Žižek* (2004)
D	*Disparities* (2016)
DI	*Demanding the Impossible* (2005)
DLC	*In Defense of Lost Causes* (2008)
DSS	*Did Somebody Say Totalitarianism?* (2001)
E	*Event* (2014)
ES	*Enjoy Your Symptom!* (1992)
F	*Freedom: A Disease without Cure* (2023)
FA	*The Fragile Absolute* (2000)
FRT	*The Fright of Real Tears* (2001)
FT	*First as Tragedy, Then as Farce* (2009)
HD	*Heaven in Disorder* (2021)
HWB	*Hegel in a Wired Brain* (2020)
I	*Iraq: The Borrowed Kettle* (2004)
IR	*Interrogating the Real* (1996)
IV	*Incontinence of the Void* (2017)

KNW	*For They Know Not What They Do* (1991)
L	*(How to Read) Lacan* (2006)
LA	*Looking Awry* (1994)
LD	*A Left That Dares to Speak Its Name* (2020)
LEN	*Lenin 2017* (2017)
LET	*Living in the End Times* (2010)
LF	*Liberal Fascisms* (2026)
LT	*Like a Thief in Broad Daylight* (2018)
LTN	*Less Than Nothing* (2012)
M	*Mao: On Practice and Contradiction* (2007)
ME	*The Metastases of Enjoyment* (1994)
MSH	*The Most Sublime Hysteric* (2014)
MW	*Mad World* (2023)
OB	*On Belief* (2001)
OSD	*Opera's Second Death* (2002)
OWB	*Organs without Bodies* (2004)
P	*Pandemic!* (2020)
PC	*The Pervert's Guide to the Cinema* (2006)
PD	*The Puppet and the Dwarf* (2003)
PF	*The Plague of Fantasies* (1997)
PI	*The Pervert's Guide to Ideology* (2012)
PV	*The Parallax View* (2006)
P2	*Pandemic! 2* (2020)
QH	*Quantum History* (2025)
R	*Robespierre* (2007)
RG	*Revolution at the Gates* (2002)
SE	*Surplus Enjoyment* (2022)
SFA	*Sex and the Failed Absolute* (2020)
SO	*The Sublime Object of Ideology* (1989)
TAF	*The Abyss of Freedom/Ages of the World* (1997)

TIR	*The Indivisible Remainder* (1996)
TL	*Too Late to Awaken* (2023)
TN	*Tarrying with the Negative* (1993)
TP	*Trouble in Paradise* (2021)
TS	*The Ticklish Subject* (1999)
UE	*The Universal Exception* (2006)
V	*Violence* (2008)
WD	*Welcome to the Desert of the Real* (2002)
WL	*What Lies Ahead When There Is No Future* (2023)
YD	*The Year of Dreaming Dangerously* (2012)
ZP	*Zero Point* (2025)

Introduction

The purpose of this book is to encourage reading Žižek and not just reading about him.[1] He is an exciting thinker whose popularity is inseparable from the sense that here is someone whose intellectuality connects with our and the world's troubling ruptures. As with any important thinker, especially a philosopher, certain concepts and ideas dominate their interests and are explored in ways that establish their originality. For Žižek, these ideas are grounded in his Marxism and in a reading of, principally, Hegel and Lacan and he interprets them with a penetrating freshness and clarity. They become part of his coinage. At the same time, inseparable from this freshness is the way he relates highbrow ideas to understanding ourselves and life more generally. These relations are not confined to the academic sphere, to be pursued in a library or in front of a laptop, and this helps to account for his appeal and his impact.

When Žižek writes or talks about a television mini-series, a current political crisis or cultural phenomenon, eureka moments can be experienced with the realization that an abstract point of Hegelian scholarship or a cryptic condensation by Lacan has been brought alive in a way not previously thought possible. What underlies this book's purpose is the venture to map the multivalent connections that Žižek is making between philosophy and everyday life; between 'high' and 'low' culture; between economics as promulgated by mainstream media and the urgency of the need to address imminent catastrophes; between public, private and the secret; between 'reality' as we know it and a quantum world that reveals something strangely different.

The connections that Žižek make are sometimes packed together in ways that can be daunting for new readers of his work. In just three pages of *Absolute Recoil* (242–4), to take an example, a multitude of ideas and tropes follow in swift succession. The subject as a result of its own failure-to-be brings in retrospection and there are references to absolute knowing, the 'spirit is a bone' and the unity of opposites, speculative truth, non-All, the big Other and God's failure to register his own inexistence. In more recent books, like *Against Progress* and *Zero Point*, the sedimentation of terms is there in supple and unrhetorical ways, but when matters do overlap and their meshing briefly touched on there is always plenty for a reader to digest.

Each of the entries in this book looks at the terms and topics that are relevant to reading Žižek. They range from crucial ones like speculative reasoning and sexual difference to vital Hegelian and Lacanian terms like retroactivity and big Other, as well as relatively less important ones like wokeness which nonetheless fits into the scheme of things.

Each entry is followed by three sets of references, the first of which is to specific pages in books written by Žižek. These references are by no means comprehensive but they draw attention to places in his texts where the topic in question is being directly explicated or emerging as crucially important and which the reader can turn to as exercises for close readings of Žižek. The references follow a chronological order of publication and are testimony to a remarkable consistency of thought over some thirty-five years. While there is, unlike a philosopher like Wittgenstein, little to be gained by distinguishing between an early and a late Žižek, there is an ongoing nuancing which brings new developments in approach to a particular area of thought. He rethinks and reformulates what has previously been said, and reading a new book or article by him becomes a stimulating experience that brings new connections and levels of interest to material previously discussed.

The second set of references are to other authors offering a critical commentary on the topic or writing more widely but in a way that directly throws light on the topic. Also referenced here, when relevant, are videoed debates, films featuring Žižek or individual articles he has authored.

The third set of references, 'Connections', is to other entries in this book that overlap with or are relevant to the topic. As networks of linked relations, this third set of references expands the meaning and significance of the subject as well as bearing witness to Žižek's fecundity of interdisciplinary thought. To take the entry on the unconscious as an example, the process of a primordial wish being arrested and distorted in Freud's account of dreamwork gains distinctiveness when Žižek contrasts it with the different process of negation of negation in Hegel's dialectic. It is not an arbitrary contrast because, by the same token and at least equally acute, it brings out how Hegel cannot encompass meaning being stalled by a failure of negation, a lack of resolution caused by overdetermination.

The boxed quotations accompanying the entries are nearly always taken from a Žižek text and they have a partly heuristic purpose by drawing attention to a salient or exemplary statement relating to the matter being considered. They are also there to foster and inspire a desire to read the author. Walter Benjamin in 'One-Way Street' observes how the power of walking along a country road is not the same as when flying over it.[2] In Žižek country this means – like the map drawn on a scale of 1 mile to a mile in Lewis Carroll's *Sylvie and Bruno Concluded* (referred to in Žižek's doctoral thesis[3]) – reading Žižek. His philosophy, about much more than just philosophy, is about living in difficult times that are hard to bear. A world where everything is what it appears to be but also its opposite – a world where, post-Holocaust, Israel commits genocide – where reality becomes a paper-thin fiction and shadows do not fade away, and where other people are a perplexing mystery. Žižek country is experiential, thought-provoking and it necessarily lacks a capital when hermeneutic borders are transgressed and speculative truths encountered in its landscapes.[4] For the reader, it holds out the prospect of a dynamic journey of self-discovery, an emergence from self and an affirmation of ideas and ideals worth actively cherishing.

How Žižek writes

Žižek's writing is characterized by dazzling, sometimes provocative analyses, arresting aperçus and an oceanic range of references. The cogency and conviction of the writing does not suffer from lapses into high-altitude, impenetrable syntax and is mercifully free of self-importance. It favours clarity, seasoned with very generous doses of theory, and is given to wearing its layers of erudition lightly. Nevertheless, readers looking for a philosopher's formal methodology may be aggrieved by a style variously perceived as habitually self-interruptive, too prone to schematization, disaggregative, excessively digressive, revelling in ideas with Bacchanalian excess.[5] The willingness to be irreverent may give the impression of lapses from seriousness but, to take his survey of different types of European toilets as a classic instance,[6] this can be approached in a severely analytic manner without sacrificing hilarity.[7] His manner of presenting an argument that occasionally upsets the protocols of a certain type of conventional discourse may be aggravating to some – particularly those blind to being courted by a crafted provocativeness[8] – but this cannot explain a degree of reluctance in some quarters to engage with the astonishing fertility of his thought. There may be some professional jealousy of his publishing success, his popularity in debates and a pronounced online imprint.[9] Terry Eagleton's gag that unlike non-realist fiction no one in real life can be in six divergent places at once except the ubiquitous Žižek[10] might suggest misgiving about success on so many different platforms. It may also betray a degree of uncertainty about what holds together his writing on so many topics and across so many intellectual disciplines.

The first entry in this book, Absolute Knowing, uses the word hodological and, as it links with the etymology of the word method, it provides a way of appreciating Žižek's methodology. Method comes from μετά (*meta* + ὁδός (hodos)), which means, according to *The Cambridge Greek Lexicon*, the pursuit of knowledge or the mode of pursuing such an enquiry. The pursuit or mode is a pathway (hodos) taken, the finding of a way, and it allows for a difference to be drawn between a single route that leads to a definitive map and the mapping of different landscapes with their own pathways.

Where indirection and circlings around a topic exist in Žižek's writing, they are intrinsic to a form of presentation and diction that combats schemas of linear progression from a starting to an end point. Form is expressive of content when, in place of a balanced flow of argument, there are cross-currents, whirling eddies and periodic reversions of the tide that allow for ratiocinative leaps into deep waters. Walter Benjamin, reviewing Döblin's *Berlin Alexanderplatz*, characterizes montage as its 'stylistic principle', mixing material in a way that 'explodes the framework of the novel, bursts its limits both stylistically and structurally, and clears the way for new, epic possibilities'.[11] Žižek's multidisciplinary and multifaceted approach is a form of such a montage, one that is pedagogically driven – it is not intellectual promiscuity or a freewheeling eclecticism – and when Benjamin adds how Dadaism brought daily life into montage, Žižek does something similar by bringing into his texts moments of everyday existence and scenes of life from movies and literature. It is not unknown for Hegel and Lacan to be shy of comprehensibility but this is not a charge that can easily be laid against Žižek.

There is a navigable flow to his written thought that is dissimilar in kind from live interviews and talks where the improvisational process of thinking, with all its hesitations and changes of direction, is on show in a remarkable way. In the writing, what may be perceived as a rapid digressiveness is not unrelated to tropes and terms resurfacing and being swiftly re-explained. When a term illustrates a particular observation, there is often a quick recap of its meaning for the benefit of readers and, where familiarity with the topic already exists, it is hasty for the reader to adduce mere duplication. In an instructional, non-performative mode, repetition is a deliberate choice[12]; not an appetitive insistence on reiteration, it is palimpsestic in deliberately recycling and reformulating ideas without erasing the earlier vocabulary or formulation.

The writing performs an intellectual spiralling around and conjugating of a set of key ideas and there is a consequent need to read across and against his texts to see how various conceptual matrices are being presented and sometimes overlaid to suit varied purposes.[13] Hegelian terms like negativity, dialectic, reflection and the absolute make up one such constellation and within it the terms light up each other. Working in a comparable way, there are Lacanian matrices where drive, desire and *objet petit a*, the symbolic and the real, the big Other and *jouissance* overlap with one another in a sometimes multifarious network. There are particular jokes (like the one about Rabinovitch), a Hegelian, Lacanian or literary locution ('*spirit is a bone*', 'there is no sexual relationship', 'I would prefer not to'), a topic like Freud's dreamwork or any one of a multitude of motifs and paradoxes that, far from being superfluous, often function as summations of propositions and as shortcuts to draw out threads between a set of main ideas. The ancient Greeks used their mythology as a tool to think with, and Žižek's honed responsiveness to pop culture allows him to do likewise, with aspects that range from Hollywood blockbusters to zombies and the fad for Western Buddhism.

The paramountcy of theory for Žižek is consistent with his remark that a good essay on a famous painting means more to him than seeing the painting in a crowded museum[14]: 'It is life without theory which is gray, a flat stupid reality – it is only theory which makes it "green", truly alive, bringing out the complex underlying network of mediations and tensions which make it move.'[15] The ironic reference to Goethe's lines from *Faust*[16] is there to refute a simple philosophical opposition between realism and nominalism. The world is more than a rich and flirting set of particulars from which abstraction finds patterns which can be given names. A nominalist approach, which can treat concepts as fictions, fails to do justice to a reasoning that traces internal connections between apparently unrelated phenomena. The word theory, coming from the Greek *theoria* (to see), contemplation rather than active engagement, is apposite for an approach that looks for relations between elements that may not be transparent but which are there for observation and open to speculative reason. The result is often not what is expected, hence Žižek's predilection for figures depicting non-orientable surfaces, like the Möbius strip and the Greimas square, for structuring relations between concepts.[17]

It is the case that Žižek sometimes reuses passages from an earlier publication but this is more revealing of a remarkable cross-fertilization of consistently held ideas than corroborating evidence for a spurious charge of self-plagiarism.[18] The opening pages of *The Sublime Object of Ideology*, the book that brought him instant acclaim, bring the dramatic news that Freud's interpretation of dreams homologizes Marx's analysis of the commodity. The procedural nature of the dreamwork is then set out for comparison with the commodity-form.[19] Nearly thirty years later, the nature of dreamwork is returned to in a section of the second chapter of *Disparities*[20] but, while its operation is described in basically the same way, the purpose of referencing Freud's account is freshly calibrated. What is now being highlighted is not the equivalence between the form of the dream and the commodity, each effacing its origins, but the similarity between the inverted movement of dreamwork and the reversal in the Hegelian motility of absolute recoil. It is this similarity that is now taken to illuminate Freud's analogy between the role of capital and dreamwork: where a quotidian hermeneutic interprets the surface dream-content as disguising a buried dream-thought, Freud maps a reverse direction of travel with the dream-thought inscribing itself up into the process of disguise. In place of an interpretive movement downwards, to the unconscious wish, there is a movement of work upwards towards the surface of the dream. The text of these three pages finds its way into *Incontinence of the Void*,[21] published a year later as part of a wide-ranging chapter marshalling material in support of Marx's analysis of capitalism. In *Absolute Recoil*, Freud's dreamwork is described once again but the context is now an extended discussion of Schoenberg's musical revolution, and it is used to give an insight into the dialectical play of form and content in the composer's *Erwartung*.[22]

In another section of *Disparities*, it is absolute recoil that is referenced once more and there is a precise framework for its use. Underway is a pushback against Robert Pippin – one of the Hegelian scholars Žižek often disagrees with but has a high regard for – and his neglect of negativity as the wellspring of substance and the ungrounded subject. What is homed in on Pippin's treatment of Hegel's breakdown of reflection into three phases is the crucially missing process of absolute recoil.[23] In order to show why Pippin's account dilutes the radical nature of Hegel's ontology, part of Žižek's explication of the reflexive movement of absolute recoil reuses some twenty-five lines taken from his earlier *Absolute Recoil*.[24] Their reuse here, directly relevant to the lengthy quotations from Pippin expressing doubts about how Hegel explains reflection, serves a specific heuristic purpose.

Comay and Ruda[25] draw attention to how, two years after publication of the *Phenomenology*, Hegel placed an advertisement in a newspaper apologizing for the haphazard appearance of the book. He advises readers that they will not make sense of it on a first reading and that only by returning to and rereading the text will they begin to make headway. As if sensing the truth of this for his own work, Žižek relentlessly carries out his own rereadings and renewals, circumnavigating back to crucial ideas in his seminal thinkers while constantly engaging with other writers who contribute to the conversation. *Surplus Enjoyment*, for instance, is structured around a set of Hegelian responses to four books that had been recently published by other authors. Looser forms of this kind of approach are to be found in many of his books.

Reiteration is essential to this process, and occasional paragraphs repeated verbatim, in changed contexts and lines of argument, is par for the course. What is being elaborated and established, a highly robust philosophy, needs a requisite methodology that, within the space of a page, can comfortably contain erudition and profanity. What might be sanitized as merely a wicked sense of humour is one element in a writing practice that strategically detonates received readings by breaking them up with interventions from other genres. The deliberate intention is to suggest unexpected but illuminating parallels, creating stations that Benjamin calls 'dialectic at a standstill'.[26]

In his writing, an ensemble of chiefly Hegelian, Lacanian and Marxist concepts are being worked through, communicated, applied, plumbed and complexified – in short, being broached dialectically. The proficiency to re-evaluate them for fresh inquiries and analyses is as remarkable as it is demonstrable proof of rigour and intellectual vision.

Recurrence is a function of the continual making of connections between ideas in Hegel, Kant, Lacan, Marx and a catholic host of other thinkers and disciplines. Congruities, as unpredictable as they are original,[27] are affirmed; between, for example, quantum physics and sexual difference. An acquaintance with the gamut of Žižekian ideas accumulates through a rhizomatic process of multiplication, replication and interdependencies in his texts and talks, with readers and listeners drawn into constellations of citations and relations. A particular nexus, like one allowing Hegel's dialectic and negation of negation to be part of an atheistic construal of Christian theology, achieves clarity when it is integrated into other aspects of Žižek's philosophy. A topic, a term, a film or other cultural reference is returned to, conceptually refined and complicated. The big Other is a Lacanian term so commonly cited in texts as to be no longer perplexing, but in *Surplus Enjoyment* it gains further depth by considering its virtual identity as *form* and as generating an 'Id-machine' that gives it a supplementary, non-virtual existence.[28] Where James Joyce spent seventeen years fusing *Finnegans Wake*, overlaying text upon text and intensifying a work method that emerged earlier in the detailed redrafting of chapters for *Ulysses*, Slavoj Žižek chooses to use his time to write another book to supplement and deepen the writing that has gone before.

Reading Žižek

Reading Žižek can seem daunting due to the number of his books and the flow of articles, videoed debates and presentations. The references accompanying the entries in this book aim to serve as navigating tools to help manage the copious amount of available material. Primary importance is accorded to texts by Žižek himself, and in places references tend to relate more to material from the time of *Less Than Nothing* (2012) onwards. This is partly because there are existing guides to earlier work, including the laudable introduction by Sarah Kay whose *Žižek* appeared in 2003. Other books providing an overview, like *Žižek: A Guide for the Perplexed* (2012) and *The Žižek Dictionary* (2014), were not able to take on board *Less Than Nothing*, let alone the score or so of new books written by Žižek since then. There are now an increasing number of texts about specific aspects of Žižek's work, as well as multi-authored ones like *Žižek Now* (2013), *Žižek Responds!* (2023), *Understanding Žižek, Understanding Modernism* (2023) and a volume of the journal *Crisis and Critique* (2025), all of which proffer different perspectives.

Reading in Žižek country on a good day is adventurous, with changes in latitude and longitude and encounters with chicanes when least expected. The vegetation is luxurious; occasional thickets are there to work through; and life forms abound. There are innumerable trails to follow, sometimes in parallel but moving through different terrains, plus intriguing detours that lead to exhilarating vantage spots. It is wise to be chary, when a route seems clear and the landscape familiar, of thinking an absolute viewpoint has been attained. The ground is never as stable as it might look and looking back becomes essential if travellers are to make sense of the territory they are going through. Signs and stepping stones may be helpful but the right pathway tends to show itself only after choosing the wrong one. It is inviting to position Hegel and Lacan as twin peaks dominating the landscapes but they are better figured as contour lines weaving across maps of the territory.

Reading Žižek as one might straightforwardly read a map and consult its legend is misleading if the nature of his thought as speculative is not embraced. Jean Copjec offers a valuable insight when she takes the idea from literary criticism of close reading and finds it outmoded for reading Žižek unless it is performed slantwise. It is not that close reading is not necessary, far from it, but it should not be experienced as an impersonal interpellation at the expense of keeping the field open for interpretation of what, as she puts it, 'does not exist'.[29]

Any nod towards something cavalier or frenetic about Žižek's work seriously downplays the sustained depth and magnitude of his engagement with Hegel and the discipline of philosophy. This is evidenced in his first book in English, *The Sublime Object of Ideology*, and in *For They Know Not What They Do, Tarrying with the Negative, The Ticklish Subject* and other works, before reaching a sinewed refinement in three books published between 2012 and 2016: *Less Than Nothing, Absolute Recoil* and *Disparities* (and continuing with *Quantum History* in 2025). Academia has been slow to recognize this, ignoring Žižek in *The Oxford Handbook of Hegel* (2017), a tome of over 800 pages from more than thirty scholars, and rating a solitary sentence in Wiley-Blackwell's 600-page *A Companion to Hegel* (2011). While the intersection of Lacanian psychoanalysis with Hegel, foundational for Žižek's thought, leaves some wary of engaging with a synthesis of ideas outside their familiar ambit, the publication of the hefty, multi-authored *The Bloomsbury Handbook to Slavoj Žižek* (Filkelde 2026) confirms the growing recognition of the stimulating importance of just such an intersection.

Kant is the philosophical springboard for Žižek's distinctive reading of Hegel. Kant argues for the unavoidability of a pre-understanding that models what we take to be reality: for example, the accepted place for gods, a real place one might say in an ancient Greek frame of reference, is not there for a modern scientific model governed by observable and measurable laws. There will always be a transcendental horizon providing coordinates of one kind or another, and Kant's exposition of this requirement provides a basis for inquiring further into vistas of meaning that affect how we view and relate to the world. With the entrance of Hegel onto this philosophical stage, a new ground rule emerges: we are also objects in a world that is presented by our point of view and our inclusion in this presented world defeats any neutral observation of reality.

A parallel at the psychoanalytic level to this inclusion that deprives the observer of a neutral status is Lacan's theory of the gaze. Unlike the commanding and subjugating look of someone with power, as with 'the male gaze', the gaze for Lacan is a partial object cast by the unconscious desire of the subject into a visual field and distorting what isthere. The gaze, says Lacan, is an 'underside of consciousness' that operates as 'a descent of desire'.[30] Lacan and Hegel, in their different ways and vocabularies, are making the same point.

The Real is real

Conceptual interactions between German Idealism, Hegel in particular, and psychoanalysis, primarily Lacan, are continually being drawn out and returned to by Žižek – this is his *activity* as a philosopher – and the confluences he charts are a hallmark of the enduring significance of his thought. It is tempting to look for philosophical bedrock, the ultimate ground that will account for the interactions and confluences being charted. This brings into prominence the Lacanian Real, with a hub or a prism coming to mind as images for the unconditional centrality of this concept for Žižek. A drawback for this way of picturing the Real is that, as material and visible objects, a hub or prism may be misleading for representing a reality of incompletion.

As a word for an unstable ontological grammar, the Real forms an 'opaque-indeterminate, abyssal, prelogical Background that is always already there, presupposed by every properly dialectical process'.[31] It is what accounts for an irreconcilable parallax and, as the gap 'that separates the One from itself, for which the Lacanian designation is the Real', is what Žižek says his entire work is circulating around.[32]

The Real, the gap that keeps apart different perspectives on reality, prevents the possibility of things coinciding with themselves. It is a pure gap that finds formal expression in a set of polar differences: those between desire and drive, the split that is class struggle, the masculine and feminine formulae of sexuation, the wave/particle division in quantum physics.[33] The incommensurability that is the Real goes all the way down, without a meta-language capable of representing the no man's land between how reality appears to us and – Kant's 'in-itself' – how it is without us. The incapacity arises because no man's land as a pure difference that comes before its oppositional terms is more than a metaphor.

For Žižek, this non-metaphorical space, the impossibility of a meta-language, finds expression in modern art and is inaugurated with Kazimir Malevich's *Black Square on White Background*. The two frames in the painting, one outside the other, denote the transcendental framing of reality and, within its own border, another frame of pre-ontological chaos. The gap between them, over which they can never meet, is crucial but so too is their interrelationship that is brought together on the canvas. The difference between the two frames is minimal at one level but this 'minimal difference' registers the discrepancy between reality as meaning and the Real as non-meaning. It is 'the difference that separates an object from itself' and it is in this liminal space that the subject becomes part of the content.[34] By marking this as a place where Hegel and Lacan converge, Žižek locates a key cartographical point of philosophical significance.

The gap between meaning and non-meaning does not leave one on a precipice, the edge of a descent into an abyssal void. Some positive bit of reality is necessary; without it 'we do not get the pure balanced Void "as such" – rather, the Void itself disappears, is no longer there'.[35] What this means, to bring us back down to earth from what might seem too highfalutin, is that we are here in the reality we create but non-meaning remains as the zero-point from where we must begin. In the world of art, Malevich's black square clears the ground and prepares the place for the elevation by Marcel Duchamp of an urinal into a work of art.[36]

Subjectivity touches the Real when trust in transcendentally constituted reality is punctuated and the empty inhuman core of our being is approached. This is often traumatic because subjectivity is the spanner in its own machinery, separating itself from the Real and relying on fantasy and other fictions to make its reality sustainable. Žižek frequently responds with infectious pleasure to punctuating moments in fiction when the fragile balance between fantasy and reality reveals itself. In *The Pervert's Guide to the Cinema* and in *Disparities*, a scene in the 1931 film *Possessed* is highlighted: a small-town woman gazes with wonder at views of another lifestyle on display through the windows of passing carriages. When the train stops and a passenger offers her a glass of champagne, it is 'as if, for a brief moment, the fantasy-space intervened in reality'.[37]

What fantasy obfuscates and helps us cope with is the otherwise unadulterated horror of knowing existence is ghastly, beyond our interpretative reach: 'Life *is* a disgusting thing, a sleazy object moving out of itself, secreting humid warmth, crawling, stinking, growing ... It should all disappear.'[38] The planet that will collide with Earth in Lars von Trier's *Melancholia* will make everything disappear and, as the film shows, people respond differently when they know this will occur. Suicide and hysteria are possible options, but the character Justine, whose tarrying with the negative has reduced her dependency on fantasy, is able to accept the inevitable and provide a non-fetishistic symbolic fiction that will help others.[39] This does not make death any less final or dreadful but it does mean facing up to negation as 'inscribed with the innermost identity of every living being, so that every destruction is ultimately self-destruction'.[40]

Ontology and Marx

Death and the 'unswerving punctuality of chance'[41] are the only certainties in a jigsaw ontology where more than one piece is missing. As a failure of completion in being itself, the picture on the jigsaw box, a projection we construct, can never match the contents inside; at its most rhetorical, there are no pieces to even begin trying to join up: 'In some sense there is only nothing and not something.'[42] This cuts across any division contrasting pre-human life with the arrival of the subject as a speaking animal. Hegel, Heidegger and Lacan[43] all note how language, enabling representation by words, effectuates a forced divorce from some fuller sense of being but Žižek resists overstating a presumed homeostasis existing before logos. He writes instead of 'de-naturalizing nature itself', finding Hegel doing this in his *Philosophy of Nature*, without diminishing the enormity of the speaking subject's break from the animal's immersion in its natural environment.[44] Nature is as riven as the human subject: 'Yes, man is a wound of nature, but literally and radically: a wound of nature itself – in man, the innermost feature of nature is registered.'[45] The inconsistency and disunity at the heart of reality, the Real, is inaccessible in itself and inaccessibility is registered by being the locus of impossibility on which the symbolic machinery founders.

How to avoid helplessness before a subjectivism that can only ever deliver a partial vision involves accepting a world that is out of joint from the start. It also brings to the fore, completing the triangulation of thinkers who have exercised most influence on Žižek, the enduring prominence of Marx. The particular interests of the proletariat, for the young Marx, are also those of society in general and this forges a universal class: 'The emancipation of the workers contains universal human emancipation.'[46] Žižek mobilizes this idea by developing the difference between the working class in its classic Marxist sense and the proletariat as a class-conscious, subjective position.[47] What is sought is alliance with a universality arising from solidarity with those excluded and marginalized from the social hierarchy. Jacques Rancière's term 'the part of no-part'[48] is repeatedly deployed by Žižek in books, from *The Parallax View* onwards. The term is used for those in society without a proper position, those who represent a place of inner dislocation that fractures a totality at a nodal point of what he calls, borrowing a term from Badiou, 'symptomal torsion'.[49] Identifying with 'the part of no-part' is the basis for choosing a side in class struggle and subjectively engaging with its position. In a prognostic move, the proletariat comes to be those who make this choice, disidentify with their given social role and commit to a feminine, non-All universal.[50] Analogies to a universality that cuts across existing demarcations are found across a wide spectrum, from St Paul's unconditional universalism (Gal. 3.28) to de Gaulle's call in 1940 for either resistance to Nazi occupation or collaboration with it.[51] Underlying this universal orbit is the recognition of the Neighbour within each one of us, the exclusion shared by all of us as strangers to ourselves.[52]

Truth and speculative thought

Any menu of the cocktails of ideas, insights and inspirations in Žižek's corpus would be a long one and the range of his cultural and political concerns underlies his status as a public intellectual in the mould of Bertrand Russell. A radical eschewal of what often passes for common sense is also something shared with Russell and it qualifies Žižek's acknowledgement that while capitalism has become the only show in town and revolutionary history – Jacobin, Communard and Communist – a catalogue of catastrophic failures, there should be no wallowing in nostalgia for lost causes and, equally resolutely, no resignation to the way things are. What he labels 'the New' is always possible, and Walter Benjamin's example of the October Revolution repeating and redeeming the failed French Revolution remains available for a new iteration because what is actual in the present does not erase other possibilities that were there in the past; there is, as Žižek puts it, '*virtuality* inherent to the past',[53] and a particular historical context can be overcome and can release what he explains are 'moments of Eternity in time'.[54] The 'Holographic History' chapter of *Absolute Progress* reaffirms how the role of contingency militates against notions of necessity when history is viewed as 'holographic'. In *Quantum History*, the principle of the holographic in quantum mechanics becomes a model for endorsing Marx's sense of history and for interpreting the contemporary political world, arising from a non-All ontology, as an arena where different universalities are in conflict.

Materialism of a purely reductive kind places causality on an inaccessible pedestal but dialectical materialism puts it within the space of a freedom that allows for its coordinates to be reset. This is judged to be represented in the political arena par excellence by Lenin and, despite repeated disappointments since October 1917, Žižek remains 'desperately optimistic', knowing that recent political failures 'might give birth to unpredictable new visions ... or horrors'.[55]

This political philosophy sheds light on an unexpected dimension to Žižek's thought. A well-known part of his modus operandi is the calling upon of a prodigious interdisciplinary reservoir of literary, cinematic, musical and humorous citations, and his adventures into the puzzling world of quantum physics is not altogether unexpected. What is a surprising conjuncture in his thought arises from a strong engagement with theology and, in particular, Christian theology. It may appear odd in the context of an anti-theism that often accompanies commitment to left-wing, emancipatory principles and he might be expected to reiterate or echo the strident atheism associated with public figures like Richard Dawkins and Christopher Hitchens. That this is not the case may have something to do with Žižek's upbringing in a secular polity where religious instruction was not part of a school's curriculum and in a home where both parents were 'resolutely atheist'.[56] What may have helped in this respect was not being exposed to the hypocrisy and shallowness of Christianity as it is so often practised in Europe, thus avoiding the negative reaction this understandably produces. The Christian inspiration for precious art, literature, architecture and so on should be acclaimed but, given the religion's institutional perfidy and the ongoing catalogue of outrages committed in its domains, one may ask why attention should be paid to its theology. The answer resides in fully acknowledging that a deity does not exist but with an equally complete embrace of the way God 'is a name for that which in man is not human, for the inhuman core that sustains being-human'.[57] The 'inhuman' here addresses an ungovernable excess beyond instinctual nature[58] and is expressive of the inadequacy of the symbolic to represent a sense of self-identity. Žižek's Christian atheism is premised on a primordial loss, the lack of complete identity of anything with itself which, paradoxically, is correlative with excess. The 'inhuman' references the acute inflections in human animalization brought about by entry into the symbolic order and its structures of signification.

Reality's zero-level is always fissured and Žižek's use of capitalizations stresses this: the impossibility of One, the absence of Beyond in the face of an ontologically disjointed, non-All reality. Paradoxes come naturally to descriptions of this abyssal level because they are a logical way of presenting the puzzling nature and consequences of an ontologically flawed world.

What needs avoiding, though, is any jump into thinking that Žižek, pursuing a new version of a discredited post-modernism, denies truth. Truth is a vitally important term for Žižek but its dimension at stake is not the one where statements of facts can be judged true or false according to their degree of accuracy. Another dimension, with an impossibility at its heart, is one where truth asserts itself through engagement and through error, where, as the possible content of an enunciation, a non-All truth emerges from the position of the enunciation. This is the lesson of psychoanalysis as set out in the second chapter of *The Sublime Object of Ideology*. There is no inevitability to truth, no metalanguage for expressing it, and this carries far-reaching consequences for social and political life.

The truth is concealed in the illusion of believing in the big Other but to break free one first has to succumb to this illusory subject-supposed-to-know. The dialectical process requires an initial failure as the catalyst for understanding and, similarly, the failure of previous attempts to conceive an absolute leads to the position that Hegel calls Absolute Knowing, a place only reached as a result of these failures. It is in this way that the inexistence of the big Other only emerges after recognizing what the failure of its existence properly means. As a fiction of the symbolic, the big Other only ever exists at a virtual level but remains operational as long as people behave as if it is really there. Only by fully assuming its inexistence can it be broken up inside us and this is what comes with the moment on the Cross ('My God, my God, why have you abandoned me') when Christ stops believing in himself: 'God exists only insofar as he doesn't know (i.e. take note of, register) his own inexistence. The moment God knows, he collapses into the abyss of inexistence.'[59] The arrival of the moment of truth is often compared by Žižek with the cartoon cat's sudden fall when it notices there is no ground beneath it. Christ dies and the Holy Spirit is born as a community of believers who pursue their project with faith but without depending on a transcendent God. This is a crux in his debate with John Milbank in *The Monstrosity of Christ*, and when Milbank writes of God appearing only incognito Žižek's response is forthright: God only appears incognito because 'there is nothing to take cognizance of here: God is hiding not to hide some transcendent Truth, but to hide the fact that there is nothing to hide'.[60] The final paragraph of *The Puppet and the Dwarf: The Perverse Core of Christianity* recognizes in this a supreme example of Hegelian sublation, a suppression that is also a preservation: Christianity can only be redeemed 'in the gesture of abandoning the shell of its institutional organization (and, even more so, of its specific religious experience)'.[61]

An image from Walter Benjamin's essay on the art of translation provides a way of understanding how Žižek approaches not just theology but philosophy as a whole. Benjamin writes how, if they are to be glued together, the shards of an object must 'match one another in the smallest details, although they need not be like one another'. His point is that a translation must follow the original language but not imitate it. The task is to make 'both the original and the translation recognizable as fragments of a greater language, just as fragments are part of a vessel'.[62] The various sites of antagonism looked at by Žižek – theological, philosophical, psychoanalytic, cultural and political – are like Benjamin's shards in this respect. The original body is fragmentary and Žižek's endeavours are uncanny acts of both breaking and putting together parts so that they are discerned as fragments of something greater but not whole. He engages with philosophies, works of literature, cinema, theology and much else besides in the way Benjamin says a translator 'must lovingly and in detail incorporate the original's way of meaning'.[63] Surprises come when meanings are found in the original work that are not immediately obvious and they lead, indirectly, to truth.

Truth for **Žižek** cannot be preordained; it must emerge from an engaged, partisan position. Georg Lukács showed how this worked for Marxism, its tenets only becoming true for those who adopt the subjective position of the proletariat.[64] Truth is never reached, only its effects reside as 'half-said', and if sought too hard, as with the Nazi intent to create a conflict-free polity supposedly blocked by Jews, the results may be catastrophic.[65]

What stymies the traditional notion of truth as something attainable is expressed by Hegel in *Science of Logic* as the '*unrest* of simultaneous *incompatibles, a movement*'.[66] There are gaps in the ecology of being and a consequence follows from this: 'Something is alive, therefore, only to the extent that it contains contradiction within itself … *Speculative thought* consists only in this, in holding firm to contradiction.'[67] The dialectical process proceeds in the way it does because it operates speculatively. It begins with an affirmative idea, statement or point of view but proceeds to engage in going beyond what looks to be a transparency of meaning. It undergoes a redefinition in the course of its own unpredictable, non-binary realization. The dialectic is open to equivocity and its speculative orbit a strange one: a truth cannot be reached directly but must encounter errors of its own making, never exhausting its possibilities. In place of a linear, telelogically driven search, a hodological approach is less about the destination and more about what is revealed on the passage. Despite sounding like a rhetorical ploy, a post-modernist celebration revelling in relativism, what matters is the achievement of truth by going beyond what might seem to be a conclusion.

Truth for Hegel is not to be confused with degrees of accuracy accruing from comparing something with the representation of it in our thought; truth, when it is not about mere correctness, has to be compared with itself, with the way it actualizes itself.[68] When this is done, inconsistencies and contradictions reveal themselves. Truth is speculative, it is discovered through mistakes, and even when something unfolds disastrously, like China's Cultural Revolution, the truth of its idea is not destroyed: 'It continues to lead the underground spectral life of ghosts of failed utopias which haunt future generations, patiently awaiting its next resurrection.'[69] Talk of eternal truths may sound quaint, rendered suspect by historicism and crude relativism, but it can be fully accepted as an antinomy and valorized as an endorsement of what is of supreme value. Any universality that embraces a truth has to be conjectured as operating in a mode that questions its claim to unconditionality: 'Emancipatory politics can only be sustained by a belief in the (in some sense obviously "illusory") axiom of universal justice.'[70]

Truths are to be found in Žižek and being speculative ones their forms sometimes lack topological stability due to their inception in a geography where the Real exists but necessarily escapes representation. Truths – when they are not surveys of available objective facts – are empirically fictional, risky and violent.[71] If this seems outlandish, it is time to recall J. G. Ballard's declaration – as guest editor in 1962 of the British science-fiction magazine *New Worlds* – that 'earth is the only truly alien planet'[72] Its human inhabitants are self-alienated but capable of separating from the big Other's prescriptions and cutting – or at least loosening – the knots that entangle them. Mapping speculative thought involves a contrapunctual grammar of thinking,[73] a speculative hermeneutic that Hegel calls absolute knowing, a form of curiosity and of unknowing; for an alphabet-based map of Žižek country there is an appropriateness in beginning with absolute knowing.

Notes

1   In the spirit of Hegel when he wrote: 'But to want to know before one knows is as incoherent as the Scholastic's wise resolution to learn to swim, before he ventured into the water' (1991: 34).
2   Benjamin (1996b: 447).
3   MSH 227.
4   One way in which speculative truths are enacted in his reasoning is through his use of examples, as shown by Robert Pfaller (2017: 69–75) in relation to a section from *The Sublime Object of Ideology* (SO 31–3) about belief materialized in social activity. Žižek's use of an example may not be to illustrate its counterpart (which is often also an example) but to 'estrange' it in Brechtian fashion and reveal what was not obvious at first.
5   See, for example, Harpham (2003).
6   PF 3–4; L 16–17.
7   Johnston (2024: 85–9).
8   Žižek's comment is also relevant: 'Yes, my jokes often do violate the threshold of "good taste", and enter the uncanny domain in which amusement turns into disgust in order to signal … what? … In contrast to the cliché of the academic writer beneath whose impassive style the reader can catch an occasional glimpse of a so-called lively personality, I always perceived myself as the author of books whose excessively and compulsively "witty" texture serves as the envelope of a fundamental coldness, of a "machinic" deployment of the line of thought which follows its path with utter indifference towards the pathology of so-called human considerations. In this respect, I always felt a deep sympathy for Monty Python, whose excessive humour also signals an underlying stance of profound disgust with life' (1999a: viii).
9   For Žižek's 'performative' rejection of the authoritative intellectual, see, for example, Burnham (2018: 26–30).
10 Eagleton (2024: 60); see also what Bar-El call Žižek's 'superpositioning' which 'attracts supporters from various, possibly opposing publics, but satisfying none of them as he reaches beyond their existing opposition' (2025: 19).
11 Benjamin (2005: 301). In a similar vein, perhaps, the editors of *Žižek Responds!* sense a 'childlike yearning to clear the table by knocking over the Lego castle and to "start from scratch"' in Žižek (Finkelde and McGowan 2023: 2). What is childlike, though, might be more progressively explained as a fearless playfulness, of the kind the editors of Žižek's *Against Progress* describe when they remark how the essays in that book – and this can be extended to Žižek's writing as a whole – 'begin again and again, from a different angle, applying a different kind of conceptual leverage, worrying away at the intractable, sometimes reeling away blood-spattered, but

always, always, returning to the fray' (AP x).

12 No more so than in *The Fright of Real Tears* where a passage in the book's introduction is reproduced later in the same book. The explanation for this is given in *Less Than Nothing* (86–7).

13 This, the topic of 'Žižek's Reading Machine' by Benjamin Noys, 'involves taking seriously Badiou's claim that Žižek is "not exactly in the field of philosophy" as the means to neither dismiss or celebrate Žižek but to grasp the provocation of his work' (Noys 2015: 73). As an example of how, non-provocatively, Žižek overlays different concepts to form a coherent position, see Žižek (2025h).

14 2020d: 107.

15 LTN 395.

16 'Grey is, young friend, all theory / And green of life the golden tree.' www.gutenb erg.org/ebooks/3023 (accessed 18 October 2025).

17 SFA 225–32, 251–8, 265–7; OWB 175.

18 'I tear a fragment out of its original context and insert it into a new context which imposes a new reading out of the fragment, sometimes even the opposite of the "original" one' (SE 346n11). What is astonishing is just how many books have been written, inspired by a core of Hegelian and Lacanian ideas and concepts, yet always in different and original ways.

19 SO 3–9.

20 D 74–6.

21 IV 184–6.

22 AR 157–76.

23 D 126–34.

24 AR 148.

25 Comay and Ruda (2018: 57).

26 'It's not that what is past casts its light on what is present, or what is present its light on what is past; rather, image is that wherein what has been comes together in a flash with the now to form a constellation. In other words, image is dialectic at a standstill' (Benjamin 1999: 462).

27 IV 50; SFA 61.

28 SE 187–93, 202.

29 Copjec (2025: 398).

30 Lacan (2024: 83, 115). Žižek describes the gaze as a 'stain preventing me from looking at the picture from a safe, "objective" distance, from enframing it as something that is at my grasping view's disposal' (LA 125). See McGowan (2025: 116–22).

31 LTN 381.

32 IR xx.

33 AR 373.

34 PV 154; see also HWB 180; QH 315–16.

35 FA 28. Žižek goes on to say: 'We dwell within the symbolic order only in so far as every presence appears against the back ground of its possible absence' (FA 28).

36 FA 34–5; ES 238, 255–6; PV 29, 85, 152, 154; LTN 712–13; AR 109–10; SE 325.

37 D 187.

38 E 193–4n12.

39 E 24–5.

40 IV 277.

41 The phrase is from the end of Thomas Wolfe's *Look Homeward Angel* and is used

in the four novels and novella of William Gaddis.

42 CA 84.

43 'The first act, by which Adam established his lordship over the animals, is this, that he gave them a name, i.e., he nullified them as beings on their own account' (Hegel 1979: 221); 'Language, by naming beings for the first time, first brings beings to word and to appearance. Only this naming nominates beings to their being *from out* of their being' (Heidegger [1978] 1993: 198); 'Thus the symbol manifests itself first of all as the murder of the thing, and this death constitutes in the subject the externalization of his desire' (Lacan 2001: 114).

44 AR 107–9, 184. Whether 'animal' is to be taken as a form of life completely immersed in its environment is not something to be taken for granted. Darwinism makes so fragile and temporary the balance between an organism and its environment 'that it can explode at any moment' (LTN 824n29).

45 AR 205.

46 Marx (1844: 34).

47 DLC 285

48 Rancière (1999: 11).

49 Badiou (2007: 18); DLC 398. 'This identification of the non-part with the Whole, of the part of society with no 1properly defined place within it (or resisting the allocated subordinate place within it) with the Universal, is the elementary gesture of politicization' (Žižek 2011a: 66).

50 DI 62–5.

51 TS 226; QH 120.

52 LET 124–5; DB 79.

53 OWB 12.

54 OWB 11.

55 HWB 11.

56 Interview with Simon Joseph Jones (2015), 'Hegel Don't Bother Me!', *High Profiles*, https://highprofiles.info/interview/slavoj-zizek/ (accessed 30 July 2025).

57 MC 240.

58 '– there is always something that adds itself to reality, that is in excess with regard to it: human life never coincides with itself' (Žižek 2023f: 284).

59 LTN 104.

60 Žižek (2009c: 236).

61 PD 171.

62 Benjamin (1996a: 260). Žižek's deployment of Benjamin's analogy for the task of the translator occurs in AR 143–4.

63 Benjamin (1996a: 260).

64 SE 294–5.

65 CA 23–5.

66 Hegel (2010a: 67).

67 Hegel (2010a: 382–3).

68 'Truth is *error as such*, what we effectively do when we commit (perceive ourselves as committing) an error, so that error lies in the very gaze which perceives the act as an error' (LTN 380). Analogously, 'the "right choice" is only possible the second time, after the wrong one; that is, it is only the first wrong choice which literally creates the conditions for the right choice' (LET 88). By making the 'mistake' of thinking the French Revolution's declaration of human rights could apply to them, the Black slaves in the Haitian Revolution thereby actualized its true meaning (D 64).

See also KNW 196–7.

69 IV 277.

70 F 217.

71 QH 116–22.

72 Quoted in Ballard (2023: xv). G. K. Chesterton is quoted in *Less Than Nothing* for his 'wonderful mental experiment' that makes a similar observation (LTN 414–15). While Chesterton is often admired by Žižek for his dialectically minded perceptiveness, his Hegelianism is also judged to have its limits (LTN 295–8).

73 A different grammar of thinking, Hegel explains in his preface to *The Phenomenology of Spirit*, carries a responsibility for the reader. Beginning non-speculatively, as one must, with 'the usual relationship between subject and predicate', the philosophically minded reader finds the result to be meagre and is called upon 'to come back to the proposition and now to grasp it in some other way' (2018: §63).

A

Absolute knowing

Basic to caricatures of Hegel are his terms 'Absolute' and 'Absolute Knowing' when they are glossed to indicate a privileged point of ultimate knowledge, a consummate Olympian position of supreme metaphysical comprehension. Žižek is not alone in seeking to exorcise a quasi-mysticism that sometimes shrouds the absolute and the way an association with esotericism obscures an understanding of Hegel.

The subject–object division – thought and external reality – is such a commonsensical distinction that a mind–world demarcation is not easily resisted. It can be fully acknowledged that views of external reality are mediated by subjective affinities and historical limitations, and this allows for a difference between subjective and objective perspectives. On the other hand, what can be ignored alongside this is the impossibility of there being a vantage position that would allow the difference to be properly clarified. Absolute knowing is not about cultural or other forms of relativism but – the opposite of what might be expected – the full acceptance of the impossibility of reaching a point where reality could be neutrally observed and judged: 'The very limitation on our knowing – its inevitably distorted, inconsistent character – bears witness to our inclusion in reality' (LTN 390).

> We reach AK [absolute knowing] not when we 'know it all', but when we reach the point at which there is no longer any external point of reference by means of which we could relativize our own position – in AK, the very fact that there is no external limit is discernible, that we do not see the limits of our world, bears witness to our limitation, to our immersion in a world whose horizon we do not perceive.
>
> (AR 244)

All-encompassing knowledge is impossible, but to absolutely know this is a paradox. Žižek (2023c: 74) refers to Frank Ruda's unriddling of this in his *Abolishing Freedom*: knowledge is unavoidably unfinished but cognisance of this cannot be formulated as another, albeit elevated, piece of objective knowledge. This leaves the absolute as a knowing about what delimits any claim to knowledge, a form of unknowing that is not equivalent to the Socratic 'I know that I know nothing'. It is less an epistemological assertion and more an informed assumption of insufficiency: 'a knowledge about giving up knowledge, about letting go of it' (Ruda 2016a: 125). Absolute knowing is not the unknowability of ultimate truths about the Thing-in-itself but the necessary unknowability of what cannot be integrated into the domain of knowing.

In this way, absolute knowing at the end of Hegel's *Phenomenology of Spirit* is portrayed by Žižek as *'the logical disposition of its previous failed attempts to conceive the Absolute –'* (KNW 100). Hegel criticizes Kant for failing to register such 'falling asunder of the moments of the absolute form' (1995: 478), and it is this 'falling asunder' that robs the Hegelian identity of subject and object of any harmony. Absolute knowledge, as Christine Malabou puts it, is a moment of release, an abrogation, 'a *sublation of sublation*' (2005: 156), and Rebecca Comay describes it similarly as an emptying out, 'an undoing or dismantling … The broken subject can no longer position itself as the creative origin of either itself or world' (2011: 146). There can be no consummation when, in the absence of an external position, 'we are CONDEMNED to Absolute Knowing' (QH 86).

Absolute knowing is a looking back from a place where the impossibility of knowing can be seen as the condition of its possibility. After the dash in Žižek's italicized quotation above, he continues with the image of a path to be followed: 'That is, with the vertiginous experience that Truth itself coincides with the path towards Truth' (KNW 100). Hodology (from *hodos*, ancient Greek for path or way), the study of pathways in geography, can also refer to routes making cerebral connections. In this sense absolute knowing is hodological, the making cognitive sense of ways that lead towards an ironic conclusion: 'There is no Outside on which we can rely, that all that remains is to compare our knowledge with itself' (CA 49). A claim to positive, independent knowledge ignores its place of enunciation and is not endowed with the neutrality it supposes itself to possess. Recognizing this is the point reached in absolute knowing. It is when the subject – no longer supposing the in-itself can be isolated from the for-itself – nevertheless pursues activities of knowing without surrendering to 'subjectivistic solipsism' (LTN 389). It is only in absolute knowing, Hegel states in his introduction to *The Science of Logic*, 'that the separation of the *subject matter* from the *certainty of itself* is completely resolved' (2010a: 29). The in-itself was deemed to be independent of the cognizing activity of consciousness – this was the '*certainty*' of the subject; but with absolute knowing – the concluding perspective of the *Phenomenology of Spirit* – this distinction is 'resolved' by seeing them as united.

The pursuit of knowledge in full recognition of the impossibility of an Olympian vision serves as a way of comprehending Hegel's famous image of owlish wisdom occurring only when day has turned to dusk (Hegel 1975: 13). This is why, opening a discussion about the book *The Dash: The Other Side of Absolute Knowing*, Žižek (2018) notes how Marx's idea that a historical agent, like the proletariat, could know in advance what they are doing is not something Hegel could readily entertain. Instead, the course of absolute knowing is its origin and its terminus.

It is the work of negativity – being's lack of self-subsistence, the absence of an organic totality wholly unto itself – that prevents the absolute from reaching a final resting place, and this impossibility carries the ontological force of Hegelian dialectical and speculative thinking. Any suggestion of a difference between how things appear and how they really are is absent when being, seemingly stable, arises within unstable appearances of itself. It emerges from a multitude of determinations, infusions of thought and the unthought, and no one determination transcends the others; there can be no reduction to total conceptual mediation. The position reached in absolute knowing is when, having subtracted material reality's moments of appearance, what might be cognized as what is really there outside appearance – the thing-in-itself – collapses and disintegrates: '[The absolute] is not a subjective notion that fits the objective (how things really are), it is the objective order which includes its subjective misrepresentations' (F 70–1). The density in this initially perplexing inversion can be simplified by saying there is no state of ultimate completion that can be understood as reality. The gap between the subject and object lies beyond the limits imposed by language and is repositioned as a gap within reality itself. The unknowing is redoubled, and Žižek likes to quote Hegel's saying that the hermeneutic secrets of the ancient Egyptians were secrets for the Egyptians themselves (LTN 128). One unabstruse context for recalling the saying is the climactic moment in John Ford's *The Searchers* when the John Wayne character becomes a stranger to himself (ADB 79; LET 119–20).

With the absolute, contradiction is fully accommodated within being and within identity. As an accommodation, it cannot be overpowered as part of a totalitarian omnipotence that has been misleadingly linked with the Hegelian absolute. McGowan (2019: 176–7) uses a banking analogy to bring out what it is and is not. In a global financial crisis, a particular bank faces a challenge it hopes to surmount by getting ahead of other banks by speedily implementing particular strategies. But systemic contradictions within the economic order make it inevitable that some banks will fail, and it needs a wider perspective to see how an individual institution deceives itself into thinking its particular difficulty can be resolved when really the difficulty is an enduring element of its and any other bank's existence. This wider perspective is one of absolute knowing.

The absolute guarantees an opportunity for transformations because it shifts the nature of the terrain. It assures openness in place of fixture, an abiding scission that releases the possibility of every identity being at variance to what it was before. 'The Absolute itself', says Hegel, 'is the identity of identity and non-identity; being opposed and being one are both together in it' (1977: 156). At the level of the dialectic, this is 'the mad dance of negativity' (AR 16), but the speculative goes beyond this with something affirmative which, taken here in opposition to the dialectic, could be termed a positivity.

KNW 67–8; ME 37–8; LTN 104, 387–90; AR 16, 186–7, 226, 242–4; D 56–7; SFA 22; F 69–71, 167; QH 84–6

Comay 2011: 146–9; Malabou 2005: 133–4, 155–60; McGowan 2013: 31–5; Ruda 2016a: 124–7; Scott 2025: 66–70; Žižek 2018

CONNECTIONS: antagonism, dialectic, enunciated and enunciation, identity and difference, infinite judgement, In-itself/For-itself, negativity, speculative reason

Absolute recoil

In *The Science of Logic*, the term 'absolute recoil' ('counter repelling' in George Di Giovanni's 2010 translation) is used by Hegel to describe a crucial moment in his account of reflection. In the book, the title of which bears the term, it is glossed as the self-determination enacted in the movement of reflection.

Absolute recoil occurs in the process of reflection an immediacy is presupposed so that something taken as a given is actually antecedently posited. This moment does not arrest movement: in the reflective act of leaving what was supposed to be a given, the posited comes to be created and its meaningfulness is assumed. To say that it only comes into existence after presupposing its givenness is an aspect of how reflection is never external to its object. Reflection can be pictured in the shape of a loop, a bending around that crosses itself by positing its own presupposition (AR 148). This finds a representation in the scientific world of quantum mechanics when an account of reality, seeming independently of ourselves, cannot exclude the observer. Unable to occupy a privileged, purely objective position, the observer also plays a part in determining what is observed (CA 101–2).

> Reflection thus *finds* an immediate *before it* which it transcends and from which it is the turning back. But this turning back is only the presupposing of what was antecedently found. This antecedent *comes to be* only by being *left behind* … the movement of reflection is to be taken as an *absolute* internal *counter-repelling*. For the presupposition of the turning back into itself – that from which essence *arises*, essence *being* only as this turning back – is only in the turning back itself.
>
> (Hegel 2010a: 348)

What might seem like philosophical magic becomes clearer when Žižek provides examples from the history of colonialism and nineteenth-century nationalism where a subject people, feeling their cultural identity under threat, look back to a fictional age where an authentic national distinctiveness functioned intact. Indian resistance to British colonialism created an image of a lost pre-colonial wholeness, where in reality there was a series of disjointed ministates, and this image is taken as a presupposed given. Then, in the process of rejecting British rule, the very national distinctiveness that had been previously been invented as something lost comes into existence. In an homologous way, it is the withdrawal from Eden that creates an awareness of what came before the Fall: 'It is the very movement of the Fall that creates, opens up, what is lost in it' (HWB 84).

Recoiling and inverting also characterizes the way the subject itself, failing to actualize itself and establish stability, compensates for the loss by retroactively assuming the causes of its existence. The subject, arising from its own impossibility, positing its own presupposition, is an enactment of absolute recoil: 'The subject as $ does not pre-exist its loss, it emerges from its loss as a return to itself' (AR 150). By coinciding with where it begins – a site of loss – the subject is said to fall back into its starting point (AR 379) and the precision here is important in serving as a concise condensation of the dialectical process where 'we begin with nothing, and it is only through the self-negation of nothing that something appears' (AR 154). The procedure carries tremendous philosophical import for when something is the retroactive effect of its own loss it establishes the rationale for writing *Absolute Recoil*. The book's undertaking is to raise absolute recoil into a universal principle for the desubstantial, unintegrable nature of reality.

SO 241–4; E 47–8; AR 1–4, 148–56; D 133–4; IV 34–5; HWB 79–80

Hamza 2016: 164–7; Žižek 2014g

CONNECTIONS: appearance and essence, dialectic, *objet petit a*, reflection, retroactivity, subject

Althusser, Louis

> What escapes Althusser in his description of the process of interpellation is the subject prior to subjectivization, to symbolic identification – this subject which is effectively the answer of the Real to symbolic interpellation but which also stands for the Real that is not simply a product of material practices but it correlative to the 'immaterial' big Other, as in effect the Real.
>
> (AR 64–5)

A theoretical cousin of Žižek, Althusser is never disowned but the term he is most associated with is given a wider ambit than it originally possessed. Althusser's 'Ideology and Ideological State Apparatuses (Notes towards an Investigation)' is read critically and revised to support a grasp of how ideology works.

In his famous *mise en scène* of interpellation – an individual on the street recognizing themselves as the person being authoritatively hailed ('Hey, you there') – Althusser presents his 'little theoretical theatre' in order to encapsulate the inescapable working of ideology. The individual, recognizing the hail as intended for them, turns around in acknowledgement: 'By this mere one-hundred-and-eighty-degree physical conversion, he becomes a *subject*' ([1971] 2001: 174). This account of ideology as a performative self-positioning is given a Lacanian saliency by Žižek, very ironic given that Althusser had been influenced by Lacan and corresponded with him. The hailed individual, before the process of self-recognition, is seen to be minimally already a subject. There is, a factor underscored more than once, a prior 'impenetrable interpellation without identification' (ME 61; AR 64; F 51).

The issue at stake is how best to account for the emergence of the subject and Althusser's account is found wanting on psychoanalytic grounds. This is brought out in *The Sublime Object of Ideology*, first by raising the difference between Althusser, on one side, and the conviction shared by Habermas and Foucault that subjects can break free of ideological straightjackets. Communicative reasoning for Habermas and self-fashioning autonomy for Foucault are emancipive routes but for Althusser this is disallowed by ideology which 'has always-already interpellated individuals as subjects' (Althusser [1971] 2001: 175). The individual is not forced into accepting the symbolic mandate bestowed on them through coercive apparatuses of government like the military and bureaucracy. Nonetheless, while there is no initial choice in interpellation, mechanisms of enforcement, without relying on the ultimate threat of force from the machinery of the state, operate in the background; internalized, they reside in the unconscious (161).

The subject as the product of interpellation is what Žižek contests when he underlines the facet crucially missing in Althusser: 'the distance separating the Real from its symbolization' (SO xxv). The big Other, as the symbolic order, is the broker of interpellation and confers on a person their encultured identity. It does not, because it cannot, represent the Real and as a consequence is penetrated by parallactic inconsistency. The symbolic, symptomatically and traumatically, leaves a remainder that remains outside its jurisdiction. This surplus is the space inhabited by *objet a* and it occasions the *jouissance* that sustains the ideological call described by Althusser. There is always resistance to the interpellative call because it cannot acknowledge the remainder of the Real and the subject is 'not an effect of interpellation, of the recognition in an ideological call; it rather stands for the very gesture of calling into question the identity conferred on me by way of interpellation' (TN 254n39). Every subject is hysteric in that it questions the symbolic identity bestowed on it by interpellation.

As an interrogational 'gesture', the subject comes out of the intrinsic failure in the process of interpellation and does so with the kind of entangled twist that characterizes Hegel's absolute recoil.

SO xxiii–xxv, 43–4, 138–9; ME 59–62; AR 51–5, 62–5; CH 211–17; F 48–51; CA 75

Althusser 2001; Kaye 2023: 78–8; Pfaller 2016; Žižek 2000d, 2024i

CONNECTIONS: absolute recoil, big Other, hysteria/perversion, *jouissance*, Real

Antagonism

Antagonism is not used as a synonym for enmity or mere opposition. The use of the term is taken from Laclau and Mouffe's *Hegemony and Sociality Strategy* where it is defined as 'relations which reveal the limits of all objectivity. Society is constituted around these limits' (Laclau and Mouffe [1985] 2001: xiv). Although he comes to qualify the definition, Žižek remains faithful to this description, classifying antagonism under the Real as the cause of the perspectival distortion limiting objectivity, the gap whereby perspectives become partial and incommensurable (LTN 48). Absolute knowing's cognition of the limits to knowledge and the impossibility of any full self-identity comes about when antagonism is accepted as a given and not as an interruption to an otherwise full coherence. It is the name for an incoherence that is indissoluble and is the reason why concrete universality, far from being a fixed given, remains open to struggle and disputation. It cannot be otherwise when, as *Absolute Recoil* concludes in its final sentence, 'there is no peace even in the Void' (AR 415).

Antagonism can be understood as 'the minimal difference', a term used by Deleuze and by Badiou, and adopted by Žižek for the immanence of rupture in phenomena. As the parallax gap, the minimal difference is what differentiates something 'from *itself*, from its own *place* of inscription' (PV 36; OWB 64).

> **Antagonism is, at its most radical, not the opposition or incommensurability of the Two, but an effect or articulation of the inconsistency of the One, of its deferral with regard to itself.**
>
> **(LTN 771)**

As an ontological nodal point, antagonism has an impact on the key areas of sexual difference and class struggle. These two deep-seated precincts exhibit their limits to objectivity by remaining outside the scope of neutral apprehension, each irreducible to a symbolized binary opposition (man/woman, us/them). There is a crucial differential but underlying the demarcation rests the irreconcilable and non-dialectical, the pure difference inherent to the Real, preceding overt disparities in fields of the sexual and social. To entertain the notion of a buried or antecedent harmony is a fond chimera: 'Such a notion is a fetish since it disavows the antagonisms that traverse the very heart of actual life' (F 137).

The Hegelian dialectic does not bring about reconciliation between opposites because the *agon* dissolves the possibility of a shared space for a synthesis of opposing positions. It is 'the self-relating of the Two which lacks any Third' (LTN 303) so that, taking law and crime as an example, their dialectical opposition is only 'resolved' when crime is recognized as a symptom of the law. Similarly 'fundamentalism is a symptom of liberalism, Antigone is a symptom of Creon, etc.' (LTN 303). Be that as it may, the absence of an available harmony is not an excuse for inaction and a collapse of agency resulting in a resigned acceptance of the status quo. Recognition of disunion is a step on the way to dealing with the underlying problem, forgoing the deceptive lure of a middle way: the source of the strain between individualism and fundamentalism, to take a currently prevalent animus, is less a clash of world views and more the discord that informs capitalism's imperial expansion, 'the antagonism at the very heart of the capitalist individualist project' (LTN 303).

The Hegelian reconciliation that is attainable points to the acceptance of a antagonism residing within a situation. An obstacle cannot be simply integrated or eliminated but should be taken for what it is and acquiesced in on this basis. Žižek's analysis of Alfonso Quaron's miniseries *Disclaimer* (QH 286–91) illuminates this.

KNW 169; OWB 60–70; LTN 302–3, 377–8, 800–1; F 100, 137

CONNECTIONS: anti-Semitism, class struggle, concrete universality, dialectic, Marx, ontology, politics, Real, sexual difference

Antigone

> The problem with Antigone is not the suicidal purity of her death but – quite the opposite – that the monstrosity of her act is covered up by its aestheticization: the moment she is excluded from the community of humans, she turns into a sublime apparition evoking our sympathy by complaining about her plight.
>
> (A xv)

Sophocles's *Oedipus* may be the most famous of the extant ancient Greek tragedies but it is his *Antigone* that holds the fascination of Žižek who, besides citing it from the time of his doctoral thesis onwards, has written his own Brechtian-style dramatization of the play. His understanding of *Antigone* is informed by other readings that share his absorption in the story: Hegel, Hölderlin's translation, Kierkegaard, Heidegger, psychoanalytic approaches by Lacan and Alenka Zupančič, a feminist interpretation by Judith Butler and Frederic Jameson's political perspective.

Little is gained by endlessly arguing over how much responsibility or blame should be attributed to either Creon for prohibiting mourning rites for Polynices or to Antigone for refusing to obey the edict and paying for this with her life. The gulf between them is the 'division constitutive of power' (LTN 323) and the source of the enigma lies elsewhere. Kierkegaard imagined a modern version of the play where Antigone is driven to death by her sole knowledge of the truth about her father, Oedipus, marrying his own mother. Her sorrow, not knowing if Oedipus himself knew the truth, is an internalized agony and she only finds peace in death. This way of accounting for Antigone's plight is deemed insufficient by Žižek because it ignores her stubborn refusal to accept the authority of the Theban state. A way of formulating the importance of this goes back to the infant's demand for love as something impossible to fulfil. The question of what the (m)Other wants cannot be answered and desire is the result of the failure of the symbolic order to provide a key. Desire is a libidinal protest against what is missing, the lack that is constitutive of the subject.

Antigone becomes 'a pure agent of the death drive' by her unconditional demand for a symbolic ritual (LTN 84). She is compared with Sethe in Toni

Morrison's *Beloved* who follows the feminine logic by not allowing for any exception whereas Antigone is unrelentingly faithful to a '*masculine* fantasy' of some supreme principle (FA 145). This demarcation is nuanced over time by Žižek and her stance comes to be seen as an assertion of a feminine universality.

In Judith Butler's antithetic view, Antigone questions gender, transgresses kinship and the symbolic order and politicizes the family. She confronts the symbolic by refusing motherhood and embracing death rather than marry Haemon, her betrothed. She stands for a 'limit' which is 'the trace of an alternate legality that haunts the conscious, public sphere as its scandalous future' (Butler 2000: 40). Žižek has reservations about a politics which, placing its radicality in terms of redefining the borders of social exclusion, 'becomes an endless mocking parody and provocation, a gradual process of reidentification in which there are no final victories and ultimate demarcations' (WD 101). Butler's politicized reading does not take cognizance of the uncanny demarcation Antigone herself denotes, the step into an unconditional 'inhuman' mode of being that exists beyond the symbolic.

Lacan, in his lengthy discussion of the play in *The Ethics of Psychoanalysis*, associates this uncanny condition with *atē*, the destructive Zeus-sent madness that the Chorus describe as having struck the family of Oedipus (Sophocles 1998: 59–61). For Lacan, beyond *atē* 'one can only spend a brief period of time, and that's where Antigone wants to go' (1992: 323), a sentence Žižek quotes when the play is mentioned apropos a Stephen King novel about 'the return of the living dead' (LA 25). Antigone's decision to insist on funeral rites for her brother, an act of absolute freedom, 'locates her, as it were, in the *ex nihilo* of the interstices of reality' (DSS 176). It places her in a space where accommodation with the symbolic is temporarily suspended, outside a space which might be open to provocative displacements. Situating Antigone in this way does not allow for the challenges and displacements that Butler wants to attribute to her and Žižek's criticism of Butler is that she fails to recognize what is contradistinctive to her own reading (TS 263–4).

Antigone clearly stands in opposition to Creon whose prohibition on burying Polynices has the full force of law in the Theban polis but what is puzzling is her motive. In the play's opening scene she speaks of acting honourably by insisting on burying her brother but in a later exchange with the Chorus there is the astounding admission that she would not be so intransigent were it the corpse of her husband or her child that lay unattended and 'mouldering' (Sophocles 1998: 87). Her singular explanation – that she could always remarry and have another child – is hardly convincing and an audience is left with the image of a decomposing body and the conviction that Antigone's behaviour 'is penetrated by obscure libidinal investments and passions' (CA 332). This is the subject matter in Alenka Zupančič's *Let Them Rot* and it is taken up by

Žižek. Law as a universal and ethics as a universal set of principles are inversed and given a Hegelian twist. Expanding a characteristic aspect of Hölderlin's late poetry (ZP 93) – beginning a line with an abrupt 'But' without indicating what exactly is being qualified by the conjunction – Antigone's act acquires the force of a primordial ethical intent. Instead of qualifying a preceding ethical state, it punctuates a pre-ethical entropy by its announcement. It is endowed with political power because it decries a status quo, reducing it to the inorganic level of something rotten, and elevates an exception (not a husband or child, only a brother) as the ground for a feminine universality of 'not all because there are only exceptions' (ZP 334). This links with Lacan's axiom about not giving up on one's desire because to do so would mean mortgaging it for an ersatz plenitude, a compromise lacking authenticity. Desire is lack and the refusal of false ameliorations and, as Zupančič puts it in the final sentence of her book, it has a name: Antigone (2023: 89). Socio-symbolically and in line with Jameson's reading, *Antigone* is a play about the nature of the polis and the contentiousness intrinsic to its makeup.

SO 130–1, 242–3; FA 142–6; DSS 157–8, 162–8, 175–8; PV 397n30; LET 104–5; LTN 566–8, 576–9; AR 144–5, 377–8; A; SE 329–34; AP 62

Butler 2000: 98–101; Jameson 2010: 79–86, 92; Kierkegaard 1971: 151–62; Zupančič 2023

CONNECTIONS: antagonism, desire, drive, event/act, not-All/non-All, reflection, sexual difference

Anti-Semitism

> No wonder that a Palestinian who left Gaza City for the South and is now asked to move again, said: 'What we wish for now is to be killed, to avoid going through all this feeling of threat all the time and being in that distress.' Can one imagine the explosion of anti-Semitism to which such scenes that circulate all around the world will give birth?
>
> (ZP 85)

It is a characteristic of Žižek's writing that a term gains traction when linked with other lines of thought that have no immediate connection with it. Anti-Semitism, exhibited in public behaviour and institutional and state practices, shows this at work when it is tied to the unconscious side of ideology as well as class struggle, *jouissance*, desire and *objet petit a*.

The surprising statement that 'Eichmann himself didn't really have to hate the Jews' is explainable because, like canned laughter in a television comedy, anti-Semitic ideology is readily out there and individuals can make use of it without having to think about their subjective beliefs: Eichmann 'was able to be just an ordinary person. It's the objective ideological machinery that did the hating; the hatred was imported' (Žižek and Hanlon 2001: 6). The film about the commandant of Auschwitz and his wife, *The Zone of Interest*, is germane here; a film that Žižek has speculatively deployed in a highly interesting way (Copjec 2025).

The libidinal undercurrent is the need of desire to compensate for its irreducible lack and sense of loss by attaching itself to something, the *object petit a*, that can be imbued with a sublimity that will make whole what is self-divided. The anti-Semite's Jew becomes a sublime object of ideology by displacing open class struggle and giving body to the antagonism by proffering a fetishistic scapegoat. The anti-Semitic figure of the Jew 'gives body to the structural impossibility constitutive of the social order' (OB 83) and becomes responsible for the social friction, the foreign element which if removed would restore some illusory harmony (AR 381; L 74).

The conflict that is class struggle precedes the oppositional terms of Left and Right. The political terms stand for clashing ways of seeing the body politic and the difference is the impossible/Real that prevents them ever coalescing. The figure of the Jew is the third element, the supplement that stands for and materializes this pure difference (SFA 133). The element that does not fit, the Jew in this case, can be constructed in other forms, like the transgender person in sexual difference, and what they share is their displacement of a bigger struggle

What fuels this displacement is the disquiet that feeds off the possibility that someone else possesses a *jouissance* that ought to belong to oneself. The anti-Semite not only fastens this discontent onto the Jew as the one who has stolen their *jouissance* but in doing so it helps create their identity as the defender of a threat to what is not there in the first place: 'As we may say … what is a Nazi without a Jew? Hitler allegedly said: We have to kill the Jew within us' (D 183).

The anti-Semitic image of the Jew sustains the identity of Gentiles but a unique irony is the Zionist figure of the 'self-hating Jew' (D 183; DLC 6). In any criticism of the racist policies of Israel, defenders of its apartheid 'always find some metaphoric or metonymic link to anti-Semitism' (MW 180) and this includes the notion of the 'self-hating Jew'. The incongruity is an aspect of a contradiction that Žižek locates in the heart of Judaism; a tension within the tradition of Jehovah that can harbour extreme violence towards its neighbours but also concern with justice and responsibility towards others. Such unpredictability reaches an unlikely apotheosis when Nazism and Zionism colluded in a plan for

Jewish emigration to Palestine (I 49–50; CH 118). The plan never materialized but it revealed a bizarre confluence of interests: Germans wanted to have Jews removed from Europe and Zionists wanted them in Palestine to outnumber Arabs: a sharing of a kind of ethnic cleansing, 'that is, a violent change in the ratio of ethnic groups in the population' (I 50).

The role of anti-Semitism has a socio-historical context which is being displaced to some extent by the figure of the refugee and by Afropessimism's positing of blackness in relation to non-blackness as the 'part of no-part'. Žižek dispute this and point to Zionist anti-Semitism – singling out the Jew who does not identify with the racist state of Israel – as indicative of its enduring toxicity. Compounding the toxicity, reflected on in *The Courage of Hopelessness*, 'is that the Jewish people themselves will ultimately pay the price for the politics of ethnic fundamentalism that brings them uncannily close to anti-Semitic conservatism' (123).

SO 48–50; DSS 149–50; I 48–50; PV 254–9; LET 68–9, 135–6, 139–50; LTN 707; D 183; CH 116–23; MW 179–82; CA 11–14; AP 61–2; ZP 70–1, 83, 83–6, 104–7; QH 192–3

Žižek 2014f, 2023g

CONNECTIONS: antagonism, class struggle, desire, fantasy, ideology, race, sexual difference

Appearance and essence

Reflection as a name for thinking about something can be pictured as consonant with the action of light being thrown back from the surface of what is encountered. A dual process, Hegel explains, is at work: 'First, something immediate, something that is, and second, the same as mediated or posited' (1991: 176). Philosophy, he goes on, is traditionally not content with the immediate standing of things as appearance and this encourages the idea that appearance is 'a sort of rind or curtain behind which the essence is concealed' (176). Hegel does not accept a dichotomy like this and he claims that essence is not a self-contained quality that abides in things behind or beyond their appearance.

In Hegel's triadic account of reflection, positing reflection presupposes a positive something where nothing substantial is there to begin with. In determining reflection, the immediacy that being seems to possess is shown to be just a *seeming*. As summarized in *Less Than Nothing*, 'all there is is the flux of illusory being, of its passing determinations, and the nothingness beneath it' (379). This is then backed up by quoting characteristically less-than-pithy sentences about the dialectic of appearance and essence in *The Science of Logic*.

> These two moments, namely the nothingness, but as persisting [*Bestehen*], and the being, but as a moment, or the negativity in itself and the reflected immediacy, that constitute the moments of illusory being, are thus *moments of the essence itself*; what we have here is not an illusory show of being *in* essence, or an illusory show of essence *in* being; the illusory being in essence is not the illusory being of an other, but is *illusory being in itself, the illusory being of essence itself*. Illusory being is essence itself in the determinateness of being.
>
> (LTN 379, quoting Hegel 2010a: 397–8)

The three iterations of what essence is not ('an illusory show of being *in* essence, or an illusory show of essence *in* being … [or] the illusory being of an other') serve to emphasize that essence is appearance, reflecting within it the gap that is supposed to separate essence from appearance. Essence, responsible for the illusion of immediate being, does not exist as something transcendent. There is only negativity and, within the economy of movement that is reflection, the essence of something is only legible in the transient becoming from the void of quantum vacillations and the void that is the subject. There is no foundational essence and Hegel takes this as licence to baffle the unwary by declaring: 'In essence, therefore, the becoming, the reflective movement of essence, is the *movement from nothing to nothing and thereby back to itself*' (2010a: 346). Putting it like this accords with Hegel's account, a couple of pages later in *The Science of Logic*, of absolute recoil as a turning back to itself and essence being 'only as this turning back' (348).

The twists and turns of Hegel's sometimes fiendishly convoluted prose strive to express the interrelatedness of being's essence and its appearance. No absolute distinction can be made between them because appearance is the effectuation of essence, its process of becoming, and reflection as light being thrown back from the surface of something becomes for Hegel a 'shining within itself' and essence is this shining of being (1991: 175). Essence is not a hidden quality that can only reveal itself with an insufficiency due to distortions that appearance brings to bear: 'The very essence is nothing but this distortion of the appearance, this non-adequacy of the appearance to itself, its self-fissure' (KNW 58). The self-fissure is the negativity of substance that does not allow for a self-subsistent essence separate from its appearance; an ontological restlessness beyond measure. Hegel, in *Philosophy of Mind*, states this in terms of spirit as 'not an essence that is already complete before its appearing, keeping to itself behind the mountain of appearance, but truly actual only through the determinate forms of its necessary self-revelation' (2010b: 5).

Appearance and essence are inseparable in a manner that is similar to the self-generation of necessity from contingency. The starting point in both cases is a contingent multiplicity and in the way contingency comes to retrospectively posit its own necessity so too does essence arise in a movement of self-mediation: essence 'sublates its presuppositions into subordinate moments of its self-reproduction (Being is transubstantiated into Appearance)' (DLC 492n40).

Žižek, echoing Hegel's image of an internal shining, writes how appearance is 'not simply the domain of phenomena but also those magic moments in which the other, noumenal dimension momentarily appears in (or shines through) some empirical or contingent phenomenon' (UE 214). An instance provided (and in TS 86 and LTN 34) is Kant's celebration of the French Revolution as an inspiring source of hope, a spectacle proclaiming moral progress. What shines through is not the noumenal as Kant's in-itself but a moment of the negativity that generates self-sublation and the emergence of something new, an eternal idea of human freedom.

Less Than Nothing begins by considering the philosophical implications and possibilities in Hegel's collapse of appearance and essence into an internal dynamic of the mind and insubstantial matter. A striking example for Žižek of a noumenal absolute appearing as appearance is taken from a scene in Jorge Semprún's *The Long Voyage* when two children, fleeing from dogs set upon them by Nazis at Buchenwald, are united in death when the older one returns to take the hand of the younger child who has fallen behind: 'The blows of the clubs felled them and, together, they dropped, their faces to the ground, their hands clasped for all eternity' (166). Transposing the moment, hypothetically, to a screen affirms 'the pure surface of such fixed images of eternity, not any deeper Meaning' (LTN 30).

The truth of Plato is that Ideas are not a concealed reality behind appearance. The movement from nothing to nothing that Hegel refers to takes place within, as entailed by negativity, the nothingness of a pure gap in being itself. The movement means that the difference between essence and appearance lies within appearance – this is the Real – and the poetic truth in the boys and their clasped hands in Semprún's novel is a truth that shines through the surface of their gesture.

The interinvolving of appearance and essence is inseparable from the reflexivity that belongs to living entities, including humans, when they interact with their environment. The particular mode of interaction accounts for their role in composing parts of reality – 'I am not just myself in my flat presence' – and in a way that appearance, not some permanent essence, becomes a part of objective reality: 'If we try to grasp a thing as it "really is in itself", this thing itself disintegrates' (F 70).

TS 59; LTN 23–48, 235; AR 153–4; SFA 137–8

CONNECTIONS: absolute recoil, contingency and necessity, negativity, ontology, Plato, Real, reflection, spirit

Aristotle

> Aristotle oscillates between two notions of the relationship between form and matter; either form is conceived as a universal, a possibility of particular beings, and matter as the principal or agent of individualization … or matter is conceived as neutral-universal stuff, a possibility of different beings, and form as the agent of individualization … For Hegel, of course, the first notion is that of abstract universality (universality as a neutral form shared by many particular entities), while the second notion already contains the germ of concrete universality.
>
> (LTN 758)

Aristotle's delineation of Ideas/Forms, which he calls Universals, appeals to Hegel and wins his praise. Žižek is more circumspect and uses Aristotle to draw out what is distinctive about Hegelian thought.

Universals/Ideas/Forms for Aristotle do not exist, as do Plato's, in their own separate realm. They are instantiated in objects, existing not as imperfect copies but as self-referential actualizations of forms. Although the actualizations are independent substances, some accord can be found between Aristotle's forms as the self-directed movement of being and processes of active, self-adequation in Hegel. There is no doubting the approval by Hegel for Aristotle's 'principal moment' when drawing equivalency between thinking and what is thought (2006: 238). Hegel concludes his *Philosophy of Mind* with a lengthy quotation from Aristotle's *Metaphysics* and, immediately before he does so (2010b: 276–7), reason is described by Aristotle in a thoroughly Hegelian manner: 'And in apprehending its object thought thinks itself. For it too becomes an object for itself by its contact with, and thinking of, its object, so that the thought and its object are one and the same' (Aristotle 1998: 1072b (f) (i)).

While Hegel accepts a similarity between Aristotle's *energia* and his own concept of actuality (1991: 214–15), there is also a gulf in meaning within the resemblance. Hegel does not share Aristotle's sense of a logical structure to being and essences as core properties essential to an entity's identity. An Aristotelian approach like this is seen by Žižek to inform Spinoza's apprehension of *conatus* as well as the young Marx's treatment of alienation. When Marx determines alienation as a consequence of labour becoming external to a worker's 'intrinsic nature' (1844: 30), there is an essentialist assumption which Hegel does not share. Actuality for Hegel does not arise from presented givens but emerges through the structure of reflection in which thought and the objects of thought inhere.

Aristotle's *energia* as a development of the *dunamis* (potentiality) residing in entities but not actual, is open to reinterpretations that challenge the consensus frame of explanation. Michael Marder does this to undermine the frenzied capitalist mentality that formulates energy as an extractable asset while Žižek derails the *dunamis/energia* axis by attesting being's failure to be itself. The idea of potentialities reaching towards actualities and sometimes failing to do so is turned on its head: 'Being as such (in the sense of a determinate entity) signals a failure, everything that is (as a particular entity) is marked by a failure' (SE 228). An ontology of rupture like this contrasts with what resonates in Jane Bennett's notion of 'vibrant matter', a vitalism possessed of 'its immanent life force or its soul (in the precise Aristotelian sense of the active principle immanent to matter)' (AR 9).

OWB 34; LTN 261, 758; AR 7–10; SE 228

Longuenesse 2007: 111–13; Marder 2017: 5–15

CONNECTIONS: concrete universality, ontology, Plato, predestination, reflection

Aufhebung

See dialectic, negation of negation, speculative reason, substance as also subject

B

Badiou

Badiou and Žižek as close philosophical and political allies – 'we make up a politburo of two which decides who will be the first to shoot the other, after having wrung from him a deeply-felt self-criticism' (Badiou 2009: 563) – is evidenced throughout Žižek's work. From a single reference to the French philosopher in *For They Know What They Do*, by the time of *Less Than Nothing* Badiou's thinking is a persistent presence and it provides the coordinates for the reading of Plato in the latter book's first chapter. Areas of variance between Žižek and Badiou help clarify distinctive aspects about how they construct their philosophies.

In a section in *The Ticklish Subject*, where views from an essay of a year earlier (1998b) are developed, key ideas in Badiou and a locus of difference with them are set out with clarity. Badiou wants to keep subject and subjectivization separate, they are not concurrent with the death drive, and the subject emerges from the engaged act of deciding that produces the Truth-Event.

In an opposition between realism and transcendental idealism, Badiou wants to provide a materialist account for the emergence of an Event and the truth that comes from it. He perceives this endeavour as imperilled if there is an ontological impasse that prevents there being a subject with the necessary consistency to maintain fidelity to the truth of an event. He needs a subject able to break through the impasse and 'force' an event by extracting it from being's existing multiplicities. The subject is able to 'force' such an event because it possesses a 'capacity of indiscernment' that obliges 'the undecidable to exhibit itself as such' (Badiou 2007: 429), bringing into existence what is latent but unrecognized.

The difficulties in this approach are probed in *Less Than Nothing* and give rise to concerns over a Kantian-like stratum, a space between Badiou's mathematically articulated ontology and a presented world of appearances. There is no ultimate ground in Hegel's negativity, an imbalance is always there in the order of being, and Žižek wants this groundlessness to be the starting point. Badiou's way of accounting for a world of appearing comes with his notion of subtraction, a movement that brings about a rupture, a space within the multiplicities of being, so that an Event which is already there comes into maximum existence. Žižek sees this subtraction as 'a kind of "negativity" that has to be somehow operative in the midst of Being itself' (DLC 397). It operates dialectically, within an excess of 'Being over World (of presence over re-presentation)' (DLC 397), and by giving it a positive spin and doubts to arise about the place of inconsistency and truth in Badiou's thought: 'a potential tension between truth as fidelity to inconsistency and Truth as enforcing a project upon being' (LTN 815). Reservations about positioning the subject as constituting itself as a result of fidelity to an event continue in *Absolute Recoil*.

Truth is an eternal idea for Badiou that imposes itself on reality and it can survive political defeat. Ideas of justice survive their transformation into injustice: Stalinism did not destroy what October 1917 stood for and China's authoritarian capitalism does not invalidate the utopian aspirations of the Cultural Revolution. Badiou insists on this and regards it as incompatible with what is seen as the Hegelian belief that a failure of an Event is traceable to a deficiency in the notion that gives rise to it. Žižek qualifies this objection: Hegel's perception that a constraint in an Idea is inseparable from a failure to actualize it in reality still holds up when the failure is linked not to an inherent insolvency but to an inadequacy in remaining faithful to the Idea.

Differences in approach between Badiou and Žižek are reflected in how they each describe what is 'inhuman' about the subject. Badiou praises Kant for theorizing reason as not only having certain limits but also a capacity for the infinite 'an excess ... that is a capacity for the inhuman' (Badiou and Žižek 2009: 76). This is what allows the subject, rising above the level of a human animal, to become a subject and the bearer of a Truth-Event. Žižek is not naysaying this and he finds his own example of this in the figure of Che Guevara. All the revolutionary's failures – in Cuba's government, in the Congo and finally in Bolivia – recede into the background against which 'the contours of his properly over-human (or, why not, *inhuman*) figure appear' (DLC 433). Nonetheless, there is a variance in the way Žižek and Badiou construe the subject. Badiou's calling upon Kant is countered by Žižek own use of the philosopher, via his explication of a negative predicate in an infinite judgement, to position the subject differently. An equivalent to saying the soul is immortal would be to say someone is undead (think Stephen King), a peculiar state of being neither alive nor dead. A state that is *sui generis* in this way best describes the subject: 'non-human not in the sense of the animalistic, but rather as the excessive dimension of the human itself' (DLC 78). What distinguishes the subject from the human animal is the unconscious, the disturbance of the Real, the realm of negativity and the drive.

Badiou does not subscribe to this. 'Ultimately', he writes, 'life is the wager, made on a body that has entered into appearing ... keeping at a distance the conservative drive (the ill-named "life" instinct) as well as the mortifying drive (the death instinct). Life is what gets the better of the drives' (2009: 509). Fidelity to a Truth-Event is the ligature that binds the subject together but, from a Lacanian-Žižekian standpoint, the subject is an 'undead' state, a surfeit that transforms animal instincts into the circularity of drive. The potential for an Event to disrupt a prevailing hegemony is hampered when a system, that is, capitalism, thrives – psychoanalytically and economically – on oversufficiency, intuiting it as its engine (DLC 394).

> **The ultimate difference between Badiou and Lacan, therefore, concerns the relationship between the shattering encounter with the Real and the ensuing arduous work of transforming this explosion of negativity into a new order: for Badiou, this new order 'sublates' the exploding negativity into a new consistent truth; while for Lacan, every Truth displays the structure of a (symbolic) fiction, that is, it is unable to touch the Real.**
>
> **(KNW lxxxviii)**

KNW lxxxi–lxxxviii; TS 127–70; OWB 103–7; DLC 393–409, 407–9; FT 127–9; LTN 805–26; AR 72–7, 265

Homer 2016: 67–83; Homer 2017; Pluth 2016: 104–7; Žižek 2004d, 2007d

CONNECTIONS: drive, event/act, infinite judgement, subject, transcendental

Bartleby's 'I would prefer not to'

In a story, a Wall Street lawyer is perplexed when one of his employees declines to carry out his work as a clerk and gives no explanation other than repeating that 'I would prefer not to'. His words, in the short story 'Bartleby, the Scrivener: A Story of Wall Street' by Herman Melville, have been given various political capabilities though none are quite the same as Žižek's.

By not saying that he doesn't prefer to do something, the predicate (the 'doing') is not negated by Bartleby. What he does is to affirm a non-predicate ('not doing'), in the Hegelian sense of an infinite judgement, and this is taken as emblematic of a necessary political stance for effective change of a revolutionary kind. The sense, not immediately obvious, is akin to a point made in *The Year of Dreaming Dangerously* about not trying to resist Fate but changing it in a way that opens up new possibilities (YD 111). A chapter's title in that book, about the Occupy Wall Street protest in 2011, called 'The Violent Silence of a New Beginning', relates to Bartleby. His refusal can be judged a futile act of passive resistance but it is also configurable as a refusal to engage in a dialogue that will not critically change anything. This emphatic silence is not that of an abject victim but 'our "terror", ominous and threatening as it should be' (LTN 1006). Its insistency is a form of violence, an Act preparing the ground for an Event.

There are situations categorically demanding that something be done, climate change being the most obvious, but there are also situations where doing something may only strengthen the system that produces the problem that needs addressing. Political debates about urgent issues tend to be conducted within a frame of comprehension that belongs to those responsible for the urgency – 'any debate here and now necessarily remains a debate on the enemy's turf' (LTN 1006) – and the outcome is usually an assimilation of the discontent that, by absorbing it, prevents radical change.

Bartleby's 'I would prefer not to' is not part of a recipe for accelerationism, a hastening towards the 'end time'. History is not linear and it is impossible to know what direction it will take. Climate catastrophes are extremely probable but such likelihood is not taken as a warrant for eschatological thinking. The future remains open, despite appalling prospects, because decisions and consequences cannot be predicted. There is no big Other directing events and pseudo-purposeful activity becomes part of the problem: 'The difficulty of imagining the New is the difficulty of imagining Bartleby in power' (PV 382).

> **The threat today is not passivity, but pseudo-activity, the urge to 'be active', to 'participate', to mask the Nothingness of what goes on. People intervene all the time, 'do something', while academics participate in meaningless 'debates', and so on, and the truly difficult thing is to step back, to withdraw from all this. Those in power often prefer even a 'critical' participation, an exchange of whatever kind, to silence – just in order to engage us in a 'dialogue', to make sure our ominous passivity is broken.**
>
> **(TP 175)**

PV 381–5; LTN 1007; AP 23–8

Beverungen and Dunne 2007; Kotsko 2008: 123–5

CONNECTIONS: event/act, infinite judgement, politics

'The beautiful soul'

See politics, transcendental

Beckett, Samuel

See event/act, literary criticism, negation of negation, psychoanalysis, retroactivity

Benjamin, Walter

Theology for Benjamin is tied by an umbilical cord to history or, as in the apologue in his *Theses on the Philosophy of History/On the Concept of History*, by the strings of a hunchbacked dwarf controlling the movement of a chess-playing puppet. An equally indelible part of Žižek's philosophical signature is theology without religiosity.

He first sets out the value of Benjamin's coupling of theology and history in *The Most Sublime Hysteric* and *The Sublime Object of Ideology* and it remains a lasting one. Its presence can be felt in the way messianism, a unique feature of Benjamin's thought, bears some resemblance to the role of contingency and the space for insurrectionary politics. The messianic, as an interruption in what otherwise might be inferred as history's continuum, is not a transcendence for Benjamin. The historical materialist, he writes, 'recognises the sign of a messianic arrest of happening … a revolutionary chance in the fight for the oppressed past' (Benjamin 2005: 396). History as pregnant with the possible arrival of the Messiah (397) is a trope iterated in Žižek's philosophy because it offers the possibility of communism: 'The past is not self-enclosed: it is open, waiting for the future' (Mossman 2024); events of the past are not to be reified and an openness, aligned with the absence of the Last Judgement and of Aristotle's teleological trajectory, is the good news that Žižek welcomes. Transitions in temporal orientation, acts of trespass, become essential to emancipatory projects.

The notion of divine violence in Benjamin's essay *Towards the Critique of Violence* does not index the economy of violence to which we have become accustomed, neither the highly visible violence typified by terrorist outrages or the largely invisible but systemic violence of the prevailing economic order. It is divine not by relying on a religious fundamentalism but by its absolute breach with the order of the big Other. Divine violence is purifying, like Bartleby's 'I'd prefer not to' it is less a means to an end than an end in itself, and this distinctiveness is what Žižek finds valuable. Benjamin's definition – 'If mythic violence is law-positing, divine violence is law-annihilating; if the former establishes boundaries, the latter boundlessly annihilates them' (2021: 57) – fulfils itself when citizens of Rio de Janeiro came down from their favelas and looted the supermarkets where they cannot afford to shop. The 'divine' was their effrontery in challenging the law's protection of the divide between the rich and the poor. Žižek's other instance of the nature of this kind of violence is found in Robespierre's rationale for demanding the execution of Louis XVI and in the revolutionary's last speech before he was himself executed (V 171–2; DLC 207). Being neither inexplicable, mystical or idealistic, it can be as blunt and brutal as the Terror (DLC 161–2).

MSH 177–85; SO 151–62; V 151–73; LTN 129, 464; AR 95; SE 319–20; AP 11, 33–4

Benjamin 2021: 39–60; Cadava and Nadal-Melsio 2023: 125–43; Kotsko 2008: 74–6

CONNECTIONS: Aristotle, contingency and necessity, dialectical materialism, Marx, predestination, retroactivity

Big Other

The big Other as the intersubjective and symbolic domain facilitating and coordinating life in accordance with a network of norms and expectations is the sea we all swim in. Unavoidable, multifarious and inescapable, it can be fictionalized as a regulatory body that is omniscient, possessed of unquestionable power and penetration into our lives. From this perspective, God is the sovereign big Other and Christian atheism confronts its theological groundlessness when Christ, abandoned on the cross at Calvary, asks his father why he has been forsaken. The good communist, asking the same question of its political embodiment in Stalin's 'Marxism', shares with Christ a loss of faith in the horizon of meaning which purported to provide purpose and consistency. The Bolshevik Bukharin, a victim of Stalin's purge in 1936, did not renege on his commitment to the communist big Other when he wrote to his wife on the eve of his execution. Calling on her to situate his personal fate within the larger picture of the USSR's great Cause, she only came to read it after the USSR had imploded (CA 211).

The big Other has a multifunctioning, often veiled presence in everyday life and a breakdown in its authority is not as a matter of course something to be welcomed; being inescapable, dignified public standards preserved in it may be replaced by ones less beneficial for the general good; Trump's assault on the customs of political discourse is a glaringly obvious case that Žižek is not alone in highlighting. When the big Other as the substance of our symbolic universe is more extremely threatened, the consequence can be severe: 'Psychotic breakdown looms when this big Other begins to disintegrate' (P2 103). When public values are worthy and necessary ones, trust in the big Other is called for; 'without it, solidarity is not possible' (SE 317).

Varied aspects of the big Other's roles – from placating to policing – are deftly illustrated with reference to films: in *Brief Encounters* where, as the friend whose chatter saves the couple from facing an unpalatable truth, it stands as a psychological crutch; in *The Matrix*, as a metaphor for our passive acquiescence, the Matrix *is* the big Other. *Blade Runner 2049* raises questions about androids and whether a digital big Other could ever discern the difference between the Freudian unconscious and neuronal or social controls which we do not consciously register (2017h). In *Hegel in a Wired Brain*, the impact of accelerating digitization and the consequent need to distinguish a digital from a symbolic/virtual big Other is addressed as an important concern.

The purpose of 'There is no big Other', one of Lacan's signature axioms, is not to demolish the need for a collective symbolic texture permeating the conduct of life but to indicate that any such texture is ridden with an enduring inconsistency. It functions successfully as a virtual reality in so far as the barred subject, $, does not acknowledge the big Other to be equally barred and, instead, treats it as the master who knows everything. The virtual identity of this big Other has a potency that resides entirely in its *form*, not its content. Instancing the fourth series of the *Vikings* miniseries, the form of the big Other is shown to articulate a veracity about intersubjectivity that transcends its particular content (SE 187–90). The truth is the way that intersubjective communication cannot directly take place between two parties when each of them is divided between their experience of personhood and their identity within the symbolic order. A third party, outside this redoubling, has to come into play and this is the big Other as a form that is virtual. The form of polite friendship established an intersubjective relation that resides as an excess, over and above Ragnar the Viking's revenge plot or any disavowed love that he and Ecbert, the king of Wessex, might have for one another. The truth resides in the form, not its content, and the form is virtual because the big Other does not exist in any substantial way.

The big Other's inexistence outside the virtual entails its lack of bodily substantiality and consistency but it can become embodied as 'a mechanism that directly materializes our unacknowledged fantasies' (SE 190). By doing so, the big Other's truth as pure form gives way to a non-virtual materialization of a repressed content. This formulation is unpacked by way of its cinematic lineage, traced back to the influential 1956 movie *The Forbidden Planet*, reaching an apogee in Tarkovsky's *Solaris* but continuing with the Icelandic television series *Katla* (SE 190–7).

Separation from the big Other involves rejecting it as a guarantor of meaning and this is one way of calibrating absolute knowing. It is also what makes radical politics possible: 'the act proper: a symbolic intervention capable of undermining the big Other (the hegemonic social link), of re-arranging its coordinates' (LET 327). Undermining is not destruction but an act of annulment, a separation, an act of creative thinking as the condition for a new order. A visual demonstration of the big Other's nakedness can be precisely dated to the morning of 21 December 1989 when Ceauşescu addressed a large audience in Bucharest only to witness a spontaneous tumult that would lead to his execution four days later (ES 46–7).

> 'There is no big Other' means … I have to identify myself as the hole in the big Other, as the crack in its edifice.
>
> (F 281)

The challenge in taking up Lacan's axiom resides in combatting the big Other's resilience and its continuing efficacy despite shows of cynical disbelief in its existence. Disbelieving subjects can believe and trust in the big Other *through* other subjects' beliefs. The big Other is not weakened because what matters is how people behave; their activities presuppose the existence of a virtual register, whatever distance from it they think is being maintained, and the disavowal is part of what sustains its effectiveness as a social collectivity. Sometimes in news items about the economy ('the market's reaction has been cautious'), the big Other is objectivized as an In-itself that is simply there, one of those 'reified mechanisms' that shape people's lives and which we believe cannot be altered because the big Other disallows it (DLC 453–4).

In the world of quantum mechanics, the big Other can be conceptualized as the facilitator between the seemingly inexplicable network of wave oscillations and the collapse of superpositions into what is experienced as a stable reality. This translates, at a philosophical level, into a performative ontological act, an indirect version of a speech act, whereby quantum processes, unmoored from any big Other, are registered/observed as moments of normal reality. An equation of this order provokes 'the deepest mystery of quantum physics … in it we find processes which we thought are specific to the symbolic universe. Collapse thus takes place neither directly in the measuring machine nor in the conscious observer but in the "big Other" which guarantees the consistency of our ordinary reality' (QH 262).

DLC 34–6, 224–7; WD 96–7; L 8–12; LTN 90–6, 262–4, 336–7661–2; AR 20–1, 346–7; SFA 167–9; HWB 52, 72, 160–1

CONNECTIONS: absolute knowing, Christian atheism, event/act, subject, symbolic order

Blade Runner

Ridley Scott's *Blade Runner*, first released in 1982 but with subsequent versions that include a 'Director's Cut' (1992) and 'The Final Cut' (2007), is discussed in the opening pages of *Tarrying with the Negative*. Deckard, the investigator in the film whose job is to track down a group of rogue androids, is taken to be a replicant himself, an identity not made explicit in the film's 1992 version. This gives portent to the question put to Deckard by the character Rachael when she asks if he has himself taken the test that can determine a person's human or android status.

The replicants are bioengineered beings with artificial childhood memories implanted by the Tyrell corporation and these help convince them they are human. Unlike cases of amnesia afflicting a hero in classical *noir*, there can be no recovery from their predicament, no integration within a community defined by stable narratives. Reconciliation is precluded because the very basis of their self-identity is shattered as they come to realize they are not who they thought they were. The film endows their plight with existential pathos, most memorably in the final 'tears in the rain' scene, but Žižek dwells on a Kantian resonance in their situation.

Kant is quoted to show that the 'I' of apperception, as an interface between self-awareness and awareness of the firmament outside, is not accessible to itself as a positive thinking substance: 'It is known only through the thoughts which are its predicates, and of it, apart from them, we cannot have any concept whatsoever' (2007: 331). This lack of a substantial identity beyond 'the thoughts which are its predicates' equates the status of the subject with the replicants; there is a blank void behind the content of the subject's being, as there is behind the implanted memories of the replicants.

One might say that *Blade Runner* is a film about the emergence of class consciousness.

(TN 10)

The possibility of some emancipatory potential to such an equation only comes with the subject's assumption of its replicant-like status. Rachael, silently crying when Deckard reveals her android nature, undergoes an intense feeling of loss, wanting to be human but knowing she never can be and, it is argued, we ourselves are most human when we confront our intermediary status between being self-directed agents and replicants implanted with ideological 'memories'. This political angle to *Blade Runner* is made clear by Žižek when describing the film's social topology as one where Capital has 'succeeded in penetrating and dominating the very fantasy-kernel of our being' (TN 10). In this way, the replicants can be seen to represent the proletariat seemingly robbed of any residues of resistance and yet still retaining the possibility of revolt. This line of interpretation is continued in his critical reading of *Blade Runner 2049* (2017h).

TN 9–12, 15, 40–2; QH 186

Neil 2020; Žižek 1993b: 210–12

CONNECTIONS: Kant, subject

Buddhism

Žižek holds a long-standing and consistently drawn-out suspicion of spiritualized Oriental motifs like the Chinese concepts of yin and yang and belief systems like Buddhism. At their pop-cultural level, he finds the optimistic promise of a balanced/holistic approach to human suffering to be facile. Christian love, with its political expression in Che Guevara's ethics (KNWL xlvi), radically contests this with an intolerant privileging of compassion. Christ does not exchange his life for us but, through an disproportionate gesture of love, erases our sins unconditionally and breaks a soulless logic that demands remuneration and sacrifice. Buddhism, on the other hand, has a calculus whereby our past acts 'trail us like shadows, and sooner or later they catch up with us: we have to pay the price' (DSS 53).

Buddhism holds out the prospect of creating a distance towards and ultimate dispassion for objects of desire and the controlling ego. It holds, like psychoanalysis in this respect, the aim of acknowledging the empty nature of the self. The critique is that Buddhism ignores drive and desire's constitutive and disruptive surplus and the libidinal stipulation of the superego to enjoy. As an ineluctable compulsion thwarting homeostasis, drive persists even if the lure of objects of desire is recognized as an illusory pursuit. Nirvana, as a transcendent capacity free of suffering and egocentric desire, is branded a deceptive ideal when there can be no state of Edenic harmony, only 'a gap of impossibility that thwarts it from within' (CA 71). The impossibility referred to here is the force of negativity that contravenes the notion of being's fullness, making unattainable the kind of beatitude and inner peace that Theravada Buddhism seeks through meditation. Felicity as a place of interiority needs to contend with what solitary introspection yields for Hegel in the much quoted 'night of the world' passage, a contraction of the self devoid of a constituted reality. This abyss of negativity, a dismembering that is violent and destructive, is an unease that needs to be tarried with because it cannot be renounced, integrated or softened into a positive mutability.

Buddhism holds fondly to the Goldilocks principle and a fairy-tale economy positing a 'just-right' amount of desire: material pleasures are not to be renounced but measured out to serve the social good and maintain a proper balance with nature; mere sensual desires are insatiable whereas authentic desires look to collective well-being and a taming of excess. Admirable as this may be in principle, it ignores an immanent difficulty: the overflow that is constitutive of desire permeates even a simple physical longing with an 'obscene spiritual dimension' that cannot be moderately satisfied (AP 19). What makes it 'obscene' is a rampancy inhabiting desire that goes beyond physical gratification, a 'limitless expansion' (AP 19) that cannot be easily contained.

When a lack of a substantial positiveness in reality is affirmed, as in Zen Buddhism, this is seen to rest on the notion of an undialectical nothingness. In a highly abstruse context of subatomic particles, Buddhism is regarded as making a category mistake by confusing the ideal of nirvana with what physicists postulate as a pre-ontological time of nothingness. The missing but necessary dialectical aspect is explored in an idea, associated with the theoretical physicist Peter Higgs, about the nothingness of empty space having its own energy and how a particle without any mass entering this zone acquires the energy.

The philosophical status of enlightenment and its assured access to nirvana, is examined in *Sex and the Failed Absolute* through the lens of Husserl's *epoche*. This signature term for a practice Husserl describes as phenomenological reduction is a suspension, a bracketing or neutralizing of the acquired presuppositions that are brought into play when experiencing the world of phenomena. Husserl found likenesses between this practice and the transcendental view attained by the Buddha and Žižek finds this intriguing when combined with ideas from cognitive science that perform their own reduction by refiguring notions of a rich, substantial self to neuronal processes in the brain. Buddhist Enlightenment may be a liberatory means of shedding the Self and voracious desires but as a destitute expanse it may also close down the capacity for compassion and empathy. In a parallel criticism, neurobiology does not eradicate ethical agency and a convenient sacrifice of personal responsibility to the demands of an anonymous fate; something that is seen to be objectionably demonstrated in Ted Hughes (PV 203–4; E 74–5; AR 318).

The Zen position of selfless awareness can become 'a perverse desubjectivization' (SFA 91), facilitating as it did a mindset of rigid submission to duty and bellicosity in Japan in the years before and during the Second World War. Nor did the attractions of inner peace and contentment prevent Zen intellectuals at the time from endorsing Japan's militarism. Then, after the war, a similar mentality helped fuel the country's rush to capitalist industrialization. In the 1990s in Bhutan, where Buddhism is a self-declared way of life, there were no qualms over forcibly expelling the country's ethnic minority in the 1990s. A particularly scathing criticism is reserved for a popular strain of fascination with Buddhism in the West, branded by Žižek as a fetish, serving as a prop for willing participation in capitalism while ensuring a clear conscience: 'What really matters to you is the peace of the inner Self to which you know you can always withdraw' (OB 15; D 176).

What is not held to be reprehensible is an authentic affinity between Husserl's phenomenological reduction and a Buddhist-inflected stance of experiencing the flux of reality 'as a dream, a totally de-substantialized flow of fragile and ephemeral appearances, to which I am not an engaged agent but a stunned, passive observer observing my own dream' (LTN 139). This engages at a metaphysical level with shifting modulations between the substance and semblance of being and non-being and the Self as a false screen projecting a perception of reality as coherently and objectively there on the outside of the observer. Responsive as Žižek is to what is interesting in Buddhism and the differences between its Hinayana, Mahayana and Theravada versions, he remains resolutely averse to a belief system that looks to overcoming desire and the enigma of the Other and ourselves. Buddhism is judged as failing when it comes to facing up to and lingering with the dissipative power of self-relational negativity (Hegel 2018: §32).

> **What this means is not that what Buddhists describe as nirvana or dharma is an illusion or a fake; it is a profound experience of subjective destitution, but it nonetheless functions as the obfuscation of a more radical experience of a gap out of which our reality appears.**
>
> **(CA 71–2)**

KNW xliii–xlviii; DSS 52–4; OB 12–15; PD 20–33; LET 99; LTN 108–11, 129–32, 304, 944–7; AR 295–9; E 55–6, 65–75; SFA 87–94; CA 55–76, 84–5; AP 18–20; QH 255–60

Žižek 2024f, 2024l

CONNECTIONS: desire, drive, negativity, 'night of the world', psychoanalysis

C

Capitalism

The devastating power and pull of our socio-economic order is so determining that when the USSR set out to create an emancipatory alternative it strove to emulate capitalism's unceasing urge to increase production, thereby paying homage to the system it sought to replace. The parasitism is traced back to Marx's mistaken belief that a new socio-economic order could reorient capitalism's expanding spiral of productivity by eliminating its contradictions: 'capitalism without capitalism' as Žižek put it at a conference (2025g). What Marx's aspiration did not take into account is how the difficulties impeding an unrestrained reproduction of capital provide a necessary thrust for it to continue on a path of increased production.

> **Capitalism is in fact not like other modes of production which fall into crisis when they encounter their limitation: the limitation of capitalism is the ground of its strength, since the more it is in 'crisis', the more it mobilizes its dynamic to get over it.**
>
> **(IV 190–1)**

There is a parallel between the self-propelled movement of capital and the self-generating movement of the Hegelian dialectic. Within each of them, something symptomatic of their restlessness and discordance becomes essential to their functioning. Extractive capitalism feeds off desiring subjects, like the machines in *The Matrix* harvesting humans' bioelectric power, with the allure of constant consumerism. The flow of commodities serves not only material needs but satisfies something that is surplus, an elusive X, the siren song of *objet petit a* that holds out the promise of filling the psychical lack that is constitutive of being-human. Compulsive consumption, keeping consumers compliant without overt displays of power, generates surplus enjoyment. Just as the Matrix feeds off the constant supply of the *jouissance* of those lying in pods silently enjoying their passive entrapment, capitalism needs what it gains through exploitation.

The instating of consumerism with humans' endemic lack fuels the flow of profit-making capital, exhibiting a frenzied dynamic that *is* capitalism, and a diagnosis points to a cure: 'Every object of desire and every commodity will fail. Capitalism thrives on this failure ... Only the turn from the logic of the lost status of the object – can move us beyond the crisis of capitalism' (McGowan 2016a: 242). Žižek concurs and a section in *Hegel in a Wired Brain* considers the psychic dimension of Capital's rule through its mobilization of the promise that a libidinal surplus awaits when the elusive object of desire is finally reached. Any anti-capitalist programme has to reconcile itself with the compulsion to defer gratification that makes a virtue of sacrifice – 'in capitalism, hedonism and asceticism coincide' (HWB 155) – and shoulder renunciation 'with no teleological justification in future satisfaction' (HWB 156). Lacan's linking of the Marxist notion of surplus-value with surplus enjoyment endorses the need to resist 'the capitalist superego pressure' of acquisitiveness (QH 303).

Capital as a form of the Real has a felt bearing on people's lives but is masked by attaining an exceptional level of abstraction that disguises its systemic violence. Contemporary finance, encapsulated by gambling on the movement of prices, 'the "solipsistic" speculative dance of capital' (F 131), can affect the lives of people and communities in ways that are less visible and personal than the violence experienced in pre-capitalist societies. When capital is personalized it arrives in economic news announcing how 'the market' reacts to events, as if it had a corporeal, non-politicized identity of its own. Any such bodily existence is eerie in nature – Žižek's term is 'spectrality' (DLC 301) – and its impersonal, fixated logic is seen as a manifestation of an endless, libidinally fuelled chase for profit with no motive other than not to stop.

Expanding the flow of self-producing capital depends on increasing the flow of commodities, now facilitated by 24/7 digital technologies and hyperactivity cultivated as the normal pace of life. The arrhythmia that Anna Kornbluh dissects as a loss of mediation in cultural forms, registered in the title of her book *Immediacy or, The Style of Too Late Capitalism*, is scored by Žižek's call to curtail the incessant pursuit for change and resist the obverse it induces, apathy. Curtailment entails control over the frenzied kinesis driving constant change and increased production, recognizing consumerism and the debt cycle it engenders as apparatus for maintaining varying degrees of people's gentrified submission Commodification itself is changing, it is noted, enlarging its scope to the experiential whereby a material product, like a wellness session or a course on meditation, turns into a purchasable ersatz item for something that is immaterial.

Žižek, in agreement with Yanis Varoufakis, regards digital neo-feudalism as symptomatic of a new stage in capitalism; a form of the privatization of the commons (though not at the same level as English laws in the eighteenth century legitimizing the enclosure of land to which small farmers traditionally had rights of access). Big tech companies do not own the internet complex but, by being in a position to charge rent to smaller enterprises for their business within parts of it, become feudal lords, capitalists of the cloud. This is noted in *The Courage of Hopelessness*, a book whose premise is the worldwide triumph of capitalism and its structural reliance on contemporary forms of pre-feudal slavery. It has done away with social repression, scoffs at master narratives and embraces multiculturalism, self-fashioning, transgression and liberal anti-capitalism as grist to its profit-driven mill. A new definition of capitalism is necessary for new modes of exploitation, including 'digital clouds' with self-learning algorithms (CA 202), financialization and forms of 'anarcho-capitalism' (TL 31–2; F 167–84).

The behemoth under whose hegemony we live and cannot easily escape – 'modernism is ultimately its code name' (2024b) – might be taken to endorse the argument that capitalism accords with human nature and is therefore ineradicable. This thesis could be supported by figuring capital as the unsurpassable 'concrete universality' of our times (DLC 181; OWB 185), its economic model founded on human weakness and susceptibility. At a historical level this is undoubtedly true – our era is witness to capitalism's success in dominating alternative economic structures and infiltrating noneconomic forms of living – but Žižek's response is to insist on historicity as a dialectic that includes the ahistorical, in this case aspects of human nature, embedded in historical change. Under the genus of human nature there is more than one species and this includes resistance, rebellion, subtraction and the possibility of transformation. Any such possibility has to contend with and answer the ontology that is peculiar to capitalism, one that feeds off worlds of meaning by accommodating itself to any cultural or religious constellation. Capitalism overcomes its own limits by absorbing oppositional positions that purport to offer an alternative: 'The enemy has now taken over the revolutionary dynamic', condemning to failure policies of 'subverting the Order … since the Order now entails its own permanent subversion' (FT 128). This is the obstacle for effective political dissent and for Žižek communism is the name for facing up to the task of dealing with the despirtualized universe that is capitalism. Calls for economic degrowth as a necessary response to ecocide are necessary but, paradoxically, are not achievable without a form of centralized control. Equally cardinal, ecosocialist degrowth has to face up to the excess that is a constitutive part of human desire and not seek solace in prelapsarian hopes of a stable ecology that could serve as the bedrock of a natural economy.

Žižek makes a point in his introduction to Michael Marder's *Pyropolitics* that always pointing to and blaming capitalism for the multifaceted antagonisms and omnicrises besetting our world has the drawback of simplistically making the economy the sole, undiluted culprit. The complexities calling for our attention – 'ecological crisis, economic imbalances, wars, chaotic migrations, the threat of AI, disintegration of society' (Žižek 2025d: 14) – are better analysed when seen through a prism for which the word capitalism serves as shorthand.

PV 55–61; FT 125–31; OB 18–21; OWB 185–6; DLC 300–3; LET 188; LTN 244–5 (and D 47), 496–7; IV 190–6, 260–3; CH 3–44; HWB 147–60; SE 241–2; F 131–2, 140–4, 167–70, 199–200; WL 134–5; ZP 46–7; AP 13–21; QH 150–4

Kornbluh 2023; McGowan 2016a; Varoufakis 2024

CONNECTIONS: communism, concrete universality, drive, politics, Real

Christian atheism

Žižek distinguishes Christianity as an emancipatory Event that breaks with Jewish and Islamic monotheism. He redescribes Christianity as a decentring of an existing One-God, separating God-the-Father from Christ. His theological beginning is the Fall, the descent into sin occasioned by the transgression in the Garden of Eden and the redemption that consequently comes with Christ's crucifixion. The Incarnation is the response to Eve and Adam's error but the causal nexus is scuttled by situating the Fall and Redemption as identical moments, making the expulsion from Eden an entrance into freedom.

The price to be paid for the loss of Eden is a dislocation, a tearing apart from what was is taken to be nature's unity, but this negative can itself be negated, sublated in a dialectical process. What this does is to make Eden's substantial positivity a presupposition, the retrospective formation of a loss that never was: it is 'the Fall itself which creates the dimension from which it is the Fall' (AR 129). A shift of perspective allows the loss to be lost, a shift not dissimilar to how it is only by Eve and Adam coming to regard themselves in a different way that allows their mortality, their nakedness and their mutuality to be registered (QH 76). In the registration, Eve and Adam accept the Fall and in their reconciliation with themselves the Fall performs the positive role of sustaining the state from which they are supposed to have fallen. They show the retroactivity that pertains to a state of freedom: 'It is not a free act which, out of nowhere, starts a new causal link, but a retrospective act of endorsing which link/sequence of necessities will determine me' (DLC 314).

The Fall becomes their redemption because the wound suffered by their disobedience is healed by their change of perspective. In the afterword to a book about his theology (Koltaj 2019: 165), Žižek explains the dialectic at work here and quotes from the finale of *Parsifal* about the wound being healed only by the spear that smote it. The Mozart reference has been made before, it is the title of a section of *Tarrying with the Negative,* and in that book's own afterword its resonance with a shamanistic-sounding statement of Hegel's – 'The wounds of the spirit heal and leaves no scars behind' (2018: §669) – is reaffirmed.

What begins in Eden ends on Calvary. The sundering of Eve and Adam from the idyll God created for them finds a redoubling in Christ's existential call, 'My God, my God, why have you abandoned me' (Matt. 27.46; Mk. 15.34). The expulsion from Eden created a split between God and humans and the cry on Calvary creates a split within God himself. G. K. Chesterton's recognition of this is quoted: 'Let the atheists themselves choose a god. They will find only one divinity who ever uttered their isolation' (PD 14; MC 48). In his subjective destitution – a term of Lacan's for the abandonment of 'the fundamental fantasy which sustains our ego' (Žižek 2024l: 14) – Christ becomes human and his anguished acknowledgement of solitude and self-disbelief amounts to the separation of God from himself: 'Only in Christianity does God not believe in himself' (Žižek 2009c: 49). In Hegelian fashion, the subject suffers complete estrangement from the substance of its being and realizes that substance is also alienated from itself. That there is no relationship between God and humans is a negative that takes positive form in the figure of Christ and 'the gap that separates man from God is asserted as immanent to god' (SE 251). God is divorced from himself and what dies on the Cross is the figure of a transcendent God and the fond belief that the big Other exists in him.

Christ's failure to connect with his Father is an epistemological obstacle that is also ontological in its nature. A theology where god is divided from itself, is a necessary step in exploding the notion of a universe that, at a meta-comprehensive level, is whole. A self-detonation of God from within his own nature is more effective than a crude, blunt atheism that attacks it from the outside.

What is born as the Holy Spirit is a collective of Christian believers, an entity enshrining fidelity to something beyond the utilitarian and existing materially as such through the combined activities of individuals. Eve and Adam leave Eden and encounter freedom, as do all humans when, after the death of God on the Cross, there is no longer any support in an onto-theological big Other. Bereft of this support, nonetheless, 'the creative act grounded in this harsh freedom is the Holy Ghost, the first figure of what, among other names, later was known as the Communist Party' (CA 264).

If the dead god were to morph directly into the Holy Ghost, then we would still have the symbolic big Other. But the monstrosity of Christ, this contingent singularity interceding between God and man, is proof that the Holy Ghost is not the big Other surviving as the spirit of the community after the death of the substantial God, but a collective link of love without any support in the big Other.

(LTN 232)

The liberatory potential of Christianity is fulfilled when the resurrection of Christ is represented as the collective spirit that survives the death of the body. 'Where two or three are gathered in my name, I will be there' (Matt. 18.20): the message in Christ's words to his disciples is not seen as either an affirmation of the Holy Spirit's presence within the Trinity or, in humanist parlance, as a monstration of the eternal human spirit. Žižek finds its political incarnation in the folk song 'Joe Hill', the immortal factor being not the reifying of some sense of a lost paradise but the solidarity within a community of believers that obstinately and actively defies circumstances working against it. What is being evoked here is not the blind faith of dogmatism but the intertie of theory and practice that brings something about through believers' commitment to a Cause. The Holy Spirit's position is a feminine one in Lacan's sense of the feminine as a demarcation in sexual difference for the non-All: non-hierarchical, non-omniscient and resistant to being totalized.

Non-theists may think that this Christian atheism – or 'atheist Christianity' as Žižek prefers to designate it at one point (SE 360n61) – is highly novel and pleasingly provocative but ultimately unnecessary when a materialist denial of God should suffice. Žižek himself poses this question – 'is it even worth spending time on religion, flogging a dead horse?' (2009c: 240; LTN 115) – and answers it by asserting the enduring worth of Christian atheism as the foundation for effective material change: 'The atheist subject engages itself in a (political, artistic, etc.) project, "believes" in it, without any guarantee' (LTN 116). It is more effective to disarm religion by undermining it from within, drawing out its atheist value to remove the notion of divinity.

It is not, à la negative theology, that God is ineffable and cannot be positively categorized but 'that the experience of the divine is, at its most elementary, a negative experience' (IV 286) and only on this basis can a materialist ethics develop. Crucial to the Christian legacy is its declaration that radical, uncompromising change is within our grasp, not by humanist calls to discover our true Self but by a reboot and a reinventing of what it means to have a Self, 'in short, *to change Eternity itself (what we "always-already are")*' (OB 148).

> Our claim is that when we will discover new aspects of reality up to alien lives, we will not cross the boundary of impossibility that constitutes our reality. We will not discover God or anything of this order ... What appears as 'God' is a reified/substantialized form of the gap/crack that makes our realities not-all. There is nothing beyond this gap, every figure of 'beyond' is already an obfuscation of the gap.
>
> (CA 51)

OB 145–9; LTN 85–6, 101–4, 112–19, 232–3; AR 125–32, 221–2; SE 250–6;
    F; 55–9, 76–7; CA 42–6; QH 392–3

Bosteels 2013; Chiesa and Johnston 2025; Hamza 2022: 180–6; Koltaj
    2019: 165–9; Mitralexis and Skliris 2019; Restuccia 2025; Žižek 2003a,
    [1989] 2008, 2009c, 2009d, 2010d, 2012b, 2021e, 2024l

CONNECTIONS: Buddhism, event/act, negation of negation, spirit, substance
    as also subject

Cinema

**The mystery is that even if we know that it's only staged, that it's a fiction, it
still fascinates us. That's the fundamental magic of film. You witness a certain
seductive scene, then you are shown that it's just a fake, stage machinery
behind, but you are still fascinated by it. Illusion persists. There is something
real in the illusion, more real than in the reality behind it.**

(PG)

Film citations and explications of theoretical ideas with reference to cinema
constitute an abundant and enduring element in Žižek's corpus up to and
including *Quantum History (321–33)*. While only two of his books directly
address a particular director – *The Art of the Ridiculous Sublime: On David
Lynch's Lost Highway* (and only then for some of its mere fifty pages) and *The
Fright of Real Tears: Krzysztof Kieślowski between Theory and Post-Theory* – a
broader cinematic landscape is traversed in *The Pervert's Guide to the Cinema*
and *The Pervert's Guide to Ideology*, two films scripted and hosted by Žižek and
directed by Sophie Fiennes. The last sentence of the first of these two films gives
expression to the importance he attaches to cinema: 'If you are looking for what
is in reality more real than reality itself, look into the cinematic fiction' (PC).

A book published in 2018 consisted of various jokes by Žižek in his books;
with a joke on each page, it comes to 168 pages. An attempt to do something
similar using his comments about individual movies would result in an unwieldy
tome of far more pages. *Looking Awry* (1991) restricting itself to just Lacanian
ideas mustered some seventy-five films in its project, and in his many books
since then it is customary to come across a film he has not previously mentioned.

The range of films highlighted is matched, to take just a few instances, by the
diversity of important reasons for looking at particular ones: an ethical act in Mark
Mylod's *The Menu* (CA 218–19) and Delmar Daves's *3:10 to Yuma* (PV 129–30),
as opposed to James Mangold's 2007 remake (LET 64–6), and the intrinsic nature

of an act in Rossellini's *Stromboli* (ES 48–53); a psychoanalytic insight in the self-beating scene in *Fight Club* (OWB 173–4; RG 250–2); a political observation with the ending of *Fight Club* (TL 81–3; F 185–6); our destitute plight under capitalism and the refusal to abnegate in *Gravity* (AR 353–6); ideology masquerading as the non-ideological in *Waltz with Bashir* (LET 58); the betrayal of October 1917 in *Burned by the Sun* (PF 74–5); subjective destitution in *Joker* (SE 322–9, 342–3); the big Other in *The Matrix* (SFA 71–2) and ontological incompletion in the same film (ES 242–8, 256–9); *objet petit a* in *Perfume* (LTN 654–5); fantasy in *Eyes Wide Open* (FRT 174–5); ideological mythology in *The Man Who Shot Liberty Valence* (CA 130–1); political violence in *The Company You Keep* (TP 209–12); law and revolution in the *Dark Knight* trilogy (Žižek 2015b: 232–43); Christian atheism in *The Rapture* (CA 46–8, 2024l: 10–11); trans denial in *Conclave* (QH 285–6).

The focus of attention may be an individual shot or moment in a scene, a genre or a film technique. The use of deep focus by Orson Welles is singled out for the way it alters the conventional placement of a character within a given visual field, exaggerating their presence through close-ups and creating for them a trancelike, 'expressionistic' background. This, by occasioning incompatible interpretations of Welles, becomes eloquent testimony to cinema's ability to explore conflicting modes of subjectivity, abbreviated in a literary analogy as 'the move from Falstaff to Prince Hal' (IV 92). A scene in Alfonso Cuarón's *Roma* is selected to query its received status with reviewers as a humanist masterpiece. The filming departs from the typically fast-paced treatment of such episodes. Using a wide long take, there are no cuts from subjective point-of-view shots of the children in the sea to ones of Cleo's efforts to save them and the resulting passivity of its depiction is taken as imparting 'Cleo's disentanglement from the pathetic role of a faithful servant ready to sacrifice herself' (LD 241).

Attention is often given to the cultural phenomenon known synecdochically as Hollywood. As an ideological dream factory, Hollywood's couple-based family narratives provide a reactionary frame for enjoyment that is surplus to the film's content, as in *Reds* where the 1917 October Revolution allows the lovers to find each other again. Steven Spielberg's movies and catastrophe films from sci-fi to *Titanic* provide other examples (as well as Chiaureli's *The Fall of Berlin* from the USSR). One of the three sections of Žižek's *Mad World* looks at Hollywood's falsely progressive movies, like *Nomadland* and *Avatar 2*, before comparing the authentic protagonist of *Tár* with the failure of Jeanne in Chantal Akerman's *Jeanne Dielman*. For 'the real Hollywood Left', Zach Snyder's *300* is extolled for the way its aesthetic form exhibits the qualities of self-discipline and sacrifice needed to combat hedonistic capitalism.

Though film references are legion, certain directors from Eisenstein and Chaplin onwards are esteemed for exploring cinema's ability to delve into and dramatize philosophical, psychoanalytic and socio-political topics. Hitchcock,

Tarkovsky and Lars von Trier, like Lynch and Kieślowski, tend to be returned to for the ways their films raise questions around illusion, reality, fantasy and how 'if something gets too traumatic, too violent, gets too, even too filled in with enjoyment, it shatters the coordinates of our reality: we have to fictionalise it' (PC). In an endeavour to pin down the peculiar impact of Hitchcock's films, certain motifs are traced that are not reducible to the diegetic content: a hand clinging to another person's hand, shadowy bodies that momentarily appear and disappear. Such moments are beheld as echoes of Lacan's term, *sinthome*, fixated moments of *jouissance* that signify nothing in themselves yet serve to inexplicably bind something of libidinal importance, in this case Hitchcock's creative imagination: they provide 'the substantial density of the cinematic texture' of his films. Another part of this density is the way gaze, central to key moments in *Vertigo*, serves to emphasize 'a place of impossible subjectivity' (ES 231); a quintessential instance, looked at in *The Pervert's Guide to the Cinema*, being the framed shot in *The Birds* of the burning Bodga Bay which then gives way, within it, to the subjectivized point-of-view shot of the birds themselves. Utilizing the camera to such uncanny effect becomes the signature of a director capable of entertaining and disturbing in equal measure. The underlying perturbations that his films examine cannot achieve closure and, adopting the way Frank Gehry's architecture strives to reconcile the irresolvable, Žižek imagines, with *Psycho* in mind, a Norman Bates motel. It would be a hybrid of the mother's Gothic edifice and with a flatly functional motel, 'a place of mediation' between extremes where there would be 'no need for Norman to kill his victims' (ES 242).

Žižek hails the cinema of Krzysztof Kieślowski for its scrutiny of the torsion between the Real and reality. Recalling the unreality of the psychiatrist in Shyamalan's *The Sixth Sense*, the actuality of the Judge in Kieślowski's *Red* is questionable, suggestive of the fictive dimension in what is taken as tangibly real: 'If we are to be able to endure our encounter with reality, some part of has to be "derealized", experienced as a spectral apparition' (FRT 68). The spectral as that which sutures the gap, filling in what would otherwise be an unendurable confrontation with the void, plays its part in Kieślowski's decision to switch from the documentary form to the fictional. Using glycerine to simulate tears is preferable – 'I'm frightened of real tears' he says – and is unsure whether he has the right to film real ones (FRT 72).

Contingent pluralities, imperfect perspectives, the role of chance and alternative realities bear witness in Kieślowski's films to the Real of an intrinsically erratic world. His *Decalogue* television series is read for its wry and transformative interpretations of the Ten Commandments, with the first episode taken as a representation of a meaningless universe. An endearingly portrayed young boy drowns when the ice on a pond thaws unexpectedly; the melting of the ice and the dripping of wax from candles (knocked over by the despairing father in a church) onto to a painting of the Virgin Mary register the trauma that always threatens to intrude upon and break apart the normality that passes for everyday reality. Hitchcock's films, especially *The Birds* and *Psycho*, similarly show how reality begins to disintegrate when the symbolic order is not able to keep at bay undesired presences: 'The big question about *The Birds*, of course, is the stupid, obvious one, "Why do the birds attack?" It is not enough to say that the birds are part of the natural set-up of reality. It is rather as if a foreign dimension intrudes and literally tears apart reality' (PC).

Vitiating criticism that Žižek operates an extractive attitude to films, taking out scenes to support or explain a theoretical judgement and ignoring the medium as a form in its own right, is the enormous and ongoing impact he has made on film studies. He does not just enjoy cinema but finds enjoyment to be a factor at work in the appeal of many films, from asinine ones to those at the apogee of artfulness, from the heyday of silent movies to the latest AI-assisted/produced blockbuster. The pleasure is of a psychoanalytic kind – it includes the pleasure of not enjoying a film – crossing into the ideological and political, and approaching cinema in this way has brought a renewed and fresh lease of life to thinking about films.

ES; LA; DLC 52–77, 253–8; PC; LTN 515n18, 654; PI; AR 289–314; IV 89–93; MW 69–133; QH 182–3

Flisfeder 2012; Žižek 1993b, 2000d, 2003b, 2006c, 2009a, 2009e

CONNECTIONS: big Other, *Blade Runner*, Lynch, *The Matrix*, Real, spirit, *Vertigo*

Class struggle

Class struggle brings into view the disseverance that prevents society ever becoming an organic, integral whole. Antagonism, preventing a totalizing picture of society taking shape, precipitates attempts to suture the social rift and mask the cause of the division (KNW 100). That 'everything is political' needs to be read not as a polemical call but the recognition of class division as constitutive of society. Wokeness, identity politics, liberalism and far-right nationalism are means of obscuring this principal split, as is any postmodernist dismissal of class struggle as regression to an outmoded pattern of thought. Recalling Groucho Marx's 'Yes Please' when asked if he'd like tea or coffee, Žižek rejects fake alternatives and affirms the primacy of class struggle and 'the new world of dispersed multiple identities, of radical contingency, of an irreducible ludic plurality of struggles' (2000c: 90). Underlying this plurality is class struggle as primary: where postulated differences between left and right are necessarily enunciated from a leftist or rightist position.

Capitalism is the singular theatre where 'the antagonism proper to class societies appears at its purest' (IV 111), cutting through organicist concepts of society. Class struggle cannot be designated as a neutral sociological fact because such a designation pits a struggle between agonistic groups, each with a set of definable qualities. This ignores class struggle as the fault line which denies society the status of being a positive order of being. Class struggle, 'the point at which subjective engagement co-determines what appears as social reality' (LET 198), is the engagement with an assumed position of truth: 'The limit that separates the two opposed sides in the class struggle is thus not objective, not the limit separating two positive social groups, but ultimately *radically subjective*' (Žižek 1998a: 1003). It is a split across the social order that divides those who take up interpellation as the exploited, the proletariat, from those who decline, deny or cannot see it. The appeal is to a feminine, non-All universal open to everyone.

To avoid an essentialist approach associated with an old-school Marxism, strife between classes is not a locus for abbreviating other struggles to the epiphenomenal. Class struggle is not 'the last signifier giving meaning to all social phenomena' (SO 184) but the inherent limit that hinders any attempt to positively totalize the social structure. Other struggles – around feminism, ecology, racism and anti-colonialism – are not subsidiary ones but without relating them to class inequalities they risk becoming smokescreens for the very division that gives rise to them. An instance of this is how liberal compassion for refugees can camouflage the underlying cause of their plight, turning a political and economic issue into a moral and cultural one. What is obscured in the process is class struggle as a concrete universal – that which over-determines and redefines the field – and when this goes unnoticed the actual functioning of class struggle remains opaque. Mere observations of a class difference, divorced from the dynamic complexity of power and exploitation, can itself be a blueprint for concealing what is salient: 'Class difference can be the fetish which obfuscates class struggle' (CH 11).

> Typically, in today's critical and political discourse, the term 'worker' has disappeared from the vocabulary, substituted and/or obliterated by 'immigrants/ immigrant workers: Algerians in France, Turks in Germany, Mexicans in the USA'. This way, the class problematic of workers' exploitation is transformed into the multiculturalist problematic of the 'intolerance of the Otherness', etc., and the excessive investment of the multiculturalist liberals in protecting immigrants' ethnic rights clearly draws its energy from the 'repressed' class dimension.
>
> (Žižek 2017c: 167, 2017e: 192–3)

Class conflict as concrete universality applies itself when faced with oppositions that are distractions from the social order's primary and immanent division. A dichotomy like multiculturalism/fundamentalism or liberalism/populism occludes the magnitude of an emancipatory politics that goes against the grain of 'official' narratives. In another discourse, a quiet erasure of the underlying class factor is revealed in the way Adorno and Horkheimer's *Dialectic of Enlightenment* prioritizes instrumental reason as an all-inclusive and ahistorical explanation for human history. What is called 'classism' is not an opposition as such because it encloses class within identity politics and moors workers as a group to their own socio-cultural traditions. In this way, exemplified in the Oscar-winning movie *Nomadland*, class struggle is pacified and permits imagining the film's subtitle as 'enjoy being a nomadic proletarian!' (SE 159).

The Me Too movement graduates to a new level when, no longer marked as engaged in a gender war and preoccupied with male aggression, it strikes a chord with women in South Korea protesting in large numbers against their sexual mistreatment. The movement becomes radically effective when sexual and economic exploitation are linked: 'Men should not be portrayed only as potential rapists, they should be made aware that their violent domination over women is mediated by their experience of economic impotence' (Žižek 2020f).

The antagonism that gives primacy to class struggle is irreducible and puts paid to any Marxist teleology that envisions an inevitable march of history directed towards radiant communism. It does not follow, regardless, that class struggle can never make progress towards disestablishing the power of the ruling class. Antagonism as the pure difference robs society of symmetry and as the Real it renders subjective any engagement with social struggle. This is exactly what opens up the space for 'the revolutionary process of the dimension of subjectivity proper, of radical cuts of the real into the texture of "objective reality"' (CA 206). Social reality is self-alienated and there can be no utopian resolution that overcomes struggle between classes but change and transformation is equally immanent and *Christian Atheism* recalls with approval what the French revolutionary Saint-Just wrote in 1794: 'Those who make revolutions resemble a first navigator who has audacity alone as a guide' (CA 206).

Žižek, never reluctant to refine and scrutinize what seems clear-cut, twists class struggle into a reflexive formulation as a thrust to reductionism. Society lacks wholeness and a statement like 'this is all about class struggle' shrinks a complexity that demands proper analysis. It is too generalizing and serves as 'a fast pseudo-totalization when proper totalization fails; it is a desperate attempt to use antagonism itself as the principle of totalization' (Žižek 2024b). What is missing from false totalizations are other elements in class struggle that displace the raw confrontation between two classes. These elements, configurable within the terms of Hegelian identity and difference, emerge as an excess that spills over the supposed duality of there being just two classes. In social practice, this third element could be the Jew, the trans subject or what Hegel classifies as the 'rabble' (1975: 150), the immiserated victims of capitalism's calculus who are decidedly hostile to the rest of society. Class struggle, in abbreviated form, 'is precisely the struggle for hegemony, i.e., for the appropriation of these third elements' (AR 378).

DLC 294–5; LET 136, 204; LTN 269–70, 800–1; ADB 61; IV 244–8; CH 10–11; TL 127; CA 202–6, 220–33; AP 41–2

Žižek 2023i

CONNECTIONS: antagonism, capitalism, communism, concrete universality, identity and difference, politics, race, sexual difference, wokeness

Commodity fetishism

> In Marx's notion of fetishism the place of the fetishist inversion is not in what people think they are doing, but in their social activity itself: a typical bourgeois subject is, in terms of his conscious attitude, a utilitarian nominalist – it is in his social activity, in exchange on the market, that he acts *as if* commodities were not simple objects but objects endowed with special powers, full of theological whimsies.
>
> (PF 135)

The attention given to the notion of commodity fetishism in the first chapter of *The Sublime Object of Ideology* is prepared for in Žižek's doctoral thesis (1982), re-edited for publication in French in 2011 and three years later in English as *The Most Sublime Hysteric: Hegel with Lacan*. Basic to both texts' accounts of commodity fetishism is the importance of Marx's analysis in *Capital*, encapsulated in his often quoted sentence: 'A commodity seems, at first glance, like an obvious trivial thing. However, when we analyse it, we see that it is very intricate, full of metaphysical quibbles and theological quirks' (Marx 2024: 47).

An orthodox Marxist account is given in *The Most Sublime Hysteric* of how the value of a commodity derives from relationships between its producers and is expressed in the form of money. Workers, at a formal level, are free citizens engaging in contracts with other free citizens to sell their labour but in reality such contracts disguise unequal relationships of dominance and servitude. Inequalities that were not concealed in feudal economies are masked in capitalism as social relationships between things that can be compared and exchanged in the form of another commodity, money. Žižek diagnoses the masking as a symptom of a social disorder because of the way unequal relationships between people in the production of commodities are repressed in the guise of relationships between things. As with Tibetan prayer wheels, he notes, beliefs can be transferred from people to things.

In *The Sublime Object of Ideology*, money as a universal representing all commodities possesses as a part of its natural property a quasi-magical attribute. In one sense, individuals know this is illusory but in everyday activities the exchange of commodities is imbued with the quality of a fetish: 'They are fetishists in practice, not in theory' (SO 28). Although a fetish is created by the hands of humans, it is worshipped as an object with a non-material quality and knowing this this brings a new purport to how ideology works. Commodity fetishism does not operate within social reality as a mental act of misrecognition by attributing magical properties to what are material exchanges between people. On the contrary, people know that the materiality of commodities represents a share of a common wealth but in their behaviour, as if unbeknownst of this, act as if the commodity, as Marx puts it, has undergone a metamorphosis. The effects are 'a performance far more fantastic than if it were to start dancing of its own accord' (Marx 2024: 48). What people are not aware of is the illusion of the 'performance' that sustains outward behaviour. With the ubiquitous use of electronic money, Žižek notes, the material form that attached itself to money's magical quality is disappearing and commodity fetishism reaches its apogee and becomes purely virtual.

In *Less Than Nothing*, commodity fetishism is referenced to crystallize how people's self-understanding has undergone an epochal change with the historical movement from feudalism to capitalism. While it makes no sense to think of a serf in medieval Europe as a peasant by profession, a person today recognizes work, whatever choice made about their own employment, as an abstract universality. They 'no longer fully identify the kernel of their being with their particular social situation' (361). The change that has taken place is a paradigm shift but, as one accompanying a deep change in the economic order, it is neither ideologically driven or an illusion in the mind. Commodity fetishism is part of 'our social reality itself' (LET 190) and affects not just social relations but how nature is viewed 'as the domain of neutral facts opposed to our subjective values' (LET 218).

In *Hegel in a Wired Brain*, considering the idea of a direct link between mental processes and a digital machine, the idea is entertained of commodity fetishism being witnessed in a way that is not open to our conscious selves. A digital big Other would register our activity and observe how 'in contrast to my professed secular rationalism, I really believe in commodity fetishism, I act as if commodities are magical objects, etc' (143).

MSH 138–41; SO 18–22, 31–4; PF 134–5; DLC 295–300; LET 189–90; LTN 44, 246 (and IV 182–3), 360–1; LET 186n8, 190, 214–15, 222–3; D 125–6 (and 276–7)

Heinrich 2021: 143–5; Žižek 2006f, 2017f

CONNECTIONS: ideology

Communism

The reality of class struggle orientates Žižek's political philosophy towards communism and overcoming the domination of market economics. Notwithstanding, 'as communists we should abstain from any positive imagination of the future communist society' (LTN 22): its actual complexion cannot be specified due to the difficulty of thinking beyond capitalism but this does not weaken the 'ineradicable, absolutely authentic *Communist desire*' (F 202). A yearning for a return to a prelapsarian harmony, the recuperation of a mythical mother earth savaged by capitalism, cannot be entertained but what remains steadfast is a call for the excluded to be included, the full participation of the dispossessed and disadvantaged that make up what Rancière calls the 'part of no-part'. This term, finding favour with Žižek, relates to 'what has to remain invisible so that the visible may be visible' (FT 101), the subtracted element which, unlike those with a place and particular interest in a system, are excluded from it. As the remainder, the part with no part is paradoxically a 'true universality … the actual existence of which is a radical division which cuts through the entire particular content' (PD 109).

Communist desire is everlasting, 'a shadow which accompanies all previous history which is, as Marx and Engels wrote, the history of class struggle' (F 203). As such, it serves to explain an essential difference between Stalinist communism and Nazism. Following Badiou, what happened in October 1917 is for Žižek a 'truth event' whereas Nazism was a 'pseudo-event' (PF 74) and this is correlated with the contrast between the groundless deceits devised by the Soviet NKVD against innocent citizens and the Gestapo's rational pursuit of active dissenters. The original communist project needed to be erased out of guilt and shame while the Gestapo were carrying out their duties as officers of state security.

One can easily imagine a new variation of the well-known line from Monty Python's *The Life of Brian*: 'All right, but apart from the sanitation, the medicine, education, wine, public order, irrigation, roads, a fresh water system and public health, what have the Romans ever done for us? Nothing!' – 'All right, but apart from universal healthcare, social regulation of the economy, free education … what will such new Communism do for us? Nothing!'

(F 256)

The authenticity of communism comes from its analytic power and its desire for a better world and the current historical situation demands reactivating and reimagining it as a wellspring of hope. There is a quid pro quo for remaining loyal to communist desire and rescuing it from the archives of vanquished hopes. It involves recognizing it as less a concrete answer to unreformable capitalism and more as an avenue for interrogating it. Žižek insists, too, on an unflinching owning of the great betrayal of what this aspiration stood for. Pointing out that Soviet communism was not all bad or that capitalism is also at fault is to avoid acknowledging the scale of its infidelity to what Lenin hoped October 1917 would inaugurate. The disappointment is not that Lenin came to realize too late the danger that Stalin represented but the cost of the contradiction between what communism cherished and what it came to embody. It stands accused by the very standards it sought to enshrine – communist regimes created the space of libertarian hopes in which their failure can be measured – and a guilty verdict confirms a vulnerability in state communism that anarchism was able to predict. Authoritarianism is implicit in state power and the abuse and corruption of power is what the history of the USSR demonstrates. Corporate capitalism poses the same danger when tremendous power is concentrated in a small number of companies, especially when there is an individual at their head – a Zuckerberg or a Bezos – who will in due course come to be replaced by another person. The obverse of this is the anonymity of power whereby, taking the case of Switzerland, it can be asked whether anyone knows the name of its government ministers and ruling party (F 210).

Žižek likes to be challenging but he identifies himself as a communist less for the sake of provocation and more to stress the urgency of problems that need addressing at a political level. There is also a wish to respect those who struggled and suffered for what it represents. Not the narcissism of the lost cause, communism has become the only name for achieving social justice and collective action against ecological disaster and looming challenges in neuroscience and biogenetics. In *A Left That Dares Speak Its Name* (2020), a revised collection of writings on contemporary political topics, from economic instability, populism and consumerism to the Middle East and China, Žižek declares the collection's premise to be the need for a communist perspective (LD 1). The same need emanates from the COVID-19 epidemic (P 56, 66–8, 103–4) and it animates the opening pages of *Zero Point*.

Orthodox communism looked to the traditional Marxist vision of an economy breaking free of capitalism's destructive energy and releasing its productive forces for the common good by harnessing a continuous expansion of productivity, Capitalism's dynamic, its restless and relentless pursuit of the profit-making flow of capital, is bound up with the libidinal urge for *jouissance* and the surplus enjoyment that accrues from the failure to attain it. Any new kind of society needs to come to terms with this, accepting antagonism and negativity as transhistorical. Marx was not fully able to take on the severance that predates capitalism. Workers are alienated in a market economy ruled by free competition and the profit motive but this is not the same as the alienation that afflicts any subject governed by the symbolic order. This deeper kind of alienation is a 'primordial trauma, the trauma constitutive of the subject' (D 22) and, as a consequence, cannot be effaced by changing the economic order. Frederic Jameson is celebrated for bringing a Lacanian awareness to questions about what will not be resolved under communism and asserting how 'precisely insofar as it will be a more just society, envy and resentment will explode' (2016h: 286). It is not allowed to harbour any fond assumption that a post-capitalist society will bring an end to the self-alienation that unreasonably turns desire in upon itself, that pursues unhappiness and aberrantly finds pleasure in repression: 'What I try to develop', writes Žižek, 'is a vision of Communism compatible with all these horrors' (SE 224). It is a vision that must grapple with the constant possibility of failure: 'It is easy to enjoy the creative unrest of the years immediately following the October Revolution, with suprematists, futurists, constructivists, and so on, competing for primacy in revolutionary fervor; it is much more difficult to recognize in the horrors of the forced collectivization of the late 1920s an attempt to translate this revolutionary fervor into a new positive social order' (LTN 798).

Whatever problems might await a transition to a non-capitalist society, the difficulties are likely to be on the scale that Platonov explored in his fiction about building communism out of a dispersed proletariat in post-revolutionary Russia (LD 32–8). Not surprisingly then, the first step should be a *moderately conservative Communism*' (HD 125) and a full acknowledgement that current prospects for even this are, to put it charitably, unpromising: 'The lesson of twentieth-century communism is that we have to gather the strength to fully assume the hopelessness' (CH xi). Nonetheless, it remains possible to imagine an ethical substance operating within the symbolic order. Rules, obligations and norms which are unreflective are not naturally inimical to communist well-being when this 'thick invisible cobweb of regulations' sustains a space without rules and norms – 'In Communism, I should be led to "trust" this cobweb and *ignore it*, focusing on what makes my life meaningful' (SE 86, 2022b: 17).

There is a stress in Žižek's communism arising from the truth in anarchism and, at the same time, the need for a strong state. It is writ large in China's transformation after 1980 that lifted millions out of poverty, achieved by an authoritarian socialist state authorizing a capitalist feeding frenzy. Unfettered state power produced Nazi death camps and Soviet gulags but left-wing libertarianism can meet its frightening doppelgänger in far-right individualism. Communism is present when the state is looked to for providing public services, controlling the market and coping with global warming but there is no party privileged to guarantee a full enactment of these basic requirements for civilization. It depends on the will of those who act in their belief in communism and in this respect it is like Hegelian spirit.

Balancing a law-based universality above class struggle and party politics with a Leninist recognition that law and justice are never neutral notions is formally impossible but struggling to achieve the balance lies at the heart of communism. It has to contend with discontent over capitalism that the populist Right is currently making better use of than the Left and Badiou's remark about the *gilets jaunes* in France is fully endorsed: ' *"Tout ce qui bouge n'est rouge"* – all that moves (makes unrest) is not red' (HD 215). If communism does emerge as a stronger response to crises, thinks Žižek, it will be through an apocalyptic danger provoking a state of emergency (CA 232).

PF 73–6; DLC 261–3; FT 86–106; HD 212–21; SE 84–6, 96–8; F 157–8, 192–6, 201–12, 276–7; ZP 3–4

Flisfeder 2014; Jameson 2016; Žižek 2010b, 2013c, 2016e

CONNECTIONS: capitalism, ecology, event, Lenin, Marx, politics, spirit

Concrete universality

In philosophy, a universal proposition asserts that some particular is a member of a class, a universal, due to some shared quality with other particulars in its class. Particulars as diverse as a London bus, a poppy and a fire hydrant can be said to share a universal in respect of their redness. Hegel refers to this kind of universal, where existing particulars with shared features make the universal appear necessary, as 'abstract'. His contrastive 'concrete universality' realises itself through a historically determined content that is a contingent particular. This kind of universality is not holistic in nature but fissured, a process that never reaches an immutable conclusion, partly because it depends on the engaged subjectivity of those involved in creating this kind of universality. Žižek brings an importance to this 'concrete universality' that is not typically found in Hegelian scholarship.

The vocabulary of genus and species that Hegel utilizes when explaining his term is not like the familiar ranking in biology that classifies species under a genus. On the contrary, the genus becomes split within itself and is also to be found in the species. What arises is a crossbred alignment that imbues any universality with a dialectical constitution: 'True ("concrete") universality is nothing but this movement in the course of which a species engenders a subspecies which negates its own species' (LTN 364). This does not make sense if genus and species are taken zoologically but the concern is with explaining how something, including a concept, is not a given but a formation subject to change. Before a change occurs, a universal is licensed as transhistorical, eternal and enduring, and it requires a particular that does not readily fit into its existing hegemony to disrupt the order. The only all-enfolding universality is antagonism, 'the Real of a stumbling block, of the impossibility around which a society is structured' (IV 273), and this is what unsettles the genus from within and affects its species: 'The very function of every "normal" state (or species of a genus) is to repress or obfuscate or cope with the antagonism that pertains to this universality' (IV 261).

Examples of how a particular inflection can overdetermine and redefine the field, without sacrificing a universal standard, range from cinema, with Krzysztof Kieślowski's move from documentary to fiction (LTN 362–3), to contemporary racism. Different historical moments engender particulars that embody a field as a whole by their predominance, as did anti-Semitism in Nazi Germany and, more positively, in the United States today when saying Black Lives Matter stands as the only valid assertion of the universal human right that all lives matter (DS 41–2; Zalloua 2020: 146–52). Similarly, in respect of Israel and the Occupied Territories, saying that Palestinian Lives Matter is the only effective affirmation of the universal value of all lives. Given that '*the universal species exists only in exceptions*' (OWB 50), it is also to be seen, unexpectedly, in the case of the Jews and Israel. The country stakes its claim to be rooted by taking land inhabited by other people but what if the absence of roots 'is the primordial state of being-human, and our roots are a secondary phenomenon, an attempt to obfuscate our constitutive rootlessness?' (HWB 9). Concrete universality would allow Jews as the exception – as the people anti-Semites accuse of not having roots – to become universal.

Abstract universality is static, an arrangement of parts under a whole whereas with the concrete there is disruption and incompletion (Žižek 2009c: 49). The antagonism that fractures every identity accounts for a strain between a universal and a particular: 'The a priori of the universal form and the a posteriori of its content' are opposites (Žižek 2011c: 224). Interplay between the two is an ongoing dynamic that translates into the speculative and this helps explain the place in *Science of Logic* where concrete universality is delineated. The primary structure of Hegel's book is triadic: Doctrines of Being, Essence and Concept (Notion), overlaid by a division into Objective Logic and Subjective Logic, and concrete universality appears in the second chapter of the Doctrine of the Concept where it is part of Subjective Logic. Concrete universality is realized through the mind's power of abstraction subtracting from a plurality and creating a universal that it endows with life through the determination of a particular. How the universal comes to be through particularity – Hegelian 'individuality' or 'singularity' – is explained by Žižek in his reading (LTN 365–7) of the paragraphs that bring the first chapter of the Doctrine of the Concept to its conclusion. The mind's subtraction that allows for the emergence of a universal is equated by Žižek with the pure I, empty of all determinations, of the Cartesian *cogito*. The emptiness it faces is negativity and the I makes itself what it is by a subjective decision that actualizes a concrete universal through willed engagement. It is a moment of historical contingency that divests the subject from complete immersion in its socio-symbolic particulars, allowing it to occupy a groundless point from where universality becomes possible as its own actuality.

At the political level, a true universality emerges through class struggle and the identification of the proletariat with those 'who lack a determined place in the social totality, who are "out of place" in it and as such directly stand for the universal dimension' (LTN 831). Dialogue from Orwell's *1984*, where Winston Smith asks O'Brien, his interrogator, if Big Brother exists in the same way as the two of them do, is used to illustrate the volatile nature of universality. O'Brien's reply to Winston Smith – 'You do not exist' – emphatically asserts the insubstantial nature of any universal in its traditional ('abstract' for Hegel) sense of a quality shared by all species of a genus. True universality does not arise in this way but manifests itself in the antagonism that splits any particular identity. In capitalism, universality reveals its presence when the 'part of no-part', those who do not have a proper place in their world, becomes all those who recognize the failure of their perceived identity.

A development of concrete universality attends Mao Zedong's major departure from the industrial proletariat to the peasantry as the agent of revolutionary transformation. It is exemplarily a dialectical movement, registering not a paradigm shift but a return, in this case to Marxist praxis, which transforms the original without abolishing it. In the introduction to *Mao: On Practice and Contradiction*, where this point is made, capitalism itself is deemed a concrete universality. It should not be analysed as an abstract universal, with various common features that can be identified, but as a form within which particulars struggle to oppose its destructive force.

Concrete universality *unsettles the identity of the particular from within*; it is a line of division which is itself universal, running across the whole sphere of the particular, dividing it from itself. Abstract universality is uniting; concrete universality is dividing. Abstract universality is the peaceful foundation of particulars; concrete universality is the site of struggle – it brings the sword, not love.

(IV 273)

TS 90–2, 100–3; PD 64–5; OWB 50–1; PV 30–5, R: xxviii–xxix; M 1–28; DLC 179–81, 413; LTN 359–67, 468–9, 763; DI 130–3; AR 260–1; IV 239–40, 273–4; HWB 8–9; CA 89–90; QH 147–8

Hegel 2010a: 548–9, 578–81; Tupinambá 2019

CONNECTIONS: antagonism, class struggle, identity and difference, negativity, not-All/non-All, politics, race, speculative reason

Contingency and necessity

In the section on Actuality in Hegel's *The Science of Logic*, the relationship between contingency and necessity is elaborated with all the intricate discriminations that can make reading parts of Hegel so maddening. He employs possibility and actuality as central modalities and harnesses them to trace the convolutions at work in his account. Possibility in the abstract has unlimited capacity: something, anything not self-contradictory, could always be otherwise than what it is or not have been in the first place. When something is an actuality, it 'has *possibility* immediately *present in it*' (2010a: 482): various circumstances and conditions exist that make something what it is and what was possible becomes real and necessary. In *Tarrying with the Negative*, Žižek expresses this transfer of contingency into necessity as a conversion at a highly formal level of becoming into being.

The topic receives close attention in *Less Than Nothing* where the ontological unrest that is becoming, it is stressed, rules out any one-way directional line running from possibility to actuality (as Walter Benjamin rules it out for the passage between the historical past and present). The conditions that coalesce to turn a possibility into an actuality already exist at a formal, abstract level but this does not make the necessity that results any less aleatory in itself. 'Necessity', says Hegel, 'takes its *start* from the *contingent*' (2010a: 484). The opposite of his caricature as the tower block-building systematizer, Hegel is the architect of the open plan where what is actual emerges, self-determined, from a pandemonium of possibilities and is only subsequently locatable in a locked chain of necessity. Actuality is never always already there as a dormant essence, waiting like a chrysalis to be made manifest, but forms itself from open possibilities which retrospectively appear to be immanently required. Žižek quotes with approval Robert Pippin's reading of Proust's *À la Recherche* because it argues against the idea that there was some inner essence to Marcel that necessarily made him the writer he became (AR 193).

Kant's infinite judgement, employing a non-predicate (e.g. 'x is undead') in favour of a merely negative predicate ('x is not dead'), is applicable. Saying everything is contingent generates an exception when happenstance itself becomes a necessity (*everything* is contingent). This is in line with the masculine logic in Lacan's formulae of sexuation but opposing this is a feminine logic where there are no exceptions, as with the infinite judgement that contingency is not-All: 'From time to time, a contingent encounter occurs which undermines all the predominant necessity (the space of possibilities sustained by this necessity), so that in it, the "impossible" happens' (LTN 369) and an event takes place.

Žižek is in full agreement with Meillassoux as regards the way necessity arises out of contingency: the regularities that account for the laws of nature are necessary in the sense that they follow certain conditions that prevail now and for the foreseeable future and this leaves them appearing absolute and eternal. Nonetheless, they remain dependent on conditions that are unnecessary because they could, reliant as they are on past contingencies, be otherwise. Despite this, when they occur they become, for us, unchangeable (LTN 637): 'The acme of the dialectic of necessity and contingency arrives in the assertion of the contingent nature of necessity itself' (ME 36). The point is seen to be at work in the film *Casablanca*: the screenwriters played with different endings for the movie, events could have taken a different turn, but the actual one arrived at on the screen appears necessary; contingency lies hidden in the 'natural' course of events, affording an ending that then seems inevitable.

> **Hegel is – to use today's terms – the ultimate thinker of autopoiesis, of the process of the emergence of necessary features out of chaotic contingency, the thinker of contingency's gradual self-organization, of the gradual rise of order out of chaos.**
>
> **(LTN 467)**

MSH 30–1; KNW 188–93; TN 153–61; DLC 179–80, 309, 315; FT 150–1; LTN 463–9; AP 105–6; QH 69–72

Hegel 1991: 213–25; Hegel 2010a: 478–88; Johnston 2018: 103–10; Rosen 2014: 377–85; Simoniti 2026

CONNECTIONS: Benjamin, dialectic, event, infinite judgement, not-All/non-All, retroactivity

Contradiction

See the introduction, absolute knowing, capitalism, Hegel, sexuality.

The 'cunning of reason'

See literary criticism.

D

Deleuze

The early chapters of *Organs without Bodies* (2004), Žižek's book about Deleuze, set out and problematize some key ideas of the French philosopher. Errors are traced in Deleuze's reading of Hegel but so too are 'subterranean' (OWB 53) links between them, despite variances in the way they understand difference and identity. In time, the links become more deeply archived and Deleuze's objections to Hegel become 'outright psychotic foreclosure' (AR 33).

Žižek pursues a materialist reading of Deleuze's concept of Becoming, using the expression Sense-Events as an equivalent. He aligns Deleuze's 'virtual intensities' and their role in generating reality's actuality with the 'immaterialism' of quantum oscillations. In *Quantum History*, such an alignment is looked at again and Deleuze's notion of pure becoming is compared and contrasted with the interpretation of quantum mechanics by Carlo Rovelli.

Although Deleuze stoutly declares his anti-Hegelian stance, the importance he brings to immanence is shared by Hegel, especially in the way Absolute Knowing bankrupts the distinction between In-itself and For-itself. An unlikely correspondence like this characterizes the way Žižek avoids shamelessly cannibalizing Deleuzian discernments and respects their value by channelling them into a broader Hegelian-Lacanian philosophy. This can be seen in the account of symbolic castration, sexuality and the emergence of matter from mind in *Organs without Bodies*.

The conversation is continued in *Less Than Nothing*, a book where Deleuze is constantly referenced and ideas from his *The Logic of Sense*, like his notion of a 'pure past', are taken on board. At the same time, his concept of the 'pseudo-cause', once affiliative with *objet petit a*, is seen to have changed by the time of *Anti-Oedipus*, co-authored with Félix Guattari. Complications are found in the way he relates the virtual and the actual and the difference between the Deleuze of *The Logic of Sense* and the Deleuze of *Anti-Oedipus* is reiterated when the topic is returned to in *Absolute Recoil*.

Two conflicting logics are detected in Deleuze's notion of Becoming, giving rise to an ambiguity that can be settled by a particular reading of Hegel. What Žižek stands against is the postulation of an original unity that then splits. The Hegelian dialectic insists on the split always being there and, instead of valorizing formlessness and the flow of desire, seeks to puncture it with an affirmation of foundational antagonism.

OWB 52–3, 55–6, 60–73, 87–93; DLC 312–15; LTN 207–16, 481–4, 619–21, 853–7; AR 372–7; QH 237–9, 241

Johnston 2018: 238–44; Kaufman 2012: 87–95

CONNECTIONS: event/act, In-itself/For-itself, negativity, predestination, retroactivity

Descartes and the *cogito*

See concrete universality, literary criticism, 'night of the world', 'spirit is a bone', unconscious.

Desire

As an elusive object of desire, *objet petit a* engenders a zone for desire to express itself as part of a human need to fill the foundational fissure in being, the out-of-jointness that is felt as lack. Unlike the need of a hungry person for food, desire cannot be satisfied. Lack remains unassuageable and, unlike an infant's demand for love, cannot be appeased. Desire, going beyond need and beyond demand, first manifests itself when the infant begins to realize that its mother's love is not as total and unqualified as is its own dependence on her. The lack experienced by the infant raises uncertainties for it about what might also be lacking in others and the nature of their own desire. Out of this enigma, occasioned by the Other, there arises desire and its resort to fantasy to stage the desire of the other. Not a physical or emotional need or a demand for love, desire is the posing of an urgent question apropos the other's desire in relation to oneself. Desire is constitutively reflexive but also inescapably intersubjective because it is always mediated by the other: 'This is why it is meaningless to search for my own "true" desire: as Lacan put it, my desire is the desire of the Other' (CA 71). What does remain as meaningful is desire's desire to be desired by the impenetrable Other and the only operational space available to desire is the symbolic order, the big Other.

The terminology of need, demand and desire is a staple conceptual triad for Lacan and in *Tarrying with the Negative* Žižek explicates it in the language of the dialectic. In time, what will become more important for mapping Lacan into Hegel is the contrast of drive with desire. The distinction between the two is congruent with a singular philosophical step that comes to the fore in *Less Than Nothing* and *Absolute Recoil*: designating desire as Kantian in its nature and drive as Hegelian. The insurmountable space between desire and the lack that is *objet petit a* mirrors the gap that for Kant exists between the subject and the thing-in-itself; in drive, the lack is embodied in the object and satisfaction is derived from circumnavigating it.

Adrian Johnston widens the surround by delineating the imperative urge that repetitively fuels the space of desire (and drive) within a field of neurophysiology and the way 'aspects of the biomaterial substance of the human organism get colonized and overwritten by swarms of psychically inscribed sociosymbolic rules and renditions' (2018: 230). For Žižek, the big Other's 'rules and renditions' can no more assimilate desire than Buddhism can quell the insistent and inconsistent nature of desire by seeking to remove its surfeit and deprive it of its unsatisfiable claims on the libido.

> **Desire drifts in an endless metonymy of lack, while drive is a closed circular movement ... desire is always unsatisfied, but drive generates its own satisfaction ... each is irreducible to the other.**
>
> **(AR 373–4)**

Desire, always deferring the reaching of the object of desire, is the 'presence of something which haunts speech ... which slides in speech but is impossible to grasp' (Soler 1995: 50), hence, for Lacan, its metonymic condition (2007: 528) as the process itself of moving from one object to another. The ghost that for Soler haunts speech is an uncanny, hysterical subject who demands to question the identity they have been given. The legitimacy of the question is what underlies Lacan's dictum that the only thing one can be guilty of is 'having given ground relative to one's desire' (1992: 392). Since every object of desire is not the plenitude being sought, it would be a betrayal to rest content with any one such object: 'Remain faithful to your hellish desire' (F 57) because to do anything else would be a compromise for the agent of desire. The negative must be tarried with and to do otherwise amounts to ethical infidelity.

The nature of desire needs to be compared with that of drive to bring out what is distinctive about each and avoid oversimplification. The stakes can be high: criticism of a political theorist, Yannis Stravakakis, in *Defense of Lost Causes* – his perceived misunderstanding of desire in relation to drive and fantasy – is seen as symptomatic of his political vacuity. Desire's excess cannot be diluted, it cannot be deprived of *objet petit a* when desire is inseparable from the object that will bring final satisfaction. It is because there will be no final satisfaction, remaining always out of reach – the lack cannot be filled – that desire begets a destabilizing overload. Even the pioneering eco-Marxism of Kohei Saito is seen to fail to take this into account and it risks bringing his agenda for degrowth uncomfortably close to the economics of Buddhism and its distinction between socially useful desires and harmful self-indulgent ones: an impossible 'enjoyment deprived of its constitutive surplus' (AP 20).

TN 120–4; TAF 80–7; DLC 326–31; LTN 496–7, 638–9, 705–6; AR 372–4;
    AP 14–20

Kaye 2023: 83–100; McGowan 2025: 66–73; Žižek 1994b; Zupančič
    2023, 85–9

CONNECTIONS: Buddhism, dialectic, drive, fantasy, hysteria/perversion, *objet petit a*, other

Dialectic

Traditionally and simplistically, the dialectic begins with an affirmed something which is then undermined by a negative of its own making. An archetypal literary case is when a tragic hero's fatal flaw, their *harmatia*, is viewed as inextricable from their heroic quality. What complicates the picture is the transformation that occurs through the dialectic's reflexive, dynamic process. It does bring about a transformation and, through a negation of the negative, a threshold is breached but the sublation (*Aufhebung*) maintains the original at a radically more open and revealing level.

No reintegration or renormalization occurs in the dialectic; no return that establishes a unity. In the place where a positive, disalienated substantiality might be expected, there is a redefinition of the term that initiated the process. The ontological foundation of the dialectic is the antagonism defining reality and what triggers its development is the pressure arising from the discord generated by a thing's non-coincidence with itself: 'Something is, *in itself*, itself and the lack of *itself* (the *negative*), in one and the same respect' (Hegel 2010a: 382). Hegel's account of absolute recoil leads to a logic in the dialectic that departs radically from traditional interpretations: 'We begin with nothing, and it is only through the self-negation of nothing that something appears' (AR 154). In *Against Progress*, Žižek writes of a dialectic analysis seeking 'to dissolve the positivity of its object' (AP 60) and avoid the mistake of investing the terms in its formal scrutiny with an unmediated, full identity. Any unity of opposites attributed to the dialectic is judged as false and, at the level of pure form, what is held to be an opposition is actually a dependence on an unmediated element. This element, a 'leftover' of the Lacanian Real (AP 60), is what supports the dialectic's distance from any kind of closure and maintains its openness.

A stress on the importance of self-negation, the energetic self-sublating possibility within every identity, is to be found as far back as *The Most Sublime Hysteric*. It is repeated in the introduction in *The Sublime Object of Ideology* and in that book the Rabinovitch joke is used to illustrate how the 'synthesis' becomes the same as the 'antithesis', a self-negation arising from something being looked at in a discrepant way. By the time of *Less Than Nothing* and *Absolute Recoil*, more than twenty years later, the dialectic's self-wrought process is seen as a supple, revelatory movement and with a non-schematic logic that proceeds from the given to the formation of something new. Terms that seem antithetical come to be imbricated, each falling into and being reinscribed into its other – as when, in a negation of the negation, Proudhon declares property to be theft (AR 269).

This activity of understanding is not that of a well-oiled piece of mental machinery. There are stoppages, resistance and the unexpected reconciliation with the apparently irreconcilable. In Hegel's famous dialectic of master-slave, the reconciliation/recognition moment is more ambiguous than harmonious: 'It is also (and primarily) that the subject recognises the decentered Other as its own site, i.e., that it recognises its own decentered character' (AR 346). The process rests on contingency, not necessity and, far from there being a teleology guaranteeing a particular outcome, a failure is immanent to the result. The source of failure resides in the endeavour of a dialectical analysis 'to dissolve the positivity of its object in the totality of its formal mediations' (AP 60). There is a meddling with terms that unites opposites by disarming apparent identities, uniting a positive with 'a remainder of the Real' (AP 60). The 'remainder' is also a reminder of the non-identity that inheres within every identity and the positive spin that the dialectic gives to the negative.

> **The Hegelian matrix of the dialectical process is thus that one must first fail in reaching the goal, as the intended reconciliation turns into its opposite, and only then, in a second moment, will the true reconciliation come, when one recognises this failure itself as the form of success.**
>
> **(AR 36)**

The failure that is part of the dialectic goes all the way down and is not to be read in the way of a self-help mantra about encountering but eventually overcoming obstacles on the journey of life. Things not only go wrong but undergo reversals, the wrong train does not irresistibly go the right station and the 'fear of erring is already the error itself' (Hegel 2018: §74). In the struggle for social justice this is seen in the way a first attempt collapses into its opposite – witness the outcomes of the French and October Revolutions – and the attempt to actualize it has to start again.

Failure resides within every apparent success (AR 36) and, as *Less Than Nothing* puts it, the only gain 'is the reflexive shift of perspective which recognises success in failure itself' (520). This kind of perspectival shift is seen to occur in the ending of Proust's *À la recherche*. Marcel discovers his vocation to be a writer because of past failed relationships and awareness of the corrosive passing of time. The bad news is the mess of his life; the good news is that he will be able to write about it and become a true writer. It is this kind of movement that characterizes the dialectical succession of Being by Essence in Hegel's *The Science of Logic*. It begins with Being, a flat and chaotic multiplicity lacking depth or meaning but, through a self-negating mediation, produces Essence – which can be taken here as thought reflecting within itself – out of its own failure to possess any inherent meaning or consistency. 'If thought was not separate from things, it would not be thought', writes Jean-Luc Nancy, but 'thought is thus itself the separation of things from thought … It runs through their separation, and it separates itself from their separation' (2002: 13). An underlying idea is how the self-undermining of identity, its ontological incompleteness, imparts a mobility to thought that non-dialectical cognition lacks.

The dialectic, especially when formulated in Hegelese, can convey the impression of a forbidding abstruseness but Žižek provides many cases of it operating at down-to-earth levels. The complaint that the imposition of the colonizer's language was foisted on India takes a dialectical turn when what appears as a cultural loss becomes the means of articulating an anti-colonial identity for all Indians: 'The English language is "denaturalized", losing its privileged link to its "native" Anglo-Saxon speakers' (AR 347).

MSH 23–5; SO viii–xi, 199; OWB 116–17; LTN 254–5, 520; AR 36–7, 262–3, 346–9

Kotsko 2008: 8–12; Taheri 2021: 23–30; Žižek 2009f: 105–6

CONNECTIONS: absolute recoil, antagonism, contingency and necessity, dialectical materialism, identity and difference, negation of negation

Dialectical materialism

Žižek does not use the term dialectical materialism lightly and it appears in the subtitles of his two more purely philosophical works: *Less Than Nothing: Hegel and the Shadow of Dialectical Materialism* and *Absolute Recoil: Towards a New Foundation of Dialectical Materialism*.

Materialism at its most basic, content with asserting that everything is matter and its movement, is assured in approaching reality as a given. Everything is reduced to some piece of matter which provides the essence of what appears as a sense-effect. The premise of the dialectical materialism Žižek propounds calls for this assurance to be so heavily qualified as to make it worthy of being discarded: 'There is no "objective" reality, every reality is already transcendentally constituted' (LTN 907). The kind of materialist ontology being advanced insists on positioning subjective perspectives, transcendental frames of understanding, *within* reality. It places us in a picture of the world that we ourselves constitute and it is this reflexive twist – the Lacanian gaze is its psychic equivalent – that forms the basis for materialism. The whole of reality is one of a 'flat infinite multiplicity' (DLC 397) and immanent impossibilities and it cannot be seen as whole 'not because a large part of it eludes me, but because it contains a stain, a blind spot, which indicates my inclusion in it' (PV 17).

Matter becomes less than matter when physicists translate their mathematical formulations into 'oscillations of the superstrings or quantum vibrations' (OWB 25). The challenge is how to account for a movement 'from nothing to something' that brings forth finite appearances, a challenge that Buddhism, content with an ontological void and reality as merely a passing play of appearances (LTN 957), is judged as failing to meet.

A conundrum that bothers Žižek is that any purchase on being's ultimate truth, including reference to a non-All universe, necessarily arises within a transcendental frame and this robs it of the universality it would claim for itself. There is a strain between what is enunciated and the standpoint from where it is made. The enunciated content of asserting non-All as a fundamental ontological vision of reality is made from a position of enunciation that claims to grasp an All. The inconsistency this gives rise to results from 'the tension between the reality we confront and transcendental horizon through which we perceive reality' (CA 26). In acknowledgement of this, the word 'theology' enters Žižek's philosophical vocabulary – as it does for Walter Benjamin – in order 'to circumscribe the obscure area that eludes any ontology, transcendental or naively realist' (SE 278). This opaque area also eludes the etherealizing of matter that imbues it with a vitalism; making it materialist in the sense that Tolkien's Middle Earth is materialist, 'an enchanted world' (AR 12) that skirts the difficulty of formulating the space where thinking and being are imbricated. The Real is a candidate for unorganized multiples of pure being but, in the play of a pre-ontological void, 'the whole point of quantum physics is that many things go on before registration', in what he calls a 'shadowy space' (AR 222). This goes some way in helping to explain why the subtitle of *Less Than Nothing* conjoins Hegel with the 'shadow' of dialectical materialism and that of *Absolute Recoil* speaks of going 'towards' a new foundation of dialectical materialism.

The dialectic is essential to materialism because it transposes the gap between the noumenal and our subjectivity into the object itself. It is not difference that distinguishes one element from another but the interstice between an element and its place of registration, between its supposedly secure identity and its place of inscription.

There is ontological incompletion but there is also the idealism of the transcendental domain, the world of meaning emerging from dialectical interactions of subject and substance. Only an infinite judgement that 'material reality is *non-All*' (LTN 742) is capable of giving domicile to these different levels. Žižek's name for his Hegelian-Lacanian position is dialectical materialism, an infinite judgement where a single predicate cannot do justice to the elements it contains.

> **Why … 'dialectical materialism', a term that is difficult to dissociate from the Stalinist tradition – a term which stands for philosophical ideology at its most stupid … Because I think what I have in mind here is ultimately unnameable, there is no 'proper' name for it, so the only solution is to use a term which signals as clearly as possible its own inadequacy.**
>
> **(SE 278)**

SO 153–62; RG 315n28; LTN 67, 260–3; SE 150–3; F 150–3; CA 25–6

Benjamin 2005; Pluth 2016; Ruda 2016b

CONNECTIONS: absolute recoil, Benjamin, Buddhism, dialectic, enunciated and enunciation, infinite judgement, not-All/non-All, ontology, transcendental

Drive

Lacan developed Freud's death drive (*Todestrieb*) into a more enveloping force, one that repetitively circles the primal void occupied by *objet petit a*. Žižek, extrapolating further, makes drive what the subject stands for and, as an ontological concept, something that is not activated by instinct and circumstance. Nor does he reduce it to a striving for dissolution and death. What activates drive is not a yearning for a return to an inorganic state but an unnatural, inhuman emptiness at the core of the subject. It is not a solipsistic cry of despair but a 'reaction to the deadlock/impossibility of sexual relationship' (D 357) and the void that is the 'night of the world'.

Drive's compulsion to repeat itself is a function of its inability to arrive at a terminus. Unlike desire, which has the illusory aim of reaching some lost object, there is no target for drive other than re-enacting its failure. If this repetition is related to the passage from animal to human existence, it is a transition that resists the narrative of a smooth evolutionary development. The measured, instinctual life of animal existence is destabilized to the point of distortion when the human animal is touched by awareness of the Real and turns to the circular territory of the drive.

Freud speculated about the source and purpose of drive and ventured that life itself was the result of some glitch, an anthropological trauma from which there is no recovery. Žižek follows Lacan in viewing a certain overload as pertaining to the human organism which, resisting integration, disrupts an otherwise familiar and reassuring life-rhythm. The 'death' in the death drive becomes not an urge to self-annihilation, an obscure longing for nothingness, but this surplus that biological life cannot contain, an indestructible 'undead' state that translates into repetition and circularity: 'The ultimate lesson of psychoanalysis is that human life is never "just life": Humans are not simply alive, they are possessed by the strange drive to enjoy life as over-kill, passionately attached to a surplus which sticks out and derails the ordinary run of things' (PV 62). Žižek aligns this derailment with the excessive enjoyment that Lacan terms *jouissance* (QH 87).

> **Therein lies the difference between desire and drive: desire is grounded in its constitutive lack, while the drive circulates around a hole, a gap in the order of being. In other words, the circular movement of the drive obeys the weird logic of the curved space in which the shortest distance between two points is not a straight line, but a curve: the drive 'knows' that the quickest way to realize its aim is to circulate around its goal-object.**
>
> **(LTN 496)**

If an instinct has a purpose, drive is motiveless, seeking to stubbornly maintain the tension sustaining its disquiet by repeating its own orbital movement and gaining some satisfaction from this. Far from seeking homeostasis, drive is the compulsion to repeat as an end in itself and this distinguishes it from desire, even though their interwovenness is such that desire can be viewed as an indication of drive. If, as expressed in *Less Than Nothing*, 'we repeat because it is impossible to directly affirm' (LTN 493) then drive and negativity are two terms for the same ontological impasse. This is confirmed when, a few pages on, the shift from desire to drive is termed a transfer 'from the *lost object to loss itself as an object*' (LTN 497; AR 237). The cartoon cat running off a cliff and defying gravity by continuing to rotate its legs is instanced to illustrate how drive perpetuates itself in a loop of its own making. This is followed by the analogy of a needle getting stuck on a groove on a scratched LP and repeating a sound over and over again. Later in the same book, in a discussion of Heidegger, drive as 'stuckness' or persistence is what, in the scene from David Lynch's *Mulholland Drive*, keeps the song going when the performer singing it collapses into unconsciousness (LTN 884).

Adrian Johnston deepens the link between drive and desire and employs the language of evolutionary biology to break down any simple demarcation between the functional operations of animal instinct and the dysfunctional nature of drive and desire. He suggests that Žižek's Lacanian demarcation is more the 'failure of evolved instincts … themselves symptoms of nature's weakness … its negligent laxness permitting proliferations of malformations' (2018: 222). For Žižek, the radical insufficiency in the order of being accounts for the existence of the drive and is coterminous with the negativity sustaining the untethered movement of the dialectic (thus giving it an impression of automation). The compulsion to repeat, symptomatic of the impossibility of ever reaching an affirmative state of unified groundedness, concerns Adrian Johnston because such an alignment might jeopardize the hard core of materialism. It could do this by becoming too metaphysical for its own good, intimating 'an ineffable Negativity floating in an inaccessible time before time and from which all existent beings somehow emanate' (Johnston 2018: 244). He looks to a neurobiological approach to the complex evolution and maladaptation of animal instinct, also stamped by repetition, into human drive. Žižek prefers to stress an ontological Hegelian infinity that cannot be contained within neurobiology and which results in an 'endless dragging of life'. Looking to the refrain in the 'Dalai Lama' song by the German band Rammstein, about having to live until you die, an ethical measure is brought to Freud's death drive by making the act of living an obligation that must be sustained despite its catastrophic nullity (HD 167–8; SE 279).

OB 94–7; OWB 24, 141–2; PV 61–5; DLC 327–9; LTN 492–3, 496–8, 546–50, 824n29, 884–5; AR 206–7; SFA 325–6; SE 224–5

Johnston 2018: 219–24; McGowan 2025: 79–83

CONNECTIONS: desire, infinity, negativity, 'night of the world', *objet petit a*, ontology, sexuality, subject

E

Enunciated and enunciation

The Lacanian subject of the enunciation ($) is also an empty, nonsubstantial logical variable (not function), whereas the subject of the enunciation (the 'person') consists of the fantasmatic 'stuff' which fills out the void of ($).

(TN 14)

Lacan draws a difference between what is enunciated, the content (*sujet de l'énonciation*), and the subject making the enunciation (*sujet de l'énoncé*). The positions that locate the subject of the enunciation and the content being enunciated are not married in the way that might be assumed. The fluidity pertaining to any particular position of enunciation can change the dynamic between the two: Gorbachev's *perestroika* and *glasnost* provide an example given from the field of politics. His intention, the position of the enunciation, was to strengthen Soviet communism but the system could not contain the enunciated content and his reforms led to the system's collapse (LET 398). Similarly, at the intimate level of private relationships, a married couple may agree to each of them ignoring sexual relations with others but when one of them explicitly draws attention to their agreement the other partner has reason to be alarmed and worry that their marriage is in jeopardy (DLC 48). The enunciated content of a theology student declaring there is an eternal life acquires a profundity when, changing the position of enunciation, it is declared by Christ (AP 64–5).

When the position of enunciation is cloaked it may become more important than what is enunciated from it. Even if Nazi claims about the Jews had been true, their anti-Semitism remains pathological because what was disavowed was Nazism's ideological need for a scapegoat and, similarly, even if Saddam had weapons of mass destruction the United States' position was still false because the weapons issue was never the real motive for the invasion (I 51).

One facet of the gap between the content and position of an enunciation is shown when the position of enunciation changes even though what is enunciated remains the same, as in the story Sam Spade tells in *The Maltese Falcon* (OWB 69). The difference that can arise in the process of repetition is a result of 'the minimal difference', true infinity and the parallax gap that reveals itself in Natsume Sōseki's novel, *The Three-Cornered World* (LTN 616–17).

Another aspect is revealed when the position of enunciation not just inflects but gives form and body to what is being enunciated; in *Less Than Nothing* this is discussed in relation to ways of representing the Holocaust and possibly far-reaching implications for the nature of speech.

The difference drawn by Lacan between enunciated and enunciation goes beyond human speech and beyond aesthetics when it informs the inaugural philosophical step taken by Kant with his notion of the transcendental. What is taken as reality cannot be equated with a pure objective determination; what can be affirmed is a subjective process in determining reality. This takes on added philosophical weight when considering the subject as a point external to what is observed: 'It [the subject] may be a tiny part of reality, a tiny speck in the "great chain of being", but it is simultaneously the singular (stand)point encompassing reality as something that appears within its horizon' (LTN 764). The puzzle and the paradox is that we know we are a part of what lies outside ourselves but we cannot locate our subjective position of enunciation within this external reality; there is no philosophical equivalent to the use of a double mirror to see ourselves looking in a mirror (Žižek 2009e: xiv). When truth appears to consciousness as a positive in-itself it needs to be recalled that it can only emerge from a subjective position of enunciation.

OWB 69–70; LTN 13–14, 23–7, 515; AP 73–4; QH 248

CONNECTIONS: antagonism, infinity, subject, transcendental

Ethics

> How I would love to be: an ethical monster without empathy, doing what is to be done in a weird coincidence of blind spontaneity and reflexive distance, helping others while avoiding their disgusting proximity.
>
> (Žižek 2009d: 303)

Like the sensuous certainty with which Hegel begins his *Phenomenology*, ethical conviction may seem transparent, expressing what it knows to be, but it turns out to be something abstract and the 'very poorest *truth*' (2018: §91).

In an ontologically disarticulated world, it may come as no surprise that ethics lacks an absolute foundation.

Ethical relativism, the polar extreme of ethical certainty, is equally vacuous and the fiction of Henry James is looked to for the inclusion of intersubjectivity in ethics. Ethical norms, educed through recognition of the claims of others, emerge dynamically and echo speculative reason. A position, far from being read off an existing situation with a guaranteed set of rules, is the result of movement of spirit: '*of "getting lost" (of losing ethical substance) that opens up the space for the ethical work of mediation which alone can generate the solution*' (PV 127). In the case of Isabel Archer in James's *The Portrait of a Lady*, she stays with her vile husband because of the claim made by 'the bond of her word' (OB 78); he is for Isabel a part of herself she does not want to relinquish. Something similar leads the character played by Brendan Gleeson in *The Banshees of Inisherin*, maintaining allegiance to the terms of his ultimatum, to sever his fingers.

Abraham is willing to follow God's command to sacrifice his son without the certainty of an ethical absolute to guide his conduct. He is sustained by faith, not by a moral dictate, and Žižek shares with Kierkegaard the importance of a 'leap of faith' where the outcome is unknown. It requires a willingness to bracket off reliance on a pre-existing norm and assume the responsibility that comes with making one's own ethical decision. With faith in the non-All out of which freedom emerges, Kierkegaard's call for a suspension of the ethical entails 'not simply the external abolition of the Ethical, it is what makes it possible for the Ethical to exist and confers its identity, its inherent condition of possibility' (AP 58). Abraham is prepared to abandon his ethical obligation as a father for the sake of something held to be more vital.

Kierkegaard is extolled for his honesty in confronting the absurd meaninglessness that takes the ground of logic away from conventional attitudes to the ethical and this is reflected in Žižek's examples of an authentic ethical position. Communists in the West who steadfastly maintained fidelity to the USSR during the Cold War are extolled not for being tragically blind to the reality of Soviet Russia but for the way their very refusal to admit what should have been obvious resonates with something essential to any ethical stance: a binding, atemporal engagement of the kind aroused in Kant by the French Revolution. What the revolution represented, the hopes it kindled, go beyond the empirical history of the event and addresses what Žižek calls the 'inhuman' core of being-human: a concurrence of lack and excess, not rationally discernible, which indexes the inadequacy of the symbolic to represent what lies obscurely between the human and the non-human. It is the abyss out of which the unconditional nature of freedom and the space of the ethical is born.

Principled commitment of the kind that informs *The Portrait of a Lady* and *The Banshees of Inisherin* is necessary but not sufficient for an ethical act and examples range from Himmler's presentation of himself as an ethical

Nazi (Žižek 2023i: 350–1) to the Scottish Parliament's decision to pursue an LGBT+ agenda which resulted in a male rapist claiming to be a transgender woman and consequently remanded to a woman's prison. In the latter case, the seemingly laudable principle of self-identifying one's sexual identity was rendered not just suspect but, in this case, open to serious criticism. In another field, the religious fundamentalism that leads to acts of indiscriminate violence is not ethical: 'The terrorist pseudo-fundamentalists are deeply bothered, intrigued, fascinated, by the sinful life of non-believers … they are fighting their own temptation' (OF 73). The unconditional ethical act displaces causality and asserts itself in its place, allowing for the unlikely pairing of Kant's rigorous notion of ethical duty with the self-justification of capricious pleasure extolled by Marquis de Sade.

The severity of this way of explaining authentic ethical behaviour is Žižek's anti-humanist emphasis on the need to acknowledge 'the latent monstrosity of being-human' and establish an ethics that can prevail after Auschwitz (DLC 166). Kant's categorical imperative, acting on a basis that can be universally applied, is not the work of a big Other's superego and it does not offer any guarantee that obviates personal responsibility for one's actions.

IR 169–73; PV 126–44, 85–90; OB 139–40; DLC 14–17, 225–6, 344–5; CA 218–20.

CONNECTIONS: Antigone, event/act, freedom

Event/act

The term event, as set out by Badiou, heralds a moment that creatively irrupts into a pre-existent order and alters the coordinates of a state of affairs. Accounting for different modes of this, without reverting to semi-religious talk of miracles, is set out by Žižek in *Event* using the metaphor of a subway trip where each stop stands for a possible definition of event.

While an act is similar, the term coming from the work of Lacan, the agent of the act undergoes a transformation: 'The subject is annihilated and subsequently reborn (or not), i.e., the act involves a kind of temporary eclipse, *aphanisis*, of the subject' (ES 51). The Fall is a Christian event and an act describes Eve's situation when her shattering decision involves an ontological alteration in how she understands herself, becoming aware of her nakedness, and accepting a now recognizably human world she is about to enter (AR 129). Staying within the Christian world, a Lacanian act is like the description by C. S. Lewis of the non-psychological moment when his religious choice is determined. What took place on the grass in Beckett's *Not I* is deemed an event (D 222–30).

However ungrounded an event or act may seem, it is not devoid of an origin if Deleuze's dynamic interaction between virtual and actual is brought into play: a 'potential field of virtualities out of which reality is actualized' (OWB 4). Badiou is pointing in a similar direction when Žižek quotes him as saying 'what composes an event is always extracted from a situation, always related back to a singular multiplicity … we must accept that an event is nothing but a part of a given situation, nothing but a *fragment of being*' (LET 201; LTN 822). This suggests a fully existing reality, out of which a hitherto unnoticed splinter or virtuality claims its actuality. What follows is the possibility that fidelity to an affirmative 'fragment' can be called upon and nominated into full existence by subjects committed to its validity. If, though, reality is conjectured as always imperfectly curtailed, then an event becomes something of its own devising, an *ex nihilo* creation, and this is closer to how Žižek deploys the term.

He ventures to explain his understanding by picturing how it is 'only through the terrorizing experience of the utter vacuity of every positive order of "normality" that a space is opened up for an Event' (LTN 835). The Real, drive and the inconsistent big Other is the context and an event/act is not an irrational abandonment of reason but an intervention in the symbolic order that forms a new norm and retroactively creates its conditions of possibility. An example is the French Revolution and how, as Kant observed, it aroused tremendous enthusiasm regardless of the fact that it was the occasion for many unpleasant incidents and experiences. As an Event, Žižek points out, it belongs to the 'dimension of the Real' (DLC 15) because it was not what took place on the ground but how the happenings appeared to observers and occasioned utopian desires. As an additional to the empirical, the utopian hopes may be betrayed by historical circumstances but they are not extinguished and lay dormant as a 'spectral Event waiting for its proper embodiment' (DLC 394).

The collage of events/acts emerging from Žižek's work includes how what happened between February and October 1917 in Russia cannot be separated from how Lenin experienced and reacted to what unfolded. Other events/acts are what Schoenberg achieved with his music (AR 157; LTN 193) and what lesser mortals go through when experiencing love. In the 1957 Western *3:10 to Yuma*, the outlaw's ethical act is his giving up the chance of freedom (LET 64–6) and, non-fictionally, it is Gudrun Ensslin's death by suicide (if it was suicide) in Stammheim Prison in 1977 after the failure of a Red Army Faction attempt to free her (ES 89). She becomes like Antigone who is the supreme case of an individual whose act unites an absolute decision where 'freedom, autonomy and responsibility coincides with an unconditional necessity' (DSS 162; IR 319). At the other end of the event/act spectrum, one of what Bruno Bosteels calls Žižek's 'intonations' of the act (2011: 175) is seen to include the non-act of Bartleby's 'I'd prefer not to'.

> If, however, we analyse it as an Event, then the ultimate factual result of the Cultural Revolution, its catastrophic failure and reversal into the recent capitalist explosion, does not exhaust its Real: the eternal idea of the Cultural Revolution survives its defeat in sociohistorical reality, it continues to lead the underground spectral life of the ghosts of failed utopias which haunt future generations, patiently waiting its next resurrection.
>
> (IV 277; LTN 389–90)

ES 35–53; DSS 162–3, 170–2; OB 83–5, 101, 112–13; LTN 34–5, 822–5; E Johnston 2009: 144–56; Bosteels 2011: 175–223

CONNECTIONS: Antigone, Badiou, drive, 'I would prefer not to', Lenin, love, predestination, retroactivity

F

Fantasy

Conceived not as an escape from reality but a necessary support for its inherent gaps and contradictions, fantasy for Lacan provides constructions for securing a sense of cohesiveness. A subject's fundamental fantasy is their psychic centre of gravity, covertly coordinating the organization of their desire. The scariness of the Mystery Man in David Lynch's *Lost Highway* is his disquieting access to the protagonist's fundamental fantasy (ARS 23). In the arena of sexual desire, the need for fantasmatic support is amusingly played with in a scene from the movie *Brassed Off*, over an invitation to have coffee (LTN 768). Fantasy takes a diabolic form in anti-Semitism where the figure of the Jew embodies a community's need to disavow internal ruptures at the heart of its social existence. Fantasy operates politically when it serves to support an ideology by masking divisions in its belief system that would otherwise expose its weaknesses. It is germane to issues of race and racism where fantasy operates to support exclusive notions of ethnic identity.

Lacan's idea is that fantasy belongs to the subject in order to sustain their fragmented but unique sense of being, coordinating their desire and managing the crux of sexual difference. The psychoanalytic status of this internal ground is clarified in *The Plague of Fantasies* by contrasting it with the philosophical role of Kant's transcendental: whereas reality in Kant is an objective state of affairs constituted through the mind's mediation – it can be said to be 'subjectively objective' – Lacanian fantasy is a subjective phenomenon, existing in the mind, but which the agency that is the first person singular is not consciously aware of; hence it can said to be 'objectively subjective'.

The subject is barred from possessing a complete sense of identity but this is screened by the libidinal gratification of fantasy which, unadmitted but operating in the background, gives form and content to desire and the *objet petit a*. This interaction of subject and fantasy is capsulized in Lacan's formula: $ <> a ($ as the barred subject of desire, *a* standing for *objet petit a* and the lozenge symbol formalizing their imbrication).

Proximity to the Other triggers intrinsically troubling questions about their desire; acutely so with the intimacy and intensity of sexual activity. This is managed by bringing the Other into the subject's fantasy; only when the physical act of copulation is supported in this way does sexuality becomes sexualized. Stanislaw Lem's novel *Solaris* is deemed superior to Tarkovsky's film version of the novel because the movie falls into Hollywood's default humanist mode yielding the couple-oriented motif whereas the novel attends to the enigma of the impenetrable Other (IV 65, 105–6; E 25–6, 14–16). The act of copulation is loosely aligned with the two views of Kafka's *Castle*: it may look like a collection of old cottages until a distanced view displays its beguiling presence and, similarly, the sexual act is a 'rather vulgar set of stupid repetitive movements' when viewed close up but when seen through 'the mist of fantasies it becomes the height of intense pleasure' (AR 198).

In *Event*, Žižek writes about Terrence Malick's *The Tree of Life* staging the fantasy of objectifying a world where the subject does not exist and contrasts this with Lars von Trier's *Melancholia*, released the same year, about a planet on course to collide with Earth and destroy the whole of humanity. The frame of fantasy as a conduit for our access to reality is maintained by Malick while its complete removal is contemplated by von Trier and it is only the melancholic character Justine in his film who is able to sanely deal with the imminent catastrophe.

Approaching a fantasy too closely may be traumatic – this is how Michael Haneke's *The Piano Teacher* is interpreted in *Welcome to the Desert of the Real* – and traversing the fantasy is a term in Lacanian psychoanalysis for a process that allows an analysand to safely acknowledge their fundamental fantasy; to approach but not possess it. Justine in *Melancholia* has traversed the fantasy, having confronted the void at the heart of existence, and is able to accept and deal with the disaster when its inevitability becomes obvious.

Taking it off the psychoanalyst's couch, traversing the fantasy can also be a political act that confronts and bestows its liberatory mark on the jurisdiction of the socio-symbolic. The racist needs to traverse their fantasy and, in *On Belief*, this possibility is valued as a legacy of Christianity's conviction that what seems immutable can be changed and that to be 'born again' heralds a new start, a new choice about who one is. Parallel to traversing the fantasy is shifting 'the underground' of fantasies (Žižek 2007c: 204), realigning the affiliation between fantasy and reality as an engine of change, making ideological fantasies a site for political intervention.

'Traversing the fantasy' does not mean accepting the misery of our lives – on the contrary, it means that only after we 'traverse' the fantasies obfuscating this misery can we effectively change it.

(LTN 477)

PV 40–1; L 40–60; PF 159 (and L 51–2); DLC 329; WD 20–1; OB 148–9; E
16–25; LTN 685–91; AR 198–9; ZP 18

Daly 2014; McGowan 2025: 122–9

CONNECTIONS: anti-Semitism, desire, Lynch, *objet petit a*, other,
psychoanalysis, race, sexual difference, subject, transcendental

Freedom

> The mistake of those who identify freedom with misrecognition (who claim
> that we experience ourselves as 'acting freely' only when we misrecognize
> the causality that determines our acts) is that they stealthily (re)introduce the
> standard, premodern, 'cosmological' notion of reality as a positive order of
> being ... Consequently, the only way really to account for the status of freedom
> is to assert *the ontological incompleteness of 'reality' itself.*
>
> (DSS 174)

Enchainments of causes and effects– whether empirical, neurological or
biogenetic – determine courses of events and the comportment of freedom has
to be found within this sphere of claims to knowledge. Hegelian retrospection
and the Lacanian concept of separation are seen to provide ways of doing so
that are not incompatible with a radicalized Kantian freedom as a traumatic state
that touches on the Real. Freedom is ungrounded, emerging from the Real like
an unexpected gift, a miracle even, and for Schelling 'a flash of eternity in time'
(IR 35).

Retrospection confers a minimal freedom by allowing for a choice of what set
of causes and effects determine our state of affairs. Something that takes place
only becomes inevitable when it actually happens, its necessity only emerges in
the process of retroactivity, and until then there is the possibility of undoing what
'inevitable': 'It is our power to rewrite the past that leads to this future' (AP 106) or
'at least, the *mode* of this linear determination' (LTN 213). Hegelian retroactivity
overlaps with an appreciation of predestination as entailing knowledge that our
future is preordained but without knowing what critical choices we will make.

The significance that Lacan brings to the notion of separation is another way
of approaching the ungrounded nature of freedom. Differing from alienation,
separation indicates the subject's awareness of the mirroring of its lack in the
big Other's own inconsistency. The two lacks, a doubling that does not allow for
reconciliation between the subject and its symbolic representation, ruptures the
status of the big Other's assumption of permanence. It allows for a puncturing

that finds expression in Paul Robeson's version of the Ol' Man River song, contesting 'the aura of unfathomable wisdom' from the inexorability of fate and revealing 'the inherent stupidity of the ideological big Other' (OWB 100).

Žižek likes drawing attention (2009f: 140, 2020c: 104–5; D 87; HWB 78) to a passage where Kant says our capacity to act freely would vanish were access granted to the noumenal realm (Kant 2015: 117–18). It supports the notion of freedom as situated in an interstice between the phenomenal and the noumenal, the space where the noumenal does appear but only within the sphere of appearance. This allows for the confluence of the impossible and the unavoidable that characterizes the Real. At one level, retroactivity only operates within the symbolic realm – choosing to inscribe the past in an alternative context does not factually change what has taken place – and we cannot escape the hermeneutic scaffolding of the transcendental that we are born into and which governs our perception of reality. At the level of the Real, reality is not consistent, it cannot be integrated within a fully determinist universe and this allows for a speculative and terrifying act of faith: 'We know that what we will do is predestined, but we still have to take a risk … we do not wait to be free, but in a short-circuit we act as if we already are free' (F 60). Theologically, it is recognition in Christian atheism of 'the explosion of freedom' that is the Fall (HWB 83) and that God was always separated from himself.

The idea of freedom being autonomous is foreign to unthinking, mechanical habit but Žižek warms to the way habit becomes for Hegel the foundational milieu for freedom. Training the body begins with essential tasks like walking – 'a man stands only in so far as he wills to stand; as soon as we no longer will to stand, we collapse; standing is, therefore, the habit of the will to stand' (Hegel 2010b: 57) – as well as language acquisition and emotions. Habit allows the body to incorporate will, create dispositions and facilitate choices: '*Thinking*, too, though wholly free, and active in the pure element of itself, likewise requires habit and familiarity' (132). A change in habit as a change in the disposition of a subject is read as a part of Hegel's dialectical and materialist account of spirit emerging from the organic.

Change in the political and social sphere combats the habitual blindness that allows unfreedom to be configured as freedom, as when the formal right to sell your labour as an equal agent in the market place is seen as proof of an individual's autonomy. There is a political equivalent of separation and Lenin is taken as the signifier for this: the 'compelling FREEDOM to suspend the stale existing (post)ideological coordinates, the debilitating Denkverbot [ban on thinking] in which we live – it simply means that we are allowed to think again' (Žižek 2000b, emphasis in the original). Lenin is not a figure of authoritarianism but the authority of a Master who pushes one towards the precipice overlooking the ground where the struggle for freedom takes place.

IR 32–5; OWB 42–3, 58, 99–101, 112–14; DLC 19–20, 70–1, 314–15; AR 68–9, 322–3; IV 232–5; F 3–65, 119–24; ZP 92–3; AP 9, 83; QH 93–4, 129–30, 160–1, 166, 216–17

Kaye 2023: 155–84; Žižek 1997: 32–6, 2009f

CONNECTIONS: big Other, Christian atheism, contingency and necessity, ideology, predestination, Real, retroactivity, Schelling, substance as also subject

Freud, Sigmund

See the introduction and drive, Marx, not-All/non-All, psychoanalysis, Real, retroactivity, superego, the unconscious, wokeness.

G

Gaze

See the introduction and cinema, dialectical materialism, *Vertigo*.

German Idealism

> This moment is the moment of German Idealism delimited by two dates: 1787, the year in which Kant's *Critique of Pure Reason* appeared, and 1831, the year of Hegel's death. These few decades represent a breathtaking concentration of the intensity of thinking: in this short span of time, more happened than in centuries or even millennia of the 'normal' development of human thought.
>
> (LTN 7–8)

The hyperbolic-sounding claim about German Idealism in the introduction to *Less Than Nothing* is argued for and its authority defended throughout the works of its author. As the book's introduction sets it out, German Idealism begins with Kant's 'transcendental turn' and leads, via, principally Fichte, Schelling and Hölderlin, to its peak with Hegel's 'ontological turn'. The least known of the quintet is Fichte and, in the chapter devoted to him in *Less Than Nothing*, difficulties, limitations and achievements in his thought come to rhyme with equivalent concerns shared by the others (LTN 187–8).

Kant and Hegel are the bookends in the developments within German Idealism and, while a bridge of whatever width between the two them has to cross a philosophical gulf, they share with the others something vitally important. In their search for a systematic philosophy, they hold in tension two seemingly opposed identifications of the subject: the subject as a self-determining agency, synthesizing potential avalanches of sensual input into meaningful units of representation, and the subject as a misaligning and negating force, beyond mediation, breaking into and divorcing unified representations. Žižek contends that the two positions are two sides of the same activity (LTN 106) working in tandem and fatally weakening trust in a pre-Kantian conception of a world, transparent in principle, available for our cognition.

German Idealism charts what remains unanswered by Kant: 'The problem is not how to attain the noumenal In-itself beyond phenomenon; the true problem is how and why at all does this In-itself split itself from itself, how does it acquire a distance towards itself and clear the space in which it can appear (to itself)' (TIR 14; TAF 15). Schelling is praised for advancing the proposition of an ontological gap but this is obfuscated by his striving for a lost unity and Hölderlin seeks to ameliorate the division that Schelling identified. Hegel, recognizing in Kant's transcendental the dethronement of a representational way of thinking, attributing actual existence to objects formed by metaphysical ideas, takes the radical step of equating the gap with an instability in being itself.

As a lens for focusing on the seminal importance of Kant and on critical differences between Hegel and Fichte and Schelling, Žižek traces a movement within German Idealism through its concept of 'intellectual intuition'. The concept, introduced by Kant, maintains a gap between the transcendental 'I' and things-in-themselves when direct access to the noumenal is only attributable to God. The self-affirming 'I' would not need the support of a transcendental capability if, as Fichte and Schelling argued for in different ways, it can provide a form of unmediated access to the noumenal. There is a level of human understanding (*intellectus ectypus*) that is not the divine understanding (*intellectus archetypus*) of God. Hegel's different approach is to return to the gap that Kant opened up but, by locating it within reality, making the antinomies part of the incompletion of reality.

The incompletion, cutting across the Kantian distinction between the subject, the 'I', and the substance of the empirical world, allows a connection to be made between German Idealism and psychoanalysis: 'It's not just that we fail to encounter the object, but the object itself is just a trace of a certain failure' (Žižek and Daly 2004: 61). Freud's death drive is an expression of this failure and the construction of a symbolic order becomes a way of dealing with it.

LTN 9–17, 137–79, 492

Gabriel and Žižek 2009; Johnston 2018: 11–20; Van Woezik 2010: 259–307; Žižek and Daly 2004: 61, 64–5; Žižek 2020c: 103–12

CONNECTIONS: Hegel, Kant, Schelling

H

Hegel

No philosopher has given rise to such vexingly contrary interpretations as Hegel but he is the seemingly impenetrable forest that intrepid travellers have no choice but to enter when travelling in Žižek country. It might be foolhardy to disagree with the erudite Adorno's abject confession that 'in the realm of great philosophy, Hegel is no doubt the only one with whom at times one literally does not know, and cannot conclusively determine, what is being talked about' (1993: 89). Despite the ravel of intricacies that define Hegel's prose, Adorno's vital qualification is that only 'at times' is there a difficulty; other occasions allow for the comfort arising from Žižek's own observation that authentic intuitions about a writer can be made by readers who have not unquestionably read all their work. He notes how a library of books exists about Hegel by scholars who have consulted all the primary sources yet manage to miss some particular insight, whereas a less comprehensive approach may touch on what is really important (LTN 280).

Central to Žižek's status as a philosopher is his forging of a Lacanian-infused Hegel. Like Michelangelo before a lump of rock, something within it is chiselled out for viewing. Though far from alone in countering the clichéd portrayal of Hegel as an obsessive thinker with a totalitarian urge to systematize everything, what distinguishes Žižek's approach is the championing of Hegel as *the* philosopher of ungrounded, incomplete Being – and in ways that find alignments with Lacanian ideas. The version of Hegel that has him engaged in sweeping up all aspects of reality into an all-encompassing act of mediation is firmly rejected because there is no substantial foundation for situating the subject and reality in this manner. A voracious appetite that eats up everything is so foreign to Hegel that the image of him as a constipating thinker is dealt with in an essay that becomes a philosophical 'dosage of a good laxative' (2011c: 231).

The Hegel that emerges in Žižek is so contrary to the caricature that an insight is to be found in the errors of interpretation and inversions that create the caricature. Like the Hegelian dialectic and the infinite judgement, it is the discrepancy between a first and second perspective, between two very different readings of Hegel, which throws up the insecure and shifting foundations of a rational order.

The introduction to *Less Than Nothing* begins with Galileo's reputed remark, 'Eppur si muove' ('And yet it moves'), made after being forced to recant his claims that the Earth moves around the sun. The heresy's ontological force, as developed across the book's thousand pages, is seen to crystallize the Real of being and the introduction goes on to sketch the context for Hegel's importance in this respect. The story starts with Kant's overturning of the presupposition that being is indubitably and objectively a coherent totality. How the totality was structured and our place in it was the legitimate stuff of philosophy but the premise for this way of thinking was undermined with Kant's transcendental, a priori categories making sense of how reality appears to us. Any conception of a totality only exists within a particular horizon of meaning that belongs to the human mind and what we take to be the real thing can only ever be approached as appearance of what ultimately cannot be fully cognized. A division between a transcendental frame and reality in itself leaves undecidable ultimate queries about the nature of reality and this opens up a space, the philosophical habitat that German Idealism moves in after Kant.

Hegel reaches a momentous position in this movement when the division identified by Kant as arising from the necessary borders of reason are relocated into the topology of reality itself: 'The void of our knowledge corresponds to a void in being itself' (LTN 149). What Hegel's dialectic shows, in the immanent failure of every phenomenon to be itself, is a disparity at the heart of matter. Kant did not go down this path, accepting that we must be able to think about things-in-themselves for 'otherwise we should be landed in the absurd conclusion that there can be appearance without anything that appears' (Kant 2007: 27).

The 'absurd conclusion' is in a way what Hegel puts forward. Identities remain abstract if relationships to other entities are removed and, when something is seen in relation to what it is not, Hegel reasons that 'as *determinateness* the negation is in the property' (2018: §73). Hegel's word for how things are what they are and not something else, determinateness, is a process of negation. Substance loses its grip as a kind of matter with its own unity when negation is at the heart of its identity and the traditional distinction between appearance as a deceptive surface and an essence that lies beneath no longer holds.

Hegel's account of appearance and essence helps establish the crucial distance between Žižek and much of mainstream Anglo-American philosophy. The air is taken out of Hegel's radical ontology and his metaphysical reach when he is read as a thinker of normativity and intersubjective agreement and countering this deflation is a sustained intent throughout *Less Than Nothing* and *Absolute Recoil*. In these books, Hegel provides the ground for conceiving materialism not in terms of some existing density of substance, beyond our notional understanding, but as 'the *subjective* moment, the most elementary "reifying" illusion of subjectivity, what the subject *adds* to the real-in-itself' (LTN 807). The subject is reflexively inscribed into substance and this undermines traditional assumptions about substance.

Hegel says there 'is nothing in heaven or nature or spirit or anywhere else that does not contain as much immediacy as mediation … [they] prove to be *unseparated* and *inseparable*' (2010a: 46). Immediacy allows for the possibility of reaching what is really there, Kantian things-in-themselves, free of the meanings we impose through representations, but the possibility is a chimera when mediation is unavoidable. Kant reasoned that immediacy was accessible but that our experience of it had to remain inside subjective structures; the distinction becomes tenuous when the difference between immediacy and mediation collapses into a coexistence. The kind of cohabitation being outlined, a unity based on two, not one, is initially as strange to become familiar with as the use of the middle voice in ancient Greek.

Hegelian scholars, including those Žižek admires in many important respects, like Robert Pippin and Béatrice Longuenesse, tend to keep Hegel within a Kantian field where substance and subject are kept separate. Longuenesse takes the example of non-contradiction, that is, A=A rules out any simultaneous A and not-A (2010a: 354–5) as a law of logic and summarizes the point Hegel is seen to be making about it. While its grammatical construction betokens a statement about a property of entities, it is actually, she says, only a 'requirement of thought' ([1981] 2007: 44). What lies within thought and what lies outside are kept separate and Pippin, in his review of *Less Than Nothing*, is explicit on this point (2015: 96n13). Pippin is judged to remain Kantian when Žižek quotes him describing Hegel's identity of thinking and being as 'not knowledge of any nonsensible reality, it is knowledge of any intelligible reality, the only kind there is' (F 67).

A different Hegelian approach is to transpose negation and the antinomies, which for Kant are strictly epistemological, into the nature of identity itself. The philosophical move explored by Žižek and others accepts the logical rule, instanced above, about the impossibility of A being simultaneously non-A, while also – and this is the crucial step – making it necessary. It is 'because opposites cannot directly coincide' (LTN 629) that development takes place and this is what Hegel establishes with the movement that begins *The Science of Logic*: Being and Nothing are and are not identical, passing into Becoming because of this impossibility (Hegel 2010a: 59–60, 83–4).

It is inconsistency in the order of being itself that underlies Žižek's disagreement with what has become an orthodox reading of Hegel as a historicist. The dialectical process as the dynamic motor of historical change, driving the emergence of one kind of society from the collapse of an earlier one, does not lend itself to antagonism as transhistorical, always-already there, dividing formations from within. Hegel's own historical awareness was limited by his knowledge of an industrialism that had not reached its advanced stage during his lifetime. He could not foresee the systemic nature of capitalism and the process whereby capital becomes a self-moving subject sublating material reality in its own interests.

> True, Kant admits antinomies, but only at the epistemological level, not as immanent features of the unreachable thing-in-itself, while Hegel transposes epistemological antinomies into the ontological sphere, and thereby undermines every ontology: 'reality itself' is non-all, antinomic.
>
> (IV 51)

Žižek's presentation of Hegel is inseparable from his own deeply dialectical and speculative way of thinking. It is what allows him to point out certain limitations in Hegel without diminishing the importance of his thought for a philosophical, psychoanalytic, political and cultural understanding of ourselves and the world. Given the parody of Hegel as grossly systematic, an omnivorous totalizer, it is ironic that Žižek's work has been accused of crafting a 'virtually totalitarian world in which everything is connected and significant' (Harpham 2003: 459) and given to a 'machinic' approach to Hegel (Osborne 2013).

SO xvii–xx; OWB 45; PV 26–8, 65–7; HWB 1–12; LTN 3–19, 200–1, 266–9; F 67–74, 130–2; AR 30–1, 181–2; QH 12–17, 97–8, 103–6

Comay and Ruda 2018: 29–51; De Boer 2010; Johnston 2018: 38–73; McGowan 2013, 2016b, 2019: 11–36; Pérez 2025; Zantvoort 2025: 158–68; Žižek 2011b, 2011c, 2011d: xv–xviii, 2016i

CONNECTIONS: absolute knowing, antagonism, appearance and essence, dialectic, identity and difference, Kant, negation, ontology, Real, substance as also subject

Heidegger

> While Heidegger is perceived as a thinker uniquely focused on the question of Being, he leaves totally out of consideration what we understand by this question in our 'naïve' pre-transcendental stance: how do things exist independently of the way we relate to them, independently of how they appear to us?
>
> (Žižek 2021d)

In *The Ticklish Subject* and *The Parallax View*, Heidegger's importance is proclaimed in the idiom of existentialism. Championed as the philosopher of our finitude and groundlessness, Heidegger's call for resoluteness in the choosing of a life that is never really a free choice is endorsed without in any measure downplaying the enormity of his political fallacy and engagement with Nazism. *Dasein*, his signature term for our being-in-the-world situation, remains undiminished in importance as a validation of our always-already presence in the world. It is a presence which does not allow for complete self-objectification.

Heidegger's 'ontological difference' (PV 23–4), distinguishing beings as ontic and Being as ontological, is highlighted in *In Defence of Lost Causes* for his failure to follow through on its own radical implications. This is later developed when Heidegger's awareness of temporality as the ultimate horizon of existence is allied with Hegelian negativity – though not understood in this way by Heidegger himself – as the mordant power of time to undermine identity.

In Heidegger's 'Letter on Humanism' language is 'the house of Being', the home where man dwells (1993: 217). The image of an abode brings into sharp relief the gap that separates Heidegger from the Lacan who describes language as what captures and tortures the subject (1993: 243). Žižek employs the difference to draw attention to a blindness in Heidegger that helps explain his susceptibility to Nazism and reluctance to see the Holocaust for what it was. Along similar lines, late Heidegger's *Gelassenheit*, a positive non-willing and releasement that in a non-calculative way lets being be, is critically examined. Heidegger is valued for highlighting a relationship to nature and technology that spells disaster and for placing it within a historical world into which we as historical actors are exposed. His deficiency was in not recognizing how this should be remedied: The paradox is thus that, in order to save Heidegger from Nazism, we need *more* will and struggle and less *Gelassenheit* (LTN 902).

For Žižek, inconsistencies and indecisions in Heidegger's thought allow terms from his vocabulary to be described in ways that give them a new magnitude. In his picturing of a world we are thrown into as one where unconcealment as the truth of being is a happening not of our making (*Ereignis*), an ambivalence is found. *Ereignis* becomes 'NOTHING BUT its own distortion', an echo of a primordial void (OB 11) but also an Event that motions 'a new epochal disclosure of Being' in a deeply historical manner (E 31; AR 93). What it registers is the emergence of a particular transcendental that governs how things appear as meaningful. Within this transcendental, entities in nature are brought out of concealment for Heidegger as 'standing reserve' (*Bestand*) and the claim they make on us as the essence of a technological view of the world is what he calls 'enframing' (*Gestell*): 'The human being reduced to an object of technological manipulation is no longer properly human; it loses the feature of being ecstatically open to reality' (E 31; AR 94). Radical thoughts about how nature might be outside of this 'enframing' occur to Heidegger but he does not pursue a move beyond the transcendental.

TS 18–20; OB 8–11; PV 273–85; DLC 117–22, 447–50; LTN 865–84, 896–
    903; AR 91–6; E 30–1; SE 263–70; QH 81–4, 87–90, 108–12

Žižek 2015c

CONNECTIONS: event/act, transcendental

Hysteria

In 'Fragment of an Analysis of a Case of Hysteria', Freud uses his case history known as 'Dora' as an example of 'the strange and wonderful phenomenon of hysteria … a disease which still remains as great a puzzle as ever' (1981a: 24). The term as used by Lacan is developed and becomes one the four intersubjective discourses set out in his Seminar XVII, *The Other Side of Psychoanalysis*. The discourses – the Master, the University, the Analyst and the Hysteric – are positioned around issues of authority, *jouissance* and knowledge. They are not as restrictive or as self-contained as the names suggest: the discourse of the University is not reserved for students and academics; the discourse of the Hysteric is in dispute with the Master's (TS 164). A hysterical position is not only open to everyone but, in a metaphysical, sense, the very status of the subject is hysterical (TIR 164).

Hysteria – neurosis is another name Lacan gives it – is the anxious questioning of one's identity vis-à-vis the desire of the Other and it arises from an awareness that the subject *is* its own loss, a failure to represent itself that cannot be allayed by the interpellation of naming and the bestowal of a symbolic identity. The self-disputing subject is not at home in language: 'The "true" word is missing, and this word is missing because I – the speaking subject – don't have a proper place within the symbolic, because I am a crack in its edifice' (AP 80). Given this cognizance of loss, the hysteric wants to know what is in them that someone else finds to be an object of their desire, what is the secret treasure that Lacan calls the *agalma*. The ancient Greek word for a votive offering, a gift to please the gods, *agalma* becomes the innermost part of oneself that sustains the illusion of a core identity. When someone is uncertain about what this might be, it is a daring perplexity and a path to learning when a satisfactory answer is not forthcoming. 'The very cry by which the *jouissance* obtained is distinguished from the *jouissance* expected' is 'that's not it' (Lacan 1999: 111). The hysteric declines to sacrifice themselves by filling in the Other's lack: 'I refuse to sacrifice the *agalma* in me BECAUSE THERE IS NOTHING TO SACRIFICE' (OB 74).

The authentic knowledge of the hysteric is available to men and women because the emptiness of the subject pertains to the failure of interpellation for a subject (DLC 344). The nature of every subject, hysterical in its unsatisfied desire, distinguishes humans from animals, borne out by the classic difference between the ape who will give up trying to reach an object out of its reach and the human who remains in the grip of an obsession for an impossible object. Hysteria defines humankind's 'installing a point of impossibility in the guise of absolute *jouissance*' (PF xvi; LTN 651). The unconscious of the hysteric displaces desires and wishes via the biological body, warping it

Of situations from literature used as displays of hysteria, the king's rejection of his designation in Shakespeare's *Richard II* (Act 4, Scene 1) is first referenced by Žižek in *Lacan*. The foundations of the monarch's identity are taken from him and, such is the affective logic, Richard is traumatized by grasping the void behind his royal title. The obverse is the monarch, in the movie *The King's Speech*, whose stuttering betrays his difficulty in accepting a royal identity. The language coach breaches the impasse when he provokes the king by sitting on the sovereign's chair and refusing to remove himself from it. The coach's success is 'a reactionary one: the king is "normalized", the force of his hysterical questioning is obliterated' (LTN 421).

When the scene from *Richard II* is looked at in *Disparities*, Phédre, in Racine's play of that name, is also seen to act hysterically when she violates her traditional identity as a mother and confesses to her stepson the passion she feels for him. His shocked response, unable to deal with being the object of her passion, also becomes a form of hysteria (D 191). In an analysis of Wager's *Parsifal*, Kundry's laughter gives body to her position as the 'true hysteric', exposing 'the fact that the master is impotent, a semblance of himself' (SFA 416–17).

Hysteria in its past association with women (inseparable from the birth of psychoanalysis) has long been upended by feminists: 'The hysterics are my sisters' (Cixous and Clément [1986] 1996: 99). This overturning is given further weight when what was called feminine hysteria is linked with a male horror of women as part of a European *Zeitgeist* marking artists like Munch, Strindberg and Kafka. These men unable to fathom a woman's change of guises and finding 'behind these masks a consistent subject manipulating them' (Žižek 1994b) are deeply disturbed as a consequence. A contrast can be drawn between a man partaking in the illusion that behind his symbolic construction there is a substantial content, the 'real' man, and a woman who knows that masks, including her own, are hollow. Lacan's statement that women do not exist is misunderstood outside of this frame but it is spelt out in Seminar XX: 'There is no such thing as a Woman because, in her essence … she is not-whole' (1999: 72–3). In this way, patriarchy's purview can be understood as the anxious containment of the hysterical depth haunting every subject.

What feminists are able to celebrate about hysteria takes on a broader political importance when the hysteric is contrasted with the pervert: 'The subject of late capitalist market relations is perverse, while the "democratic subject" … is inherently hysterical' (TS 248).

> What differentiates hysteria from psychosis is their different relation to the 'enjoyment of the Other' (not the subject's enjoyment of the Other, but the Other who enjoys [in] the subject): a hysteric finds it unbearable to be the object of the Other's enjoyment, she finds herself 'used' or 'exploited', while a psychotic wilfully immerses himself in it and wallows in it.
>
> (LTN 92)

TIR 162–5; TS 247–8; OB 73–4; L 35–6; AR 150, 159–61; D 190–3, 211–13; CA 29–31, 36–8, 182–7

Bailly 2009; Kaye 2023: 144–8, 160–2; Žižek 2024e; Zupančič 2023: 82–3

CONNECTIONS: fantasy, *objet petit a*, other, perversion, subject, unconscious

I

Identity and difference

Identity and difference underlies Hegel's dialectic and a related nexus of formulations, from antagonism and negation to infinite judgements, concrete universality and speculative reason. It relates to Lacanian ideas about the nature of the subject, sexual difference, the plight of the hysteric and the Real. Psychoanalytically, it informs issues of race and anti-Semitism and the reactionary force of identity politics and far-right nationalism. The dialectic of identity and difference possesses this breadth because it constitutes the nature of being, hence its role in the analysis of being and nothing at the beginning of Hegel's *The Science of Logic*.

Identity as a principle of thought, a requirement for its consistency, does not for Hegel depend on a one-to-rule that equates thought with a given, a fact, that ontologically precedes it. It does not involve intrinsic qualities but does require the movement of reflection in order to construct identity, not some prior, individual self-announcing essence. Recognizing diversity, the distinguishing of one object of thought from another, arises in a similar way from the development of reflection and there is unison in their ways of ascribing identities. Hegel stresses – this not being a uniform allocation – how only the 'thoughtless examination of them enumerates them *one after the other*, so that they appear unconnected' (2010a: 356). Connectedness resides in the cohesion of identifying with differentiating; the activity of one is the activity of the other. Identity and difference are irreducibly unified and both are determined by thought. The determination of things rests on an indeterminate plurality and Hegel mocks the idea of individual essences determining difference. He recalls the story about Leibniz, propounding this idea, prompting court ladies to search among trees for two identical leaves (366).

Difference, says Hegel, 'is the negativity that reflection possesses in itself … It is the *difference of reflection*, not the *otherness of existence*' (2010a: 361). What follows are not just the determinations of things' identities but the difference that pertains to any particular identity in itself: 'A thing's difference from all its particular properties (each of which can be shared by other things): a thing "is" not its properties, it "is" a unique receptacle of its properties' (F 99). The radical implication is that difference now acquires a pure status of its own, one that transcends it being just the difference of the symbolic ordering that accords unalike identities. This is why, when looking at class difference and sexual difference, the opposition within each of them is never merely binary. If the dissimilarity were simply a difference between two classes or two sexes then there would not in principle be anything preventing a steady concord. There has to be a third element that exists as pure difference in itself 'irreducible to symbolic differentiality' (F 100). In sexual difference this element is positivized as the transgendered subject –for anti-Semites as the Jew, for unadulterated nationalists as the refugee – functioning as a disavowal of the antagonism that is difference.

KNW 33–48, 87–8, 141–2; TN 130–4; F 99–100

Cole 2014: 9–23, 50–7; Longuenesse ([1981] 2007): 54–6

CONNECTIONS: antagonism, anti-Semitism, concrete universality, hysteric/ pervert, infinite judgement, negation, ontology, race, Real, reflection, sexual difference, speculative reason, subject

Ideology

<blockquote>
The affected subject, the subject addressed by an ideological edifice, does not take ideological injunctions seriously, he mocks them, dismisses them cynically, but this very 'resistance' is in advance taken into account and serves the reproduction of the ideological edifice.

(D 60)
</blockquote>

The nature of ideology, first examined in *The Sublime Object of Ideology* and *For They Know Not What They Do*, remains central to Žižek's critical thinking. The soft power of ideology is seen to immunize effective objections to capitalism's ascendancy by assimilating apparently critical beliefs about the status quo. Consumerism, individualism and satirical derision, more efficient than the hard power of overt oppression, facilitate the way 'ideology appears as its own opposite, as *non-ideology*, as the core of our human identity underneath all the ideological labels' (FT 39).

There are states of 'constructed ignorance', typified by the liberal's espousal of Martin Luther King's 'I have a dream' speech which conveniently ignores the full import of what he stood for. Ignorance is crafted, not so much conspiratorially on behalf of vested interests but at a level that escapes the consciousness of those accepting an ideology. Under Nazism, denigrating Jews functioned openly in the political and social terrain in ways that meant a subjective investment was not required of anti-Semites. People can behave in ways that conflict with their consciously avowed beliefs, as is the case with commodity fetishism, without it bothering them.

It is insufficient to treat ideology as a colonizing of the mind, projecting false beliefs and deceptions which can be unmasked through a hermeneutics of suspicion. Climate change and ecological disasters are not secrets being withheld from the public and the disavowal that irrationally allows the situation to grow worse points to ideology operating like a fetish – held on to for succour in the face of an unbearable truth (OB 14; DLC 296) – rather than a straightforward false consciousness. Cynicism, creating a distance between professions of disbelief in the big Other and actual behaviour signalling the opposite, is now an integral part of how ideology works. The contrast, put succinctly in *Hegel in a Wired Brain*, is that ideology is less a conspiracy of lies fabulated by the ruling class and more 'stories invented by subjects to deceive themselves' (ADB 89; HWB 23).

Ideology's reign over people's behaviour and the denialism that oils the machinery of political control becomes more explicable when *jouissance* is taken into account. Its libidinal appeal is part of 'our self-proclaimed postideological universe' (WD 70) where guilt is absolved. *Jouissance* facilitates the paradox of finding satisfaction in suffering, the symbiosis of pleasure with unpleasure so palpable in the scenarios that catastrophe movies excel in depicting. An unexpected homology is found in medieval scholasticism when Thomas Aquinas proffers a dubious rationale for saved souls in Heaven being able to see the damned being tortured in Hell. The unspoken supposition is that enjoying heavenly bliss is not enough (AR 219; LD 227) and needs to be supported by the surplus pleasure of taking a look at the suffering of others. Such thinking becomes ideological when extended to real life involving political choices, though enjoyment in the planned destruction of Palestinian life 'no longer dwells in the obscene underground' (CA 250). In Israel's genocidal war on Gaza, it stands exposed as an undue supplement for many citizens of that country.

SO 15–16, 27–8; KNW 241–53; AR 209–10, 218–20; D 59–64; TP 66–71; F
    32–3, 144–8; TL 134–5; CA 76, 250–1

Kaye 2023: 67–81, 131–5; Zalloua 2020: 10–13; Žižek 1994a

CONNECTIONS: anti-Semitism, commodity fetishism, *jouissance*

Infinity

> Life (even at its most elementary as a living cell) is the basic form of true infinity since it already involves the minimal loop by means of which a process no longer is simply determined by the Outside of its environs but is itself able to (over) determine the mode of this determination and thus 'posits its presuppositions'.
>
> **(OWB 117)**

Hegel distinguishes two ways of comprehending infinity. What he calls 'bad' or 'spurious' infinity is akin to the common sense of something finite, limited in extent or scope, being followed by another finitude and so on without end. Infinity's potential as an endless set of multiplicities is unbounded, always continuing beyond the current finitude. Each logical atom is non-dialectical, taking its place in a continuum and giving way in linear fashion to a process of becoming, ending and succession.

Finitude as something bounded by some other is contested by Hegel's 'true' infinity which 'consists in remaining at home with itself in its other, or (when it is expressed as a process) in coming to itself in its other' (Hegel 1991: 149).

A 'remaining at home' does not collapse infinity and finitude into a single identity. It involves the work of negativity and its compulsion to repeat, unfolding infinity from the failure of what is finite to remain statically itself as a singular, positive something:: 'Finite things *are*, but in their reference to themselves they refer to themselves *negatively* – in this very self-reference they propel themselves beyond themselves, beyond their being' (Hegel 2010a: 101). Jean-Luc Nancy expresses this by saying 'the negative is the prefix of the *in*-finite, as the affirmation that all finitude (and every being is finite) is, in itself, in excess of its determinacy' (2002: 12).

Infinity as the movement of what is finite, continually ceasing to be by giving way to another finitude, like the painting contained within the painting or the map within the map (MSH 227), only becomes 'good' when eternal repetition is interrupted by a self-determination that is not inert, creating its own limitation and the capacity to go beyond itself.

The idea of a self-limitation creating its own precinct is found 'the moment a cell's membrane starts to function as a self-boundary' (OWB 117). In *Organs without Bodies*, accounts of autopoiesis and emergentism in biological sciences help explain how true infinity is a process where each finite moment pushes beyond itself. Autopoiesis is given a dialectical amplitude when a form of self-negating reversal is recognized in descriptions by thinkers like Francisco Varela about what is going on when a cell forms a membrane that separates its inside from its outside. For Varela, a network of molecules organizes for itself the boundary that identifies it as a cell. It produces its own set of causes by way of reversing something given – biochemical reactions – into a new formation that is its own opposite, a self-positing cellular entity. It becomes possible, then, to understand aspects of nature, in this case a biological process, in a way that is structurally similar to Hegel's notion of a true infinity.

The difference between 'bad' and 'good' infinity becomes fertile ground for philosophizing. Crosscutting the Lacanian with the Hegelian, drive's compulsion and the opposition between finitude and infinitude are seen to both rely '*on the blockage of direct positive affirmation*' and how 'we repeat because it is impossible to directly affirm' (LTN 493). On a Kantian plane, yearning for the thing-in-itself results in 'bad' infinity as one finite piece of phenomenal reality succeeds another whereas 'good' infinity can be achieved with a Hegelian change of gear from elusive Being to dynamic Becoming. The Absolute becomes not some infinite cloud of the ultra-rational, clear of recurrent encounters with phenomenal finitude, but the unceasing process itself: 'In other words, *true infinity is nothing but finitude as such*, its immanent limitation which pushes it into a constant self-overcoming' (AR 352). The constancy here, the unremitting activity of 'self-overcoming', is the continuation of the restless subject. This also ministers to a way of philosophizing time that explains a situating of eternity, the immanence of becoming in being, as an 'infinite virtuality' within the finitude of temporality (OWB 11). An abstruse formulation like this is a result of speculative reason.

If all this seems too rarefied for its own good, a down-to-earth example is found in the first codename, Infinite Justice, for the United States' post-9/11 campaign against terrorism. As 'bad infinity' it indicates an endless task of combating one terrorist threat after another. In the true Hegelian sense, infinity involves a reflexive 'remaining at home' that 'has to ask how we ourselves, who exercise justice, are involved in what we are fighting against' (I 66).

OWB 11, 69, 117; LTN 157–8; AR 351–2

Hegel 1991: 149–52, 2018: §§161–3; Houlgate 2006: 394–9

CONNECTIONS: dialectic, drive, negativity, speculative reason

Infinite judgement

There are two ways something can be negated to affirm a reality that does not fall within the scope of a given concept: a straightforward negative judgement ('she is not dead') or – and this is Kant's infinite judgement – by affirming a non-predicate ('she is undead'). A negative judgement allows the possibility of determining something by first ruling out a particular property, 'deadness' in this case, but the domain remains open for some other positive judgement. Kant's infinite judgement leaves the field indeterminate by failing to positively determine a property. With 'she is undead', some reality is left over, that of an undead being, but attaching a positive status to its nature cannot be established. Matters are left uncompleted and it is this deficit that Hegel and Žižek find fruitful.

A tautological statement, like 'it is what it is' or 'a rose is a rose', is akin to Kant's infinite judgement as one where the copula 'is' only serves to defer the predication. 'The *being of spirit is a bone*', a statement of Hegel's in *The Phenomenology of Spirit* (§343), can be read as an infinite judgement but not in the way Kant termed a judgement to be infinite. It goes beyond Kant by making indeterminacy meaningful: what is contradictory about spirit being a bone encapsulates a negation of the negation that turns an obstacle, here the reconciling of completely oppositional terms, into a positive affirmation of unfinishedness: 'Absolute spirit comes into existence only at the point where its pure knowing of itself is the opposition and flux of itself with itself' (§671). The insufficiency brought to the surface in a tautology is an inherent inadequacy pertaining to every identity.

Grasping 'the true not just as *substance* but just as much as *subject*', from *The Phenomenology of Spirit* (§17), is another infinite judgement. It also knots what seems patently incompatible and finds meaning in an apparently blatant discrepancy. The meaning is not that substance shares in the self-consciousness associated with substance for this cannot be the case – the terms are different because they are taken to oppose one another – but that the inability of substance to be subject is internal to it, part of its non-identity with itself. The impossibility of substance to be itself, to be self-subsistent, is the impossibility of affirming substance to be also subject. At one level this is Alice-in-Wonderland nonsense but of the kind that Lacan was drawing attention to about the nature of language whereby, as Žižek puts it, an elephant 'is "more present" in the word which evokes it than in the immediate physical being' (KNW 120).

The difference between negative and infinite judgement marks a change in form whereby the predicate is no longer a property or quality that in itself can be denied ('this is not representable art') and becomes, by contrast, a property or quality reflected within itself ('this is non-representable art'). The sublation that denotes the difference is utilizable in different spheres and, for instance, it clarifies the nature of sexual difference when the not-All in Lacan's formula for female logic is read as a Kantian infinite judgement. It allows for woman as 'not man' to be redefined as woman is 'non-man' because it 'not only does not bring us back to man but leaves behind the entire field of man and its opposite' (LTN 785). Similarly, the move from 'there is no sexual relationship' to 'there is a sexual non-relationship' traverses the difference by ditching any semblance to traditional motifs of conflict between the sexes in favour of a non-predicate that conveys a radical deadlock.

A political wing of infinite judgement finds expression in Bartleby's 'I would prefer not to' when, by its negating of the negation of not-wanting-to-do-it, it becomes a site of resistance by affirming the non-predicate of wanting-to-not-do-it: 'This is the gesture of subtraction at its purest' which 'opens up the space for the New' (LTN 1007). Žižek formulates an infinite judgement of his own, accommodating the New in the fullest sense possible, with 'material reality is *non-All*' in opposition to the negative judgement that 'material reality is not all there is' (LTN 742). Kant's infinite judgement is here affiliated with the female formula of sexuation for a refined materialism which does not succumb to the metaphysical cliché about a higher spiritual scale that is implicit in the negative judgement.

> **And one has to go to the end here: the supreme figure of Evil is therefore God himself insofar as he stands above creation, judging us. This is why true reconciliation happens only in Christianity, which enacts the infinite judgment 'god is a mortal man', an absolute contradiction.**
>
> **(Žižek 2024j)**

KNW 119–21; ME 43; LTN 534–5, 788, 796–7, 1006–7; SFA 152–3

Kant 2007: 108; Ruda 2015b: 156–73

CONNECTIONS: 'I would prefer not to', negation of negation, not-All/non-All, sexual difference, speculative reason, '*spirit is a bone*', substance as also subject

In-itself/For-itself

The contrast in the terms being in-itself and being for-itself, associated with phenomenology and Sartre's *Being and Nothingness*, can loosely serve as shorthand for the commonsensical distinction drawn between contingent, space-filling, self-relating things (in-itself) and things developed in relations to other things, including ourselves (for-itself). Hegel, responding critically to Kant's differentiation of a 'thing-in-itself' from its appearance to us, uses the terms in more than one way and complicates the relation between them.

Hegel states that there is consciousness of objects external to it but that consciousness is also aware of itself: 'It is consciousness of what, to it, is the true, as well as consciousness of its knowing of the true' (2018: §85). In his next two sentences, the source of the complication is laid out: 'While both are *for the same* consciousness, consciousness itself is their comparison. It is an issue *for that consciousness* whether or not its knowing of the subject corresponds to the object' (§85). The problem, he goes on to say, is the difficulty of distinguishing any 'in-itself' from 'for-itself'. They affect each other and become inseparable even through the distinction between them remains.

The terms collapse in Hegel's Absolute Knowing when an objective comprehension of 'in-itself' and 'for-itself' is clearly not available. The gap in reality, in the in-itself, its lack of a transcendent core, is what accounts for the Real and it warps the notion of an in-itself: 'The real is not the In-itself but the very obstacle which distorts our access to the In-itself' (QH 86). The mathematicized formulae of quantum physics approach the in-itself but, Žižek notes, subtlety resides in recognizing the subjective involvement of scientists that leads to advances in quantum physics. The in-itself and the for-itself cannot be kept apart, they overlap internally, and Absolute Knowing is the full acceptance of this inextricability. Occasions when the passage between in-itself and for-itself reveals themselves are found in the experience of falling into love (TS 54) and the falling out of it (TS 74).

Meillassoux's *After Finitude* is applauded for its philosophical panache in presenting the utter contingency that informs the In-itself and making this the very source of our knowledge towards it. What has been viewed as a cognitive constraint, access to the in-itself being hindered by the gap between facticity and the finitude of our reason (hence the title of Meillassoux's book), becomes the gap that is intrinsic to the Absolute. Meillassoux's achievement in this Hegelian move is qualified nonetheless by his attachment to thinking that reality as it really is remains available to the subject. This is why Meillassoux places such importance on what he calls the 'arche-fossil', evidence of 'ancestral' reality 'anterior to terrestrial life' (2008: 10). Žižek's rejoinder is to indicate what he regards as a failure by Meillassoux to locate the non-correlation between subject and object within 'the real INSIDE the subject' (SFA 38). The subject, emerging from the antagonism that is the Real, is inaccessible to itself. In what comes across as a timely philosophical pun, the true 'fossil' becomes the bone that Hegel calls spirit (LTN 645) because the In-itself cannot be unswervingly reached. A transcendental correlation between reality and a subjective position is, contra Meillassoux, unavoidable but it resides within the self-movement of the In-itself. The gap between in-itself and for-itself 'is immanent to the In-itself' (LTN 906).

> The dialectical buck stops here: the subject can no longer play the game of the 'experience of consciousness', comparing the For-us with the In-itself and thereby subverting both of them, since there is no longer any shape of the In-itself available as a measure of the truth of the For-us.
>
> (LTN 389)

IR 47–8; TS 74–5; LTN 389–40, 632–6, 644–5, 906, 958–9; SFA 37–8

Hegel 2018: §§82–6

CONNECTIONS: absolute knowing, Real, '*spirit is a bone*', subject

J

Jouissance

Underlying the difference between desire and drive is the *jouissance* that comes from the drive's failure to reach a foreclosed object of desire. Desire's metonymic journeying from one object to another in an endless search for satisfaction is resolved by drive deriving satisfaction from the fruitlessness of the search. Desire purely desires but drive is motored by a structural imbalance in the order of existence. It is not a procreant urge but it does result in an excess that expresses itself as *jouissance*, a term laden with a meaning by Lacan in ways that fall short of its translation as enjoyment.

The sense of an out-of-joint life force as one of the modalities of the Real overlaps with *jouissance* as an unreachable but ineradicable point of enjoyment. Possessed of an oversufficiency, it can disrupt the body and in *The Metastases of Enjoyment* paintings by the Pre-Raphaelite artist Holman Hunt give visual expression to this carnal excess: in his *The Hireling Shepherd*, 'the all too vivacious red and green palette stains the entire painting with a repulsive tone, as if we were dealing with a putrid overripe nature' (ME 113; Žižek 2025j). The bodily disturbance, its lack of equilibrium, is *jouissance* in its lack of purpose, serving nothing, without meaning and devoid of interpretation. Hunt's paintings insinuate a biologism that is echoed in Lacan's use of the word *lamella* for an amoeba-like organ that thwarts corporeal stability. This also finds painterly expression in Francis Bacon's portraitures where, under the dictatorship of the body, eldritch matter seeps out through the skin and begins to spread itself (AR 358). The 'overripe' colours in Hunt's painting, like the formless stains in Bacon's work, bear witness to *jouissance* as an 'intervention' whereby 'a human animal becomes properly mortal, relating to the prospect of its own extinction' (QH 87).

At a pre-ontological level, *jouissance* emerges from a rift in being and the unassuageable plight of the subject arising within it, aghast at its own failed existence (SE 228). It permeates the body, exceeding the requirements of socio-symbolic rubrics and, outstripping the resources of the big Other, is realized in the *jouisseur* through a *sinthome*. A Lacanian neologism for 'traces of affective intensities' and 'a figment of obscene enjoyment' (OWB 5, 143), a *sinthome* is 'the only positive support of our being' (SO 81). Traction for what is being described by these 'intensities' is found in the case of someone contentedly engaged in life with a partner and friends but who unaccountably succumbs to a lure – gambling, perhaps, or alcohol – that risks utterly derailing their happiness. The *sinthome* is a prop for subjectivity, a self-sustaining knot by acting as a libidinal equivalent of what T. S. Eliot called an 'objective correlate'; not a way of representing an emotion in a literary text but a source of satisfaction that anchors a person's fragile sense of being.

Jouissance's peculiarity is the engendering of enjoyment out of displeasure, 'a self-sabotage of pleasure' (CA 66), and this extends to deriving an enjoyment in being subordinated and oppressed. When taking this particular form, it is an additional pleasure of its own unbalanced make-up as if the body finds a way of rewarding itself for not finding pleasure in more normal ways. Lacan calls this surplus enjoyment and Žižek finds its representation in a scene from Brecht/ Weil's *The Threepenny Opera* where the music reverses an expected course and moves from a slow, sermonizing style articulating life's capacity for joy to a lively, gratifying expression of its failure to do so. The oddity of the gap between the subject and the content of enunciation gives voice here to the strange way satisfaction can be accrued from suffering (SE 237–8). This gap between the content of enunciation and subject of enunciation reaches an obscene level with Nazi executioners' perverse *jouissance* while killing in the guise of duty. Hannah Arendt, reporting on the Eichmann trial, famously wrote of the 'banality of evil' but this is inadequate when it simplistically contrasts a bureaucratic mindset with the horrors of the Holocaust. Eichmann's defence was not just a convenient fiction for evading responsibility and, in particular, 'this "bureaucratization" was in itself a source of additional *jouissance*' (PF 69–70).

'I' am in a place from which a voice is heard clamouring 'the universe is a defect in the purity of Non-Being'.

And not without reason, for by protecting itself this place makes Being itself languish. This place is called *Jouissance*, and it is the absence of this that makes the universe vain.

(Lacan 2001: 351)

Objet a is conceived by Lacan as surplus enjoyment and the link this provides with surplus value in Marx is not accidental for either Lacan or Žižek (SE 6).

Jouissance in itself is historically and ideologically indifferent but, as a part of what used to be called the human condition, close encounters with *jouissance* characterize personal relationships. At an intimate level, there are occasions in any authentic relationship with an other that bring one traumatically close to their 'moment of *jouissance*' (PF 61) and the uncanny gap between any two people.

Being too close to someone but not as part of a loving relationship can be a source of discomfort and this Other, conceptualized as the Neighbour, exhibits aspects of their culture that can be felt as gesturing towards a manner of excessive enjoyment. Their enjoyment may be just different to ours but, convinced of our own inadequate enjoyment, we magnify it into a conviction that their enjoyment is fuller and superior. This then acts as a source of antipathy. *Jouissance* as a state that cannot be satisfactorily attained is inherently problematic, experienced by the subject as the presence of an intrusive enigma. Though irresolvable, a palliative method in the psychoanalytic realm allows dissatisfaction to be relieved by transferring onto an Other what is out of reach for ourselves. There is an Other deemed able to revel in full enjoyment, 'a utopia of full *jouissance*' (D 181), but this is difficult to accept and jealously can melt into hostility and racism. Refugees must be denied asylum because they will smuggle in a *jouissance* being denied to the indigenous population and Trump's supporters stormed the Capitol in 2021 to have returned to them the rightful enjoyment taken from them by others – to 'stop the steal', the theft of their enjoyment (Žižek 2024d; ZP 8).

'Lacan's key name for the Real is *jouissance*' (F 161), meaning for Žižek that the hollowness at the heart of the human animal is bound up with drive's insistent circling around the primal void of what is not there. The repetition of failure provides its only source of enjoyment and the superego demands that enjoyment must be relentlessly pursued. Occupying the core of the subject is the 'fantasmatic kernel of enjoyment' which lies beyond its reach and 'the subject can only stare, with a cold, transfixed gaze, at the kernel, unable to fully recognise itself in it' (AR 166).

PF 60–3; TS 291; PV 188–90, 308–17; CZ 113–14; D 180–3; ADB 74–5; SE 236–46; F 86; ZP 122

McGowan 2025: 73–9

CONNECTIONS: anti-Semitism, drive, enunciated and enunciation, neighbour, other, race, Real, superego

K

Kafka, Franz

See fantasy, hysteria, literary criticism, other, *Vertigo*.

Kant

There are entries for Kant in the indexes of most books by Žižek, testimony to an unshakeable influence rooted in an agreement with Hegel's judgement that Kant irrevocably undermined traditional metaphysics. Kant's notion of the transcendental is accepted as marking a pivotal division in the history of philosophy (OWB 45; LTN 9; QH 88). After Kant, inquiries not previously considered could be asked about *how* we make sense of reality. Pre-Kantian philosophy itself becomes readable as a hermeneutical orientation that assumes there is a complete, non-antagonistic ontology. Kant's greatness lies in his recognition of this assumption's failure.

Kant's achievement was to direct attention away from a putative transcendent reality that lies beyond the quotidian appearance of things and consider in its stead what conditions are necessary to make possible the way things appear in the way they do. Objects of the senses are 'mere appearances' but this is the extent of our knowledge of them and 'we thereby admit at the very same time that a thing in itself underlies them, although we are not acquainted with this thing as it may be constituted in itself' (Kant 2004: 66). This is not to say that phenomenal reality is a subjective misapprehension; it is the way things effectively appear. When a perceptual error occurs and something is mistaken for something else 'what is wrong is not that I am unaware of how things "really are in themselves" but of how they "really appear" to me' (OWB 44; Žižek 2020c: 106–7). The 'really' here is doing a lot of work, underlining the way appearances are not 'merely' appearances. They could not appear in any other way because, phenomenologically speaking, this is reality and any deviation is a subjective misapprehension, capable of being corrected.

> **In a way, one claim that it is only with this idea of Kant's [the transcendental] that philosophy reached its own terrain; prior to Kant, philosophy was ultimately perceived as a general science of Being as such, as a description of the universal structure of entire reality.**
>
> **(LTN 9)**

Kant's transcendental requires embedded categories of conceptualizing thought that process empirical data but which cannot provide direct cognitive access to the sources of the data. The noumenal things-in-themselves that are the sources are inaccessible to the human mind.

This inaccessibility is a circumscription that causes problems when the immanent forms of thinking are taken beyond their permitted role and applied to what is not directly experienced. Kant's position is that ideas of reason lead to antinomies (SFA 108) when, to take one of his examples, the notion that everything takes place according to the laws of nature comes up against the notion that nature must have its own special and spontaneous beginning that is not determined by the causality that determines everything else. Each position can be arrived at through impeccable reasoning and the antinomy is not traceable to a flaw in the categories themselves. The antinomy arises by forgetting that they relate merely to appearances and not things-in-themselves.

By introducing an unbridgeable breach between our knowledge of entities as they appear to us and as they really are in themselves, Kant prepares the ground for later philosophers. Most crucially for Hegel, that antinomies exist is 'one of the most important and profound advances' in modern philosophy but Kant's solution lets him down and reveals 'a tenderness for the things of this world'. Kant is to be reprimanded for thinking that 'the stain of contradiction ought not to be in the essence of what is in the world; it has to belong *only* to thinking reason' (Hegel 1991: 92). Kant's 'tenderness' prevents him locating the antinomies in reality itself. Hegel does locate them there and they indicate a rupture that he subjects to a metastasis by investing them with the disorderly force of negativity. What to Kant is a limitation in our knowledge that produces inconsistencies becomes evidence of a fractured reality. As Žižek puts it, what was an epistemological constraint becomes an ontological actuality: entities exist, they are not merely appearances, but only in the sense that 'they cannot fully exist' (IV 52). The noumenal reality that Kant tenderly presupposes and holds fast to is there as an antinomy writ large: 'He *already has what he is looking for*' (LTN 267). When

Kant writes how the concept of a noumenal is 'a merely *limiting concept* … only of negative employment' (2007: 272), because the noumenal is unreachable and places a limit on the phenomenal, the words are read literally to radically reverse Kant's intended meaning. It now serves as a pointer towards the power of negativity that signifies all phenomena as self-limiting. It is not that some pure transcendent can only be figured in its negative capacity: 'On the contrary, every positive figure of the In-itself is a "positivization" of negativity' (LTN 282). None of this denies the reality of existing entities – their quiddities and processes – but it does do away with the need for a positively existing noumenal realm and a transcendental schematism. What stands in its place is a non-holistic and self-limiting jurisdiction within phenomenal reality. This jurisdiction, nonetheless, accommodates human freedom as a state transcending the causal realm of phenomenal reality. For Kant, ironically, it is the inaccessibility of the noumenal that guarantees our freedom: if the noumenal realm of '*God and eternity with their awful majesty*' were to appear before us, we would do what is right out of fear not moral worth and become 'mere mechanism in which, as in a puppet show, everything would *gesticulate* well but there would be *no life* in the figures' (Kant 2015: 117–18).

OWB 41–5; PV 20–3, 90–5; LTN 9–11, 266–9, 280–3; AR 9–11; IV 50–2; SFA
    120–3; SE 263–6; QH 123–5

McGowan 2025: 9–17; Žižek 2020c: 103–7, 112–20, 2024k: 16–19

CONNECTIONS: *Blade Runner*, freedom, German Idealism, Hegel, negativity,
    transcendental

Kierkegaard, Sören

See Antigone, ethics, Lacan, love, Marx.

L

Lacan, Jacques

The topic 'Lacan and philosophy' can be adequately approached only when we avoid the trap of the clear line of demarcation between the two: psychoanalysis as a specific clinical practice on the one side, philosophical reflection on the other.

(IV 4)

Žižek has long been explaining Lacanian ideas for general readers as well as academic audiences and today's ready availability of reliable guides to Lacan is partly an effect of Žižek's success in popularizing the French psychoanalyst and teacher.

On first acquaintance, Lacan's discourse is still capable of producing an aura of enigma and obscurity and in the past this invited ridicule. In 1989, the year when Žižek's first book in English appeared, Noam Chomsky was dismissing Lacan as a charlatan producing nonsense for the sake of it. Žižek countered the charge of unaccountability in *Enjoy Your Symptom* (1992) and *Looking Awry* (1994) with numerous examples from films, literature and everyday life designed to shed light on Lacanian categories which, stated abstractly and encountered for the first time, can fail to convey their meaning.

Terms like the big Other, fantasy, *objet a*, Real, the subject and the symbolic no longer come with the bafflement once attached to them. Accompanying this, Freudian terms like drive, desire, hysteria and superego have been invested with distinct Lacanian articulations. The drawback to encapsulating Lacanian vocabulary in simple definitions is the preclusion of the complexity brought over the course of his teaching to developments in Lacan's own conception of his key categories.

An obvious entry point to Lacan is our fluency with situating the subject as a by-product, a construct, of larger-than-I networks of various socio-symbolic kinds. Thrown into and nurtured by a particular life-world, historically determined, the decentred subject is cut adrift from possession of an inalienable identity. Unresolved traumas are pushed into hiding, the Freudian unconscious, where they wait to make themselves felt in myriad ways. Lacan's impact on all of this is what underwrites Žižek's investment in his thought and central to this involvement is reading Lacan through Hegel. A philosophical link is established through the way Lacan works with his own categories and the Hegelian dialectic 'as a kind of short circuit between level and meta level, where you reapply a movement of a category onto itself' (Žižek 2022c). In the preface to the second edition of *The Ticklish Subject*, Žižek sees this dialectic helping to explain Lacan's advance over Heidegger in their understanding of language. Lacan does not consciously set out to apply Hegelian processes and sometimes, as when he intentionally evokes Hegel's Absolute Knowing, a misinterpretation is made (LTN 522–3). Far more vital, there is in the late Lacan a position reached which is unequivocally Hegelian in the weight of its meaning. In a lecture given on 12 May 1971, 'Class on "Lituraterre"', part of Lacan's Seminar XVIII (Lacan 2024) and later published as a chapter in a book, he describes a conceptual space by the word 'littoral'. It stands as a term for the positing of a space which cannot be called a frontier because it rules out reciprocity. Existing between *jouissance* and knowledge, its shape is that of a curve, never a straight line which he says is only found in the inscription that is writing. As a curve, the 'littoral' bends towards 'S (the symbolic semblance) and towards J (the Real of *jouissance*' (LTN 819) but never reaches either: a truly Hegelian convergence of the irreconcilable that is 'sustained by their very divergence … it is the very intersection between the two fields which constitutes them' (LTN 819).

The development of early into late Lacan complicates compact summations of his thought due to ambivalences and tensions that he brings to his own thinking. His focus of interest moves from the symbolic to the Real and what he comes to claim for psychoanalysis is likened by Žižek to the unconditionality that Kierkegaard brings to his theological understanding of Christ. The psychoanalyst does not become a Socratic figure of enlightenment, the midwife who cures the analysand by aiding them to recollect a past trauma and rescue it from their unconscious. A staged re-enactment, via transference to the analyst and eventual assumption of responsibility for what is being spoken though their symptoms, gives way to a repetition that has to be experienced by the analysand as if for the first time (AP 70–5). The goal is not 'to assume the meaning of his speech, but for him to assume its non-meaning, its nonsensical inconsistency' (LTN 515).

Bailly 2009; Homer 2005; Leader and Groves 2005; McGowan 2025; Neill
     2023; Taheri 2021: 18–22; Žižek 1994b, 1996, 2016j, 2022d; LA; L; ES

CONNECTIONS: big Other, desire, drive, enunciated and enunciation, event/ act, fantasy, gaze, hysteria, *jouissance*, not-All/non-All, *objet petit a*, Other, perversion, psychoanalysis, Real, sexual difference, subject, superego, the symbolic, the unconscious

Law

See antagonism, Antigone, Benjamin, cinema, communism, Shakespeare, superego.

Lenin

A radical political phenomenology emerges when a step is taken out of the prevailing economic and social order, suspending its hold over what is thought possible. A different future is seen but the past cannot provide a map or agenda for its implementation. The contingency of the moment is fraught with uncertainty and, with full awareness of the jeopardy involved, a subjective decision is made to engage and intervene in a situation. This is what Lenin did between February and October 1917, crystalized in the moment when, heading for the Smolny Institute where he would head the planning for a second revolution, he boarded a bus on 24 October and asked the conductress if there was any fighting going on in the city centre (RG 197); he simply didn't know.

The February revolution in Russia deposed tsarism and a provisional government was established but there was no agreement as to the way forward. Most Bolsheviks, like everyone else who looked to Western Europe as the cradle of revolution, were taken by surprise. The big Other of history had taken leave of absence when Lenin audaciously read aloud his 'April Theses', named after the month of his arrival in Petrograd and his call for a second revolution. Along with his other 1917 texts, collated and edited by Žižek in *Revolution at the Gates*, Lenin is seen responding to a unique situation with an equally unique intervention. Caricatured as a figure of stubborn dogmatism, Lenin becomes a hero who, thrown into a political situation where Bolshevism's existing compass points were of limited use, found himself having to reinvent what revolution meant.

The Lenin of *Materialism and Empiriocriticism* (1909) – unceremoniously dismissed by Žižek (QH 2–3) – had clung tenaciously to a static epistemology, a deeply un-Hegelian type of materialism that insisted cognition of an objective reality was possible, even if not completely attainable. Knowledge of what exists independently outside our minds ignores how minds are part of the reality they are claiming to be able to objectively observe and this imparted to *Materialism and Empiriocriticism* an 'utter philosophical worthlessness' (OWB 23n28).

The Lenin who arrived in Petrograd in April 1917 was different, convinced that orthodox pieties about necessary stages of historical development was a chimera, that simple certainties had to give way to contingencies. This change had been fostered by Lenin's turn to Hegel in the period after the outbreak of the First World War. In despair at the capitulation of left-wing parties to nationalist pro-war euphoria, he immersed himself in *The Science of Logic*. After reading Hegel, Lenin's intuitive grasp of the whoosh of history led him to criticize a vulgar materialism that is not based on a dialectic, a 'living, many-sided knowledge (with the number of sides eternally increasing), with an infinite number of shades of every approach and approximation to reality' (Lenin 2008a); through his reading, Lenin 'transformed himself' (Kouvelakis 2007: 182).

Lenin, like St Paul and Lacan in this respect, reinscribed an existing belief and practice – Marxism, Christianity and psychoanalysis respectively – not by pragmatically modernizing it but by radically changing some if its presuppositions.

The call for a return to Lenin (RG 11) does not come from a nostalgic longing for barricades on the street but from the exigent need to originate an emancipatory project for the new historical conjuncture that is the early twenty-first century. The impulse itself is not a monopoly of the Left, as evidenced in Margaret Thatcher's ability to redraw the UK's economic landscape and rightly claim that her greatest achievement was New Labour. Lenin is a reminder of the urgent need for 'a Thatcher of the Left' who could repeat her gesture in the opposite direction, transforming the entire field of presuppositions shared by today's political elite of all main orientations' (Žižek 2013d). One of the orientations that Lenin opposes – as did Marx before him (2024: 148–9) – is liberalism and its reliance on a notion of freedom that ignores the structural inequalities of capitalism. In this respect, Lenin's scathing criticism of formal freedoms, like freedom of the press, is matched by Žižek's disparagement of liberal multiculturalism and wokeness. Freedom of choice which only exists inside existing relations of power and domination is as open to criticism as is the idea of a vanguard party claiming to objectively know what is best for those it claims to represent. What Lenin represents is the aspiration to break with the falsity of a liberalism that fails to question issues of power and economic control. The call is to return to the possibility of authentic change 'and accomplish the fateful step from ludic "postmodern" radicalism to the domain in which the *games are over*' (RG 311).

There is a tension in any emancipatory project between imposing what is necessary while desiring to orientate events in terms of autonomy and becoming. Writ large in the history of the USSR is the exercise of power and administration of government sliding into a betrayal of the dream that gave it its existence. The tension, between the means and the end, can grow into an antinomy and Lenin is seen to embody this. In his *State and Revolution* there is a utopian anarchism – 'Under socialism all will govern in turn and will soon become accustomed to no governing' (quoted in F 206) – but there is also the apparent authoritarianism of his *What Is to Be Done?* stipulating subordination to Bolshevik diktats. He died while trying to maintain the thin line between these standpoints but part of his greatness is how, in 1923 after realizing a pan-European revolution would not occur, he persisted in the hope of creating 'the fundamental requirements of civilization in a different way from that of the West European countries' (quoted in LEN xlviii).

Lenin continued working towards communist solutions despite having to make concessions to a market economy and private property when the scale of the problems facing the country became apparent in 1922. The civil war had brought victory to the Bolsheviks but at great cost and Lenin called for 'strength and flexibility "to begin from the beginning" over and over again in approaching an extremely difficult task' (LEN 33). The moral Žižek draws from Lenin's persistence and fortitude is that October 1917 came to its end with the implosion of the USSR in 1989 and now is a new time and a time to begin again: 'Although sublime moments like the Jacobin climax of the French revolution and the October Revolution will forever remain a key part of our memory, that story is over, everything should be re-thought, one should begin from the zero-point' (SE 27).

Complimenting *Revolution at the Gates*, a selection of Lenin's writings from the last two years of his active life have also been pooled and edited by Žižek in *Lenin 2017*. The two collections provide a basis for evaluating Lenin – but only when a step back is taken from the dystopian shadow of the Stalinism that emerged in the 1930s. It is difficult to subtract from the present its embedded perception of the past – a contemporary Russian perspective is likely to see Lenin's revolution as an unmitigated disaster that paved the way for Stalinism – but Lenin needs to be looked at in his own time, inclusive of all the ambiguities, mistakes and triumphs. What he stood for is the truth that emerges from an engaged, often minority position. Like de Gaulle's refusal to accept the defeat of France in 1940, Lenin made an 'undemocratic' decision. While that which grounds a truth is the subject's position of enunciation, no criteria for establishing the truth are written in stone. What follows is the element of risk and uncertainty and this edgy lack of a guarantee is what deregulates an authentic truth from the declarations of all fundamentalist zealots (LEN xxv).

What emerges from the historical Lenin is a political lesson for today's world where discontent and unhappiness over the state of capitalist society reaches points of revolt that burn themselves out in their acts of expression. Movements like the Yellow Vests in France or the earlier Occupy Wall Street protests in New York, while eminently worthy of support, 'soon run of breath, unable to reach the "Leninist" stage of an organized force with a clear program' (Žižek 2021c: 16). The scare quotes for 'Leninist' indicate the need not to replicate a revolutionary past by means of a new Bolshevik party but to build a systematic form of opposition in the spirit and long-term resolve of Lenin. It is a radical project which draws a line in the sand between left-wing liberals and communists and Žižek's testimony to the divisiveness provoked by *Revolution at the Gates* (Badiou and Žižek 2009: 91) bears witness to this.

> As a result, *repeating* Lenin does not mean a *return* to Lenin – to repeat Lenin is to accept that 'Lenin is dead', that his particular solution failed, even failed monstrously, but that there was a utopian spark in it worth saving. Repeating Lenin means we have to distinguish between what Lenin actually did and the field of possibilities he opened up, the tension in Lenin between what he actually did and another dimension: what was 'in Lenin more than Lenin himself'.
>
> (RG 300)

DSS 113–17; OB 1–5, 113–14, 121–2; RG 3–12, 168–205, 292–312; IV 211–13, 240–2; LEN vii–lxxx, 171–83; F 47, 206–10; ZP 9133; AP 47–50; QH 2–6, 119

Budgen, Kouvelakis and Žižek 2007; Žižek 2021b

CONNECTIONS: class struggle, enunciated and enunciation, event/act

Literary criticism

> The modern uneasiness, unfreedom in the very form of formal freedom, servitude in the very form of autonomy, and, more fundamentally, anxiety and perplexity caused by that very autonomy, reaches so deep into the very ontological foundations of our being that it can be expressed only in an art form which destabilizes and denaturalizes the most elementary coordinates of our sense of reality.
>
> (SFA 455)

A neat and pleasing anthology could be constructed by collating Žižek's literary criticism, beginning with his comments on Shakespeare's *Hamlet*, Sophocles's *Antigone* (two texts repeatedly returned to) and Jane Austen's *Pride and Prejudice* in *The Sublime Object of Ideology* before continuing with insights into a world library of novels, short stories, drama and poetry. A book edited by Russell Sbriglia has been published, *Everything You Always Wanted to Know about Literature but Were Afraid to Ask Žižek*, which is divided into essays about his contributions to literary theory and a series of readings, influenced by him, of literary works from Chaucer to Gaétan Soucy.

Looking Awry, when not examining movies, uses works of fiction, like the detective story genre and Patricia Highsmith stories, to illuminate Lacanian concepts. As with the film criticism in that book, there is a balance between a connoisseurial enjoyment in writing about literature and a more instrumental use of literary texts. Reducing a literary work to a concept it happens to illustrate tends to detract from the pleasure of conjoining the affective with the cognitive. This does not occur when particular parts of a text attract Žižek's attention for the acumen of their philosophical or psychoanalytic observations. The scene in Proust's *The Guermantes Way*, when the narrator uses the phone for the first time and talks to his grandmother, anticipates the Lacanian object that only ever appears partially. In its fragmentary form, the partial object's libidinal force, motioning towards a presence immeasurably more intimate than the whole body to which it belongs, holds out the promise of a return to a prelapsarian bliss that was never possessed. Proust, *avant la lettre*, evokes this precisely. When the voice of Marcel's grandmother on the phone is subtracted from the person he has become accustomed to feeling so affectionate towards, he cannot return to her company without seeing an elderly, frail woman. The frame through which he used to see her, built up from childhood, loses its support: 'We are no longer engaged participants in the world, we find ourselves confronted with things in their *noumenal* dimension' (LTN 676, 2009e: viii).

Literary texts also serve to illumine Hegel and a particularly precise instance of this is the reading of Dickens's *Great Expectations*. The Hegelian Cunning of Reason has been traditionally understood as an idea about reason silently achieving an end unbeknownst to the human actors bringing it about. Todd McGowan dexterously presents a very different interpretation (2019: 146–9), one that accords with Žižek's rejection of reason's 'secret guiding hand'. What takes its place is 'a trust in un-Reason, the certainty that, no matter how well-planned things are, somehow they will go wrong' (LTN 510–11). This is what happens in Dickens's novel when its title only fulfils itself through the failure of its realization in the way customarily expected. The 'great expectations' attributed to Pip are only truly realized when he turns his back on worldly success, failing what was expected of him but succeeding at another, higher level that endows him with a certain greatness. The novel's final paragraph is read as exemplifying the ambiguity of Hegel's notion of reconciliation: 'What changes in the course of the hero's ordeal is not his character, but also the very ethical standards by which we measure his character' (PV 27; LTN 519). The cunning of reason can also be read as a figuration of the big Other (LA 77–8).

Žižek's literary criticism, attuning to the weft and warp of language, surveys what cannot be resolved when what is meaningful is the absence or displacement of meaning. Sometimes this is actualized in the form of narrative fiction, as with Mary Shelley's *Frankenstein* where the French Revolution's revolutionary hopes and their collapse into terror are realized in the conflictive and disruptive elements of its genre (DLC 73–81). With Edith Wharton's *Ethan Frame*, these elements are the clues to what the novel – any novel – cannot directly express, the trauma that is the Real that only emerges obliquely through its narrative voices (F 90–4). The obstacle a literary form faces is trying to accommodate what cannot be integrated into the symbolic – a obstacle which is one way of defining the Real – and G. K. Chesterton is praised for registering this in the distortedness that characterizes the 'realist' style of Charles Dickens (D 185–7). This difficulty that possesses language when it comes to representing the trauma of the Real is how Žižek begins *Less Than Nothing*. There, the temporal twists in Jorge Semprún's *The Long Voyage* express the impossibility of representing the Holocaust other than by inscribing the unattainability into the skewed form of the narrative (LTN 23–9).

Žižek's literary criticism is especially alert when what claims his attention is not language as an expression of a fictional character's interiority but language itself. The impossibility of giving expression to the inexpressible is a cliché of Samuel Beckett commentary and this is seen through a Lacanian lens when the protagonist in his novel *The Unnamable* is contrasted with the *cogito* of Descartes. The 'I think', serving for Descartes as *terra firma* for trusting in reality's structure, becomes in Beckett's novel a being who 'finds himself in the black box of his own consciousness' (HWB 111), struggling with language as an inescapable imposition. The predicament posed in the novel is one of being caught between the silence that came before language and, now that it is broken, the uncorrectable and omnipresent post-silence state of existence. The same dilemma is at work in Beckett's *Not I*, when the uncertain role of the Auditor becomes the big Other as 'a silent impotent witness which fails ... and the speaking subject itself is deprived of its dignified status of "person" and reduced to a partial object' (D 224; Žižek 2015a: 278).

Kafka is another literary figure with a recurrent presence in Žižek's work but not in the way his fiction is customarily evoked. A figure like Odradek, the enigmatic creature in his short story 'The Cares of a Family Man', is usually seen as part of a nightmarish complex traceable to anxieties of social or parental origin. But Odradek can also represent that lop-sided and disruptive life force that Lacan calls *jouissance* and when this interpretation is given (Žižek 2005b: 163–4; PV 114–18) it is in a context that looks to recognizing the 'inhuman' side of ourselves that is displaced when expediently embodied in the Other as the monstrous neighbour. There is a self-serving that facilitates ideological hegemony, as when the fantasy of a bureaucratic nightmare – crystallized in the use of the word Kafkaesque – helps manage the entrapment that comes from believing there is no means of escape (SO 34–7). This accounts for the interest in the Orson Welles movie of *The Trial* (Žižek 1996: 95–7; LTN 687–8) and the way it overturns orthodox readings of the novel. In *Quantum History* (140–1), by way of another approach to Kafka, the ending of the story in *The Trial* about the door of the

Law is read as consonant with the principle in quantum mechanics that what is observed as objective reality includes the role of the observer.

Nor does a Lacanian-inflected approach to literature preclude a Hegelian-Marxist percipience that reads a text's content as inseparable from its form. The first 'interlude' in *The Parallax View*, 'Kate's Choice, Or, The Materialism of Henry James', includes a reading of *The Wings of the Dove* along these lines. The concerns of the novel become a reflection of Henry James's probing of capitalism's impact on the ethical and Samuel Beckett's work is also valued for the way it finds a form for expressing the desolation accruing cumulatively from this impact. In his late play, *Catastrophe*, Beckett's sense of the futile predicament that is closing in around us becomes acute: 'Nobody is simply innocent, nobody is totally exempted', concludes Žižek, and a bankruptcy in what passes for politics demands a requisite response (SFA 457–8). The kind of response required is found in the poetry of Shelley and his refusal to succumb to leftist melancholy when the French Revolution gave way to the Terror. His resolute conviction is that setbacks in an emancipatory project do not presage the ultimately inevitability failure of revolutionary endeavour but reinforce the need to repeat the attempt and achieve a different and more radical outcome (DLC 394).

SO 66–7, 130–1, 135; LA 3–66, 8–9, 134–6, 154–5; PV 125–44; E 116–19; LTN 672–6; D 218–30; HWB 109–15

Thompson 2016

CONNECTIONS: Antigone, Bartleby's 'I would prefer not to', Shakespeare, symbolic

Love

In *Looking Awry*, there are too many films and texts featuring the nature of love to make a list of them. Love becomes Žižek: its unpredictability, unconditionality and disruptiveness discloses something autonomous and momentous about life. Love creates the possibility of the freedom that allows us to choose the reasons that will define us. There is a mystery about love that allows for the word miraculous to describe how it occurs; it is not cajolable. It is said to be like one of the tales from *The Arabian Nights*, about the wandering hero who enters a cave and finds within three wise old men who, awakening from a deep sleep, inform him that they have been waiting three centuries for his arrival (MSH 26). Like the political message of Marx's Thesis XI, about changing the world and not just interpreting it, love requires a special kind of commitment to effect its truth value. Like the proletariat, the lover must believe in and own their decision in order to change their reality. Love, usurping the place of the deadlock in sexuality, is an absolute engagement that makes it an Event. The cadence of normal life is ruthlessly altered and the virtual measure pertaining to the past also undergoes a deep change. My present love creates the past which occasioned it, giving legibility to what until then comes to seem like a period of confused indecision. The experience of love feels like destiny fulfilled, something that was always there: 'Once it *is* here, it was *always already* here' (LET 29). Love is peculiar in the way it defies representation through signification, a phenomenon witnessed on the screen in a scene from *Four Weddings and a Funeral*. The faltering muddle of the hero before his beloved as he tries to give voice to his love is proof of his authenticity. It is the failure of language to express our will that bears witness to the truth of our intentions. A smoothly composed love letter in elegant words can raise a suspicion of artificiality in the writer; a too graceful articulation may bespeak a lack of genuineness (LTN 259).

In the film *Vertigo*, after Scottie recreates Madeline in Judy he comes to see how it was Judy who had been pretending to be the Madeline that he purportedly loved. He had been adoring a fake and with this realization that mystery quality that had engaged his rapture crumbles away: 'His discovery *changes the past*, deprives the lost object of the *objet a*' (LET 29). It does more than this, revealing a spurious element of his love: 'If his love were true, he should have accepted the full identity of (the common, vulgar) Judy and (the sublime) Judy' (IV 271).

Being an event, love creates its own grounds for existence; they only emerge retrospectively. Someone is not loved due to some particular of their appearance or character; such aspects are cherished *because* they belong to the beloved. What sets a person's love in motion – it is, after all, a state that is 'fallen' into – is a contingent moment where, putting it brusquely, indifference receives a libidinal investment arising from a disposition of the will. This is the setting for Žižek's interpretation of T. S. Eliot's 'love' of Emily Hale during the years when his wife, Vivienne, was confined to an asylum. In the wake of Vivienne's death, Eliot's desire for Emily came to an end. It was as if both women were never truly loved and Emily was a 'symptom' (LTN 772) of this. With authentic love, the impurity of the contingent moment that is its point of origin is taken up by those involved and comes to be owned by them.

The retrospective causality at work in the person truly in love is not dissimilar to the way the Christian grounds the reasons for their belief only after the experience of faith. Given the interest in Christian theology, it is not altogether surprising to find words by St Paul, from Cor. 1.3, being quoted to bring out the peculiar status of love in relation to Lacan's term not-all and his masculine and feminine formulae of sexuation. Love does not follow the male logic of sexuation by being the exception to the All, in this case the All of complete knowledge. St Paul's claim that without love I would be 'nothing' does not just mean that with love I am 'something'. In love, '*I am also nothing*, but as it were a Nothing humbly aware of itself' (IR 308) and it is this attentiveness to lack that accounts for the vulnerability that characterizes the person with the capacity to love. The paradox of love is that a deficiency, a not-all, emerges as more worthy than complete knowledge. If science was able to completely identify and isolate the biochemical nature of sexual love, there would still be something autonomous about love as an event (IR 71). The love that the Old Testament demotes to 'carnal knowledge' has nothing to do with the 'abyssal decision' to love someone (OWB 162). Love is a comedic fusion of sublimation – imbuing a loved one with all one's libidinal capital – and a desublimation which unreservedly accepts the body of the beloved in all its grossness: 'True love doesn't idealize' (HWB 162).

Love and sex are not the same and when they do overlap it is not a straightforward convergence. Marriage is a cure for intense love in so far as it puts sex in perspective and the joke told to illustrate this (CA 82) reaffirms Žižek's own self-mocking joke in an interview where he declares that he is unable to have one-night stands: 'In my city, Ljubljana, you can tell exactly which women I've slept with, because I married them' (2016g).

Kaleidoscopic aspects of the disjunction that divides love from sex are discussed in *Incontinence of the Void*. Distilling the purity of love and applying it to one's life would be, as Kierkegaard presents it, to love one's neighbour; the unchosen person who happens to be there. Such love would attain a level of perfection, unadulterated by distinguishing features that are usually associated with the beloved. This religionist position is chastened by Žižek putting forward Don Juan as a 'properly *Christian* seducer' (IV 269) for he also does not care about particular qualities. From their very different but equally exalted perspectives, what Kierkegaard and Don Juan fail to see, what they cannot plumb, is the importance of imperfection in love, the role of the contingent and arbitrary quality that is *objet petit a*. The disjuncture characterizing love and sex is crudely depicted in a graphically literal scene from Catherine Breillat's film *Romance*. It is taken as testimony to the 'impossible/real' of love and sex coinciding as an absolute. Sex is irrelevant to love, it can be enjoyed without the superego making demands; it does not at a deep-seated level really matter. In *Surplus Enjoyment*, John Huston's *The Night of the Iguana* is lauded for affectingly dramatizing this in a scene that is the opposite of bathos. The Deborah Kerr character, beginning her narrative with 'grandfather went up to bed and I went out in the sampan with the Aussie underwear salesman', goes on to describe a strangely serene 'love experience'.

The serenity of this scene has to be augmented by the one of the eponymous narrator opening Astra Taylor's film *Žižek!* with a statement of his belief in the universe as a void, suffering a cosmic cataclysm whereby 'things exist by mistake'. Love, he goes on, is 'precisely this kind of cosmic imbalance' due to its convergence on 'a small detail, a fragile individual person, I say, "I love you more than anything else". In this quite formal sense, love is evil'.

> Psychoanalysis can perform its reductionist analysis demonstrating how what attracted me to a person was some feature repeated from (my memory of) my mother or sister, but the act of falling in love proper cannot be reduced to such a libidinal process since it involves a move beyond the qualities of the beloved person, a move of unconditionally accepting the abyss of the beloved Other as a subject beyond all qualities.
>
> (HWB 321)

LA 76–7, 103–4; IR 171–2, 308–9, 370; LET 28–30; AR 21, 71–2, 74, 274–5; E 80–2, 133–6; D 108; IV 268–73; HWB 44, 162–4; SE 165–72; QH 210–11

Taheri 2021: 36–42; Tutt 2016: 203–5

CONNECTIONS: event, not-All/non-All, sexuality

Luxemburg, Rosa

See retroactivity.

Lynch, David

> Therein lies the lesson of David Lynch's *Straight Story*: what is the ridiculously pathetic perversity of figures like Bobby Peru in *Wild at Heart* or Frank in *Blue Velvet* compared to Alvin Straight's decision to cross the US Midwest on a lawnmower to visit a dying relative? Measured against this, Frank's and Bobby's enraged outbursts look like the impotent theatrics of old and sedate conservatives.
>
> (AR 185)

Exploring what is kept at bay within the articulations of the symbolic order, the madness that haunts it, sustains the pulse beat of Lynch's films. The close-ups of a burning match in *Wild at Heart*, the extreme violence of Sailor at the film's start and the later excessive presence of Bobby Peru, or in *Lost Highway* the inordinate response of Mr Eddy in the tailgating scene, fuse together into a persistence of too-muchness and its association with drive.

If this is taken as licence to characterize the movies as symptoms of cultural malaise – Hollywood excursions to the dark side of the human soul, albeit it with tremendous visual panache – critique remains at an uncomplicated level. For, unless put away in a drawer as excess kitsch, the apparition of an angel towards the end of *Wild at Heart*, or the dream about robins in *Blue Velvet*, possess a rapturous tonality not to be reduced to the level of a whacky moment in a Wes Anderson film. As indicated in the title of Žižek's short publication on *Lost Highway*, they couple the sublime with the ridiculous in a way that cannot be shrunk to the merely zany

The compact account of the David Lynch universe in chapter five of *Metastases of Enjoyment* pictures it as an undoing of the seams that separate the homogeneity of 'normal' life from its disturbing undercurrents and keep apart the body's smooth surface from the horrific goo beneath its skin. The philosophical context for this is briefly sketched as a tensile opposition, between 'a pre-symbolic depth and the surface of events' (ME 124), evident in Deleuze, Alexius Meinong and early Wittgenstein. Psychoanalytically, it is the Lacanian role of fantasy that comes to the fore when five of Lynch's films are discussed in *The Pervert's Guide to the Cinema*.

Žižek's optic distils the complex narrative structure of *Lost Highway* into a paradigm of the psychoanalytic process: Fred, a sexually confused husband, murders his wife (or fantasizes the deed) before collapsing into psychosis. He is only able to return to reality when, within his hallucinogenic state of mind, his sexual angst is therapeutically repeated. The Mr Eddy character is for Fred the obstacle to his sexual happiness but this fantasy comes to disintegrate and the impossibility of resolving the deadlock that has spawned his torment comes with the words whispered by Alice, his wife's wished-for doppelgänger, 'You'll never have me'.

Certain scenes from particular Lynch films are returned to for their dramatic psychoanalytic force and none more so than the violent and mental assault by William Dafoe on Laura Dern in a motel room in *Wild at Heart* and the exchange between Isabella Rossellini and Dennis Hopper in an apartment in *Blue Velvet*. Both scenes are readable as powerful enactments of the fantasy screen that supplements the sexual act by providing a necessary substitute for the deadlock inherent to sexual relations. The *Blue Velvet* scene, when examined in *The Pervert's Guide to the Cinema*, is looked at from the fantasmatic perspective of all three characters and it is the oscillation between their fantasies that accounts for the potency of the dramatization. In the *Wild at Heart* scene, 'the fantasy is forced out, aroused, and then abandoned, thrown upon the victim' (PV 69, 237).

ES 131–3, 148–9; LA 40–1, 172n6; ME 114–21; PF 237–8; TS 77–8, 299–300; ARS; FRT 96; PV 69–70; PC; QH 107–8

Ravetto-Biagioli 2010, Žižek 2025j

CONNECTIONS: fantasy, sexual relations, sexuality

M

Marx

Žižek's early writing on commodity fetishism and ideological fantasy follows Marx in seeing exploitation as emerging from a state of domination and servitude. In *The Parallax View* the Japanese philosopher Kojin Karatani is found wanting for ignoring Marx's central point that a commodity's use-value uniquely produces an increase in its own value and this surplus-value accrues only to capitalists. Basic propositions like these remain closed to negotiation by Žižek and, when analysing the 'virtual' aspect of financialization, Marxism is not seen as redundant but in need of being formulated more radically to take this development into account.

What is not taken on board is the young Marx's attribution of a teleological urge, an Aristotelian striving by the agent to fulfil its potential that is present in *Economic and Philosophical Manuscripts* (1844) and *The German Ideology* (1846). This is deemed too simplistic, too un-Hegelian, as is Lukács's *Marxist History and Class Consciousness* even though it propounds the idea of a subject's conscious allegiance effecting a change in perspective that alters reality. What is missing when Lukács construes the proletariat as a self-consciously determining agency is the condition of a retroactivity that does not allow history to programme its future and Žižek notes (QH 168) how the late Marx comes to recognize this. The future is unknowable but, as Benjamin conjectured and as may be discerned in Marx, possible futures are to be found in the past where they wait to be redeemed; freedom resides in our choice of what will necessarily determine us.

Marx, though criticizable at times, remains an absolutely critical presence in Žižek's thought. In *Living in End Times*, the weight of Hegel is brought to bear on Marx's analysis of capital and the commodity form. Problems with the labour theory of value are discussed in *Incontinence of the Void* and, in *Absolute Recoil*, a category mistake is seen to arise from Marx not integrating into his revolutionary thought the reversal at the heart of the dialectic. There is a need to begin again after an initial failure – a failure like the movement from October 1917 to Stalinism – and actualize emancipatory goals that at first will be defeated. There can be no immediate resolution that will reconcile all previous antagonisms.

> **Marx does determine proletariat as *substanzlose Subjektivitaet*, but in his scheme, substanceless subjectivity (a worker reduced to pure capacity-to-work since all substantial content is taken away from him by the capital) is reduced to a moment of extreme alienation which announces the revolutionary reversal by means of which the collective subject will re-appropriate its alienated substance. In Hegel and Lacan, on the contrary, substanceless subjectivity is subject as such, its constitutive negativity, and the only way it can 'overcome' its alienation from its substance is to pass from alienation to separation, i.e. to perceive itself as an effect of the crack, disparity, in the substance itself.**
>
> **(HWB 168)**

In *Disparities* and *Freedom*, the weakness in early Marx is traced to the mistaken, un-Hegelian assumption of an organic underpinning from which people have become unyoked. This facilitates the classic Marxist trope of the proletariat as the subject that, deprived of a sustainable social existence, recognizes its alienation and seeks to reappropriate through revolution what has been taken away from it. What this sidelines is that 'there is no actual life external to alienation which serves as its positive foundation' (F 137); alienation is the very ground from which the subject surfaces. A similar reservation finds expression in *Surplus Enjoyment* as the need to avoid conceiving of capital as external to the positive substance of life, feeding off it like a vampire (Marx 2024: 205) and leaving the worker disenchanted. An inherent antagonism prevents the postulating of a positive substance: the Hegelian movement between subject and substance has the subject emerging through the self-alienation of substance. This is at odds with thinking of the proletariat as the alienated subject of history who recovers its unalienated fullness of being through revolutionary action.

What these reservations about Marx share arises from the need to locate a rift in being that predates capitalism. What Freud calls death drive is a disruption to animal rhythms of biological life that cannot be appeased. The rift divides nature from culture and comes before any economic order: 'In short, capitalism is NOT the source of the asymmetries and imbalances in the world, which means that our goal should NOT be to restore the "natural" balance and symmetry' (SE 63).

Žižek has not lost faith in the political force in Marx's metaphor of the proletariat as the gravediggers of capitalism – the possibility of working-class revolt has not been eliminated – but there is a refusal to find refuge in the fond notion of an ordained agent of revolution. What is judged equally fond is Marx's mistake in not realizing that capitalism's dynamism, 'the mad dance of its unconditional spiral of productivity' (AR 37), cannot be preserved in a communist economy

Accepting Marx's mistakes does not weaken a valorizing of his insight into the selfless and insatiable greed propelling capitalism's motor. He 'opened up a new theoretical field which sets the very criteria of veracity' (AP 72) and, while demonstrating a dogmatic quality, revealing such a field creates a prominent place for Marx in Kierkegaard's category of an apostle: an authority, 'the medium of Truth' (HWB 166; SFA 147), carrying a message which cannot be ignored. .

PV 57; LET 198–228; LTN 220–1, 245–6, 260–1, 464–6; AR 36–40; D 36–8; IV 175–82, 188–92; SE 38–42; F 137, 153–8; AP 65–6, 72–4; QH 162

Žižek 2017d

CONNECTIONS: antagonism, Aristotle, Benjamin, capitalism, commodity fetishism, communism, dialectic, retroactivity, substance as also subject

The Matrix

See big Other, cinema, capitalism.

Meillassoux, Quentin

See contingency and necessity, In-itself/For-itself, retroactivity.

'Minimal difference'

See the introduction and antagonism, enunciated and enunciation.

N

Neighbour

The neighbour (capitalized on occasion) is the person who causes discomfort arising from the recognition of their unfathomable otherness, an alterity which is part of what Žižek calls the inhuman. Not as an index of some essential bestiality in people, inhuman is being used here by way of Kant's differentiation of a negative from an infinite judgement. To say that the neighbour is non-human would be to locate their nature in an animal, divine or alien kingdom whereas describing them as inhuman allows for a positive but unspecifiable property that lies somewhere between the human and the non-human. This indeterminate state is 'the terror constitutive of our being-human, the inhuman core of being-human' (LTN 830), a monstrous abyss that Hegel calls and describes as the 'night of the world'. The amplitude of this is missing from the way the philosopher Levinas sees the call of ethical responsibility in the human face of the anonymous neighbour.

What is seen as unassimable in the neighbour is not inseparable from what we avoid confronting about the non-integrable, impenetrable void of our own subjectivity. We cannot properly account for ourselves and this lack of self-transparency lies in the background of encountering the neighbour as someone who, like us, is a mystery to themselves. Shared participation in the symbolic and customary forms of behaviour help make this acceptable but at other times the neighbour's alterity provokes repugnance that cannot be gentrified and their face becomes a mask hiding the abyss of the Other. An uncanny creepiness arises from the enigma of their *jouissance* and the opaqueness of their desire and this can interpenetrate forms of racism and racial hostility: 'The feature which disturbs the racist in his Other (the way they laugh, the smell of their food …) is thus precisely the little piece of the Real which bears witness to their presence beyond the symbolic order' (PF 200). The character played by John Wayne in *The Searchers* is propelled by racism to kill Debbie but at the juncture when this becomes possible he discovers the neighbour inside himself, shielded until now by his self-image as the seeker of vengeance (ADB 77–9; LET 119–20).

The face as a mask effacing the monstrosity of the neighbour kindles a social space for sharing human vulnerability and facilitating empathy. It also serves to explain the anxiety that can be occasioned, in the West, by women wearing garments that cover the face, including Islamic veils such as the niqab or burqa. The face that is covered 'confronts us directly with the abyss of the Other-Thing, with the Neighbor in its uncanny dimension' (LET 2). More positively, the concept of the neighbour does not lead to a non-universalizable blockage in any encounter with others. Acknowledging the neighbour within ourselves is, on the contrary, a basis for a non-exclusive identity and a universality that grounds collective, emancipatory acts. Liberals who try to foreclose it through a carefully guarded multicultural tolerance 'share with the anti-immigration advocates the need to keep others at a proper distance. The others are OK, I respect them, but they should not intrude too much into my own space' (2014f: 10–11).

That's why the privileged way to reach a Neighbour is not that of empathy, of trying to understand them, but a disrespectful laughter which makes fun both of them and of us in our mutual lack of (self-)understanding (inclusive of 'racist' jokes).

(ADB 79)

PF 199–200; L 42–4, 46–7; PV 113–14; DLC 16–17; FT 46; LTN 830–1; ADB 73–80; QH 323–6

Žižek 2005b

CONNECTIONS: infinite judgement, *jouissance*, 'night of the world', other

Negation of negation

The term is used by Hegel for a movement in the dialectic he calls sublation (*Aufhebung*). It occurs when an estimation of something, previously taken as fixed, becomes unstable and insufficient. What causes this loss of certitude is seeing how the something in question has another meaning and one so different as to be its opposite. This first-order negation leads to a second one: sublation as the negation of negation, an overcoming of the initial understanding which is not simply cancelled but taken on board and radicalized as part of a more inclusive and perspicuous comprehension. It is what happens to Pip in *Great Expectations* when he turns his back on London life and it is what Muhammad Ali displayed when he held the Olympic torch at the 1996 Olympic Games.

The moment of reversal that brings an unexpected radicalization is the realization in Mozart's *Cosi fan tutte* that 'one love counts as much as the other, [so] the couples can return to their initial marital arrangement' (OSD 152). Or, in a different orbit, it is when terms implicit in the legal truth of an employment contract reverse their meanings through a shift in perspective. A worker and an employer enter without coercion into a work agreement on the basis of freedom and equality and on this footing aspects of a contract, like rates of pay for overtime, can be disputed and, at this level, negated. When looked at from outside the legal framework, freedom and equality are broad terms that can generate very different meanings. When the notion of a voluntary contract is criticized, its untruth allows a disguised truth to be made explicit. From the perspective of a different social organization of production, the legal truth of an employment deal would fulfil itself in a way opposite to what was intended. In the language of Hegel, the contract would truly realize its notion – but only as part of a different political economy. Left to itself, it becomes a misrepresentation of what freedom and equality could mean.

Another example, from *Less Than Nothing*, deploys the debunking of nature as a balanced state of order to illustrate a shift in the horizon that negates the negation. The apparent negative, environmental damage as a defilement of the natural order, is turned on its head and it is the very idea of Mother Nature that becomes a violation of the Darwinian truth that nature is about contingency not harmony. The space of negation of negation is 'twisted' due to it residing 'in the decisive shift from the *distortion of a notion to a distortion constitutive of this notion*, i.e. to this notion as a distortion of itself' (AR 268–9).

In *Absolute Recoil*, in a chapter titled 'Varieties of the "Negation of Negation"', torsion is applied by going beyond a shift in perspective or a meeting of opposites to a doubling that becomes a renewal of a failure. A model for this, 'a weird kind of *negation of negation*' (AP 330), is then provided by Lacan's conjoining of alienation and separation. Alienation for Lacan arises from subjection to an already existing linguistic symbolic order. It is a negation of freedom and, crucially, is concomitant with the infant's realization that the mother/other has desires that are focused elsewhere. The infant experiences lack and the shock of also sensing a lack in the other – 'One lack is superimposed upon the other' (Lacan 2004: 215) – and neither is able to be completely filled. Negation of negation takes place in what Lacan calls separation, the consequence of the other's lack making itself felt as an unfathomable enigma for the infant. The assumption of a place for us in the symbolic is never complete: the desire of the other can be queried, the big Other's command has its own gaps and our determination by it is not hermetic. The subject emerges from the failure of the symbolic to fully represent us. The old-fashioned algorithm for the dialectic that would result in the restoration of a higher state, through the sublation of the original position, breaks down. The positivity that was first negated through alienation cannot be reappropriated; and in the doubling of the first alienation in separation, out of which the subject arises, a negation of negation occurs.

After characterizing the result as a 'less than nothing' (AR 331), this line of thought is then taken to another level. Using a term taken from a book about Hegel and Shakespeare, 'downward-*Aufhebung*' (Bates 2010), a sublation in reverse leads to a drastically peculiar formulation of negation of negation by way of ghosts and the undead. The ghost's initial resistance to sublation prepares the way for a negation of negation, a strange extension that finds a parallel in Hegel's theory of repetition in history where an event repeats itself but with a different outcome. Shifting between *Hamlet*, Sophocles's *Antigone* and the dialectic in comedy, Hegel's negation of negation inherits an additional and highly original scope. The complex ambiguities that consequently evolve from reiterations of failure form a discussion around Edith Wharton's *Ethan Frame* and Tana French's *Broken Harbour*. The two novels also suggest that a downward spiral is the 'true secret' of the dialectic, unlocking the possibility of rereading Hegel 'from the perspective of Samuel Beckett's late short texts and plays which all deal with the problem of how to go on when the game is over, when it has reached its end point' (F 98).

In political thought, Mao Zedong's failure is conceptualized through his categorical dismissal of negation of negation and, in its place, reliance on a 'bad infinity' of recursive negation, as in the Cultural Revolution. This failure is then contrasted with Margaret Thatcher's free-market reforms in the UK, a negation of the existing more liberal order. It required an apparent ideological opponent, Tony Blair, to achieve a negation of negation by seeming to be different but actually normalizing and cementing what she had achieved.

SO 199–200; LA 160–1; TS 70–5; PV 27; M 1–28; LTN 292–304; AR 330–6, 339–43; IV 232–4; SFA 421–2; F 89–98

Lacan 2004: 210–15

CONNECTIONS: dialectic, Lacan, other, subject

Negativity

Negativity is what robs every entity of a consistent identity, from subatomic particles to super-sized planets. Everything undergoes temporal and spatial developments and a kinetic self-differentiation is immanent to the order of being. It is what distinguishes the nature of true infinity.

Negativity as a persistent self-cancelling that prevents being ever holding on to a positive self-affirmation possesses a generative force. In the preface to *The Phenomenology of Spirit* Hegel describes it as 'the energy of thinking' (§32) and calls for the need to look the negative in the face and tarry with it. Negativity is what facilitates the absolute.

> The negativity just considered constitutes the *turning point* of the movement of the concept. It is the *simple point of the negative self-reference*, the innermost source of all activity, of living and spiritual self-movement; it is the dialectical soul which everything true possesses and through which alone it is true.
>
> (Hegel 2010a: 745)

Other philosophers are used as a foil to bring out the singularity of negativity's unruliness. In *Organs without Bodies*, Spinoza's espousal of the striving of every entity to actualize itself, of expressive substance as univocal and hence undialectical, is contrasted with Hegel where what prevents full actualization comes not from outside but from within the entity. Deleuze's opposition to Hegel is seen to arise from this inclusion of negativity within positivity, a catholicity that is instanced by a Sherlock Holmes story where the dog not barking during the night is a negative but curious fact that brings with it a positive import. A similar, non-fictional case, where negativity assumes a positive force, is seen in the United States' removal of the reproduction of Picasso's *Guernica* behind the speaker's podium when the country was promoting an attack on Iraq to the UN Security Council in 2003. One could add Elizabeth Hardwick's essay on Faye Dunaway as another, though more endearing, example: 'She arrests the attention by many negations, by what she is not. The face almost flat, with a peculiar flat smoothness. She does not possess a large mouth or round, floating eyes to be insisted upon as the identification that announces presence' (Hardwick 2022: 62).

Less straightforwardly than with Spinoza and Deleuze, Kant is deployed speculatively by adopting some of his formulations of the noumenal and reading them as intimations of Hegelian negativity. In *Critique of Pure Reason*, Kant describes the noumenal as 'a merely *limiting concept*' and 'therefore only of negative employment' and this, taken together with how he continues, is taken, or stretched, by Žižek to indicate a limiting that is internal to the phenomenal and the absence of anything beyond this self-referring, intransitive negativity.

Heidegger's criticism, that the origin of negativity is not accounted for by Hegel and thus uncritically taken for granted, is acknowledged and dealt with by Žižek in a novel way. Heidegger's objection is accepted but then undermined by seeing in negativity something – death drive – that Hegel himself could not have formulated. Freud's death drive has the force of an unavowed origin and its repetitive nature is confirmation of being's incapacity to claim any positivity. Drive shares its structure of repetition with the negativity functioning in the dialectical process but there can be no sublimation. This introduces a non-dialecticizable nucleus into the dialectic.

TS 29–31; OWB 33–5, 52; LTN 281–3, 492–3; AR 89

Kant 2007: 271–2

CONNECTIONS: absolute and absolute knowing, Deleuze, drive, Hegel, identity and difference, infinity, Kant, quantum physics

'Night of the world'

> The human being is this night, this empty nothing that contains everything in its simplicity – an unending wealth of many representations, images, of which none belongs to him – or which are not present. This night, the inner of nature, that exists here – pure self – in phantasmagorical representations, is night all around it, in which here shoots a bloody head – there another white ghastly apparition, suddenly here before it, and just so disappears. One catches sight of this night when one looks human beings in the eye – into a night that becomes awful.
>
> (Hegel's 'Jenaer Realphilosophie', www.marxists.org/reference/archive/hegel/works/jl/ch01a.htm; ME 145; TAF 8; ES 58; TS 29–30; PV 44; LTN 353, 389–90; E 93; CA 73; Žižek 2024k: 11–12; QH 105)

A passage from Hegel's 'Jenaer Realphilosophie' of 1805/6 using the term 'night of the world' is quoted on a number of occasions as a vivid description of what is identified as the *cogito* of Descartes – 'I think, therefore I am': a deep divorce from immersion in existence, animal or human, a contraction that affects links with the world outside. This divorce marks the existential abyss of negativity, out of which a symbolic world has to be constructed to survive the trauma of being touched by the Real. The abyss can be seen as a form of madness but, in a characteristically Žižekian reversal of expectations, madness is more properly the crossing into the rationality of the symbolic order and its exclusion of the excess that is the place out of which, in an act of separation, it emerged. Lacan's declaration about the gods belonging to the Real (2004: 45) is understood as recognizing this separation as a traumatically violent cut of the kind that Sophocles dramatized in *The Bacchae* (AR 245–8).

The symbolic world is a projection of a stable reality, an antidote to a chaotic proto-reality: 'Without symbolization, there is no Real, there is just a flat stupidity of what is there' (CA 23–4; Žižek 2024l: 8). As *logos*, symbolization ushers in the power of language to designate a part of the pre-symbolic with a name. In doing so, the subject as a being of language inaccessible to itself emerges: 'Thus the symbol manifests itself first of all as the murder of the thing, and this death constitutes in the subject the externalization of his desire' (Lacan 2001: 114). The 'night of the world' is 'the ground on which our universe thrives' (Žižek 2024k: 8), representing a necessary middle stage between total immersion into a natural environment and the space for a symbolic constitution of reality that will be manageable.

Far more than a transitional moment, the 'night of the world' becomes the basis for conceiving of something as having limits or form. The radical negativity that finds expression in the Bosch-like apparitions of the 'night of the world' is not abolished but *it assumes determinate form*' (ES 58). Žižek is referring here to Hegel's term, at the start of his *The Science of Logic*, for what issues from the unstable unrest that is the coming-to-be and ceasing-to-be of pure being and nothingness. The determinateness has a positiveness but one inescapably limited by its negation, by non-being (Hegel 2010a: 83–4), and this resonates with a passage from the preface to *The Phenomenology of Spirit* praising the power of the faculty of understanding (§§32–3). In that passage, understanding involves a breaking-up and separation of what seems whole and Žižek links this with the Lacanian symbolic order as a constraining, classifying network of signifiers with the capacity to structure organic life processes as symbolic fictions and rituals: 'What we forget when we pursue our daily life, is that our human universe is nothing but an embodiment of the radically inhuman "abstract negativity", of the abyss we experience when we face the "night of the world"' (ES 61).

ES 57–61; TS 92; E 90–5; LTN 339; AR 182–7; P 2; CA 72–4

Žižek 1998c: 258–70, 2009f: 116, 2016f: 190–1, 2024k

CONNECTIONS: negativity, ontology, Real, Schelling

Not-All/non-All

> The 'universal exception', according to Lacan, is the fundamental feature of the symbolic order (the 'big Other') as the order of universality: each universality is grounded in its constitutive exception. This feature is to be supplemented with its no less paradoxical obverse, the so-called 'not-All [pas-tout]': an order (or rather, a field, a signifying space) with no exception that is eo ipso not-all, and cannot be totalized. These two features – formalized by Lacan in his 'formulae of sexuation' – are the two aspects of the inconsistency of the big Other: the symbolic order is by definition antagonistic, thwarted, non-identical-with-itself, marked by a constitutive lack, virtual – or, as Lacan put it, 'there is no big Other'.
>
> (UE x)

Lacan's term (*pas-tout*) not-All or non-All and its contrast with an order of universality that requires an exception for its functioning is set out with clarity in Žižek's preface to the paperback edition of *The Universal Exception*. Not-All emerges in Lacan, across Seminars XVIII–XX, as an important part of how he determines the underlying structure of male and female sexuality.

Freud's invented myth of society's origins, the nature-culture passage featuring a proto-human horde and the murder by the followers of a primal father who reserved for himself sexual access to the women in the group, is used by Lacan in a novel way. Prohibition – the followers in their remorse prohibit themselves from enjoying the incestuous sexual freedom of the primal father – is linked with a lack that comes with entry into the symbolic order and this loss is figured as 'symbolic castration'.

Lacan devises a set of four formulae for sexual difference. For an assertorial male logic in the set, all x are subject to castration: $\forall x$, where $\forall$ means 'all'. The exception to the rule is that there exists one who is not castrated – the primal father never suffered the prohibition his followers demanded of themselves. The formula of female logic, on the other hand, claims that not all x are castrated – $\overline{\forall x}$, where the line over the top negates what is below it – and, with no female equivalent of the primal father who escapes the prohibition, there is no exception to this.

Castration, as the lack that comes with prohibition and the symbolic order, is something that women are not subject to in the same way as men. In lieu of trying to fill in the anxiogenic lack by submission to the symbolic, women acknowledge the lack and by crafting it a source for their own *jouissance* make not-All their constitutive own. Like men, they must remain inside the symbolic order but subversively so; outside the full reach of castration as the all ($\forall$) of the male logic that men cling on to, longing for a phantasmatic return to the primal father's sovereign enjoyment.

What needs stressing is that for both Lacan and Žižek the male/female differential is not reducible to biology but, instead, bespeaks oppositional positions, identifications, that can be taken up in response to the symbolic order and *jouissance*. Irrespective of anatomical attributes the feminine logic that denies a universality rooted in exception is available to men and women. It is philosophically freighted as a description of the ontological incompleteness that Kant registered as the deadlock that results when reason tries to go beyond the boundaries of the symbolic and reach reality as a whole in-itself.

Bailly 2009: 146–51; Leader and Groves 2005: 156–61; Neill 2023: 77–80

CONNECTIONS: sexual difference, sexuality

o

Objet petit a

Sometimes referred to as just *objet a*, Lacan's *objet petit a* ('object small a') – 'a' being the small *autre* (other), as opposed to the big Other – is in a symbiotic relationship with the subject to an extent that makes them inseparable. The subject, lacking the self-identity and completeness that would give it positivity, desires what in a psychoanalytic sense Lacan calls an *objet* (object): 'a point of imaginary fixation which gives satisfaction' (1992: 140). It brings to his mind seeing a collection of identical matchboxes decorating a wall of a friend's house on a visit some twenty years earlier. France had been conquered by the Nazis, his friend was living in Vichy France, and Lacan realizes that an object as simple as a matchbox can become something more than its use value. It becomes a 'Thing' (140–1).

In the early 1960s, Lacan stops using the words Thing and *das Ding* (German for 'thing') but important features of these terms are recognizable in what he begins to call the *objet petit a*. The 'object small a' gives body to the subject by ascribing to it a material form but, given that the subject is a void without substantiality, *objet a* is a bewitching chimera. The paradox in materializing what cannot be manifested lies behind Lacan's reference to anamorphosis and Holbein's *The Ambassadors* (1992: 166–7). The empty subject cannot be straightforwardly represented but it can be enrolled into the field of objects as a distorted image that appears normal only when viewed in a particular way. More precisely, it is the subject's desire that causes the distortion and this is strikingly brought out by Žižek in his book *Lacan*. There, lines from Shakespeare's *Richard II* are used to dramatize the imbrication of subject, desire and *objet petit a*.

Lacan describes the Thing as 'that which in the real suffers from the signifier' (1992: 154), referring to how language and the symbolic order effects a breach between the body and the psyche. Corporeal needs can be satisfied, as when a parent gives milk to a baby, but continuing and maintaining the affective attention that usually accompanies this immediacy is more a matter of desire than need.

Not seeking biological sustenance, desire is a permanent demand but expressing this is thwarted by the symbolic order and its intersubjective network. There is a gap between 'embodied gestures' (OWB 86) by primates, including humans, and a linguistic system based on the distribution of phonemic differences. Things are substituted by words standing in for them but there is something that cannot be symbolized by a signifier or provided for by the big Other. The consequent sense of loss and displaced wholeness is *objet petit a* as lack and this is what denotes it as the cause of desire. It provokes a search for something able to assuage the subject's sense of loss.

What is sought by the subject cannot be recovered because, being correlative with the subject, it is 'an object the entire being of which is an embodiment of its own impossibility' (D 81); 'a kind of negative correlation, an impossible link, a non-relationship' (AR 359). The failure of complete signification allows for a place of detachment by the subject from a symbolic order unable to fully represent it and in this sense *objet a* becomes an auratic piece of the Real. While not actually the Real, 'it deceives by posing as a shadow of the underlying Real' and 'the lost substance of *jouissance*' (TN 36–7). What cannot be signified is left over as a remainder, an excess that cannot be contained within the symbolic, and this is what *objet a* designates, 'that which remains of the Thing after it has undergone the process of symbolization' (PF 105). It may be a simulated enticement for a *jouissance* denied but the topology is such that it inhabits 'the place of the Real, which is why there is more truth in unconditional fidelity to one's desire than in a resigned insight into the vanity of one's striving' (LET 72).

What would fill in the gap in the subject is invested with a libidinal force that initiates the capacity to desire, thus becoming its *cause*, but it is also the *object* that offers the rapturous but delusory promise of completion. Lacan's example is the lady of the knight's earnest mission in courtly love and one of Žižek's is by way of the joke from Lubitsch's *Ninotchka*. The waiter in the film – enacting what Hegel calls 'determinate negation' – cannot serve a coffee without cream but does offer the customer a coffee without milk. A coffee on its own, however, will not do, something that is missing to complete its identity has to be added: 'Coffee is in itself not One but a One plus something' (AR 404). Any object, a coffee or matchboxes or something else, acquires the sublimity that elevates it to *objet petit a* only after it has been etched in the space of desire; it is a retrospective positing (SO 221).

When coffee is enjoyed without cream or milk, it functions 'as its own supplement –it itself fills the void its mere existence creates' (SO 221). This dual functionality, both the cause of desire and the object desired, is bound up with *objet petit a*'s relationship to the role of fantasy; encapsulated in Lacan's formula: $ <> a ($ as the barred subject of desire, *a* the *objet petit a* and the lozenge symbol for their interconnection). Fantasy offers the prospect of bringing a substantiality to the void that is the subject; the allure of the *objet a*, its siren call, is that it will transform the prospect into reality. It becomes an object of fantasy, believed to possess some special quality that endows it with potency, like the family's noodle soup and the sacred Dragon Scroll in *Kung Fu Panda* (2008). The soup, it turns out, has no unique ingredient and the Dragon Scroll is blank.

To 'break the spell of *objet a*, to recognize beneath the fascinating *agalma* (the Holy Grail of desire) the void that it covers' is what Kristin, in the likeable television mini-series *Station Eleven*, is able to accomplish (Žižek 2025c). She comes to live with the knowledge that the eponymous comic book does not possess the sublimity that Tyler attributes to it.

> **When we define the *objet a* as the object which overlaps with its loss, which emerges at the very moment of its loss (so that all its fantasmatic incarnations, from breast to voice to gaze, are metonymic figurations of the void, of nothing), we remain within the horizon of *desire*.**
>
> **(AR 237)**

The duality in being the cause and the object of desire is an engagement of two gears that ratchets the subject into the object. It is the subject's encounter with the place where it should find itself but fails. It is an impossible convergence because subject and *objet a* – the $ and *a* of Lacan's formula – are like the opposite sides of one coin that can never meet face to face. Žižek's simile for this impossibility is the peculiarity of a Möbius band (AR 403) where the same point on its surface has opposite sides. A coming together that is also a keeping apart is what Lacan means by 'extimacy', his invented word for an 'intimate exteriority' (1992: 171). The subject is formed through both its close attachment to the Other and by its recognition that the Other is also not whole. Their common alterity, a mutual self-estrangement, brings them together but also separates them. Although Lacan uses his neologism only a few times, it has taken on an importance of its own as a concept informing psychoanalytic theory and the role of *objet a* (Bou Ali and Singh 2025).

There is a crucial difference when *objet a* serves as the object of drive, not desire. No longer the goal of a quest for the semblance of a fullness of being deemed to have been lost, its status changes from the nostalgic and it becomes the void around which desire moves. As an object of drive, it is the push in the movement towards staging the loss itself through repetition. It is not what blocks the drive from attaining its target, slipping out of place at the last moment so that it has to repeat its movement. It is 'purely formal ... the curvature of the space of drive' (IV 19) that allows drive to repeatedly designate loss, not by moving towards the object in a straight line but by orbiting the empty space and ratifying its absence. This is not the domain of desire and the fabrication of a lost object that characterizes *objet petit a*. Desire futilely searches for a lost object while drive elevates this futility into endless motion around a lost object. *Objet a* mirrors the parallax effect arising from their different ways of dealing with the lack of fullness at the heart of existence: the object of desire is the externalization and materialization of the void while drive derives satisfaction from circulating it (SE 235–6); no rapprochement is possible.

Philosophical resonances of *objet a* are traced in both Kant and Hegel. Kant's case for the antinomies of reason and the unknowability of how things in themselves really are is countered by Hegel's line of reasoning whereby the deadlocks indicate the non-All nature of reality as a whole. In the movement from Kant to Hegel, pitching the elusiveness of a thing within the thing itself – an epistemological difficulty becoming an ontological fact – a site of similarity is found with what Kant calls the 'transcendental object' (Kant 2007: 137). This puzzling and sometimes confusing concept is neither empirical or noumenal and, for Kant, is 'thought only as something in general = x' (134). *Objet a*, being both beyond the symbolic but also not the thing-in-itself, has a similarly intangible and in-between status, acquiring its sublime status when an ordinary object is empowered by the libidinal force brought to it by the subject. It becomes similar to the Kantian transcendental object 'since it stands for the unknown X, for what is "in you more than yourself" ... it exists only – *its presence can be discerned only – when the landscape is viewed from a certain perspective*' (IV 54). This 'positing' is matched by the transcendental object being the object's general form that is given an intelligible unity when moulded by the a priori categories.

Objet a's Hegelian aspect is more problematic. Although Hegel is aware of the commonality that is the lack of both subject and substance, he is not able to see *objet a* as the result of this; as the positivization of what is not expressible as a signifier, as a 'nothingness' (LTN 599). Despite this limitation, the logic of *objet a* becomes acutely Hegelian when read as a 'negation of negation'. As that which cannot be received by the symbolic, a left-over refusing integration by the big Other, *objet a* is the first negation. But as the element that gives a necessary consistency to what is essentially inconsistent, in this case filling the void that is the subject, a second negation occurs.

TN 17–18, 35–6; L 66–73; LET 68–70; LTN 598–603, 660–6; D 43–4, 81–2; IV 52–5; QH 124

McGowan 2025: 110–16

CONNECTIONS: desire, fantasy, subject, unconscious

Ontology

Ontological questions – inquiries into the ultimate stuff, the substance of reality, outside of human mediations – loom large and dig deep in Žižek. The puzzle that is grappled with begins with trying to establish what form mind-independent entities might per se possess.

Far from there being a secret that can finally be revealed, Žižek's conclusion takes a negative form: substance has no full identity; not fully realized, it is unsutured, unlinked from itself, thwarted from within. This is very much at odds with views of Hegelian scholars like Robert Pippin for whom claims about holes in the fabric of reality amount to a 'gappy ontology' (Pippin 2015: 99). What is unacceptable for Pippin is a first principle for Žižek: there is something fundamentally unspecifiable and not fully determined about the nature of reality. It is only expressible in the formulas of quantum physics, a mathematicized language that cannot amount to what would be understood as a realist ontology. If mathematics is ontology at its purest, as Badiou presents it, the question that presses is how appearance, the world as a focused state of facts, arises from being's elemental flow of becoming. The German Idealists, primarily Schelling and Hegel, are seen as providing a better answer than Badiou (LTN 808–9; AR 384–5).

There is no unidirectionality behind the emergence of the symbolic and its *ex nihilo* advent becomes homologous to 'speculation in quantum physics about the virtual Void out of which (particular) reality emerges through the collapse of the wave function' (AR 226). There is no pre-existing positive for the symbolic to work on and give expression to, only an immanent negativity that the symbolic actualizes within its own order.

That there are gaps in the order of being is taken to be of primary significance and it underlies an approach to Hegel's dialectic in terms of parallax, discrepancies in the position of an object caused by shifts in the site of observation. Ascertaining the 'correct' position of an object causes an epistemological difficulty and this is mirrored in a gapped ontology: 'The parallax gap goes down to the bottom' (F 105); the void itself is 'divided, split in itself' (CA 85).

Parallax pictures a necessary move of the dialectic – 'the reversal of epistemological obstacle into ontological impossibility' (IV 3) – and this is the kind of ontology Žižek proposes. The impossibility that is its base is what is registered in the Real. If the symbolic matrix becomes sufficiently out of kilter, a sense of the ungrounded, fissured nature of reality becomes available and it can be traumatic if encountered in an extremely visceral way. This is expressible as touching the Real but not in a literal sense because there is nothing tangible there: its status 'is purely parallactic and, as such, non-substantial' (DLC 127). In the language of quantum cosmology, such non-substantiality is the quantum void and its transient electromagnetic waves and particles. If this is the closest science comes to a condition of nothingness, Žižek refines it into 'less than nothing' by stressing the profound instability and impermanence that defines it as a vacuum state or zero-point field (QH 58, 376–7). It is barred from completing itself: 'not the void pregnant with virtualities but the void of the pure self-contradiction, of the utter tension crushing a One which persists as its own impossibility' (IV 20). To say reality is not-One, in the form of Kant's infinite judgement – attesting a non-predicate rather than simply denying a predicate – serves to underscore the non-availability, the impossibility, of attaching any notion of balance or neutrality to an ontology premised on 'extreme antagonism, tension, self-contradiction' (IV 23). The premise, in one Hegelian word, is negativity and an acceptance of this is contrasted with the philosophy of Spinoza where any antagonism or obstacle always comes from outside and is never immanent. When 'all that he admits is a purely positive network of causes and affects' (OWB 35), what cannot be countenanced is the lack or absence of negativity in Spinoza.

> **A is just not-B, it is also and primarily not fully A, and B emerges to fill in this gap. It is at this level that we should locate ontological difference: reality is partial, incomplete, inconsistent.**
>
> **(D 21)**

It is because reality is not-One (SFA 119), that is, lacking coherent wholeness, that the Real can never be something transcendent, the X marking the buried treasure on an ontological map. On the contrary, reality as the ground of positively existing entities only becomes possible through a subtraction of the Real (LTN 958). Saying reality is not-One could be regarded as regression into a totalizing of its own, a comprehensive point of view only possible from an all-knowing, neutral position. If so, agnosticism should prevail and leave open the chance that some ontological coherence might later emerge. This argument is addressed in *Christian Atheism* and met with a Hegelian answer: the crack in reality that truncates it does not allow for exceptions and agnosticism only keeps open the illusion that the gap is fillable. Hegel's remark about there being nothing behind the curtain unless we go there ourselves (2018: §165) is quoted to indicate that only fantasy formations like God can fill the gap in reality and make it seem whole. When the subject goes behind the curtain, 'he is bringing with him the very thing that he will find' (MSH 23).

The ontological enigma that Schelling tried to resolve, his uncompleted *Ages of the World* being testimony to the problem's intractability, is posed by Žižek as the question as to why there is something rather than nothing (LTN 925). His interest in quantum physics is indicative of the wish to establish an answer to the question that dogs many of his philosophical reflections and inquiries. In *Sex and the Failed Absolute*, taking the case of cognitive science, there is no way brain processes themselves can explain the mind's self-awareness. What is left open is the strong possibility that at some primordial level matter possesses a degree of consciousness.

LTN 957–61; D 13, 21; SFA 379; CA 48–51, 84–5; QH 100–2, 35–66, 375

Johnston 2008; Pippin 2015: 99; Žižek 2013e, 2021f

CONNECTIONS: Aristotle, Hegel, infinite judgement, In-itself/For-itself, negativity, quantum physics, Real, Schelling, transcendental

Other

Experiencing the (sometimes capitalized) other is a minefield of imponderable desires, inaugurated by the infant's shattering discovery that a mother's love, synonymous with the other, is not total. Unconditional love had been taken for granted – 'the unfathomable desire the child discerns in maternal caressing' (OWB 101) – but the mother becomes inscrutable when found to have needs of her own. When the mother's want is moved to another place or person – temporarily directed elsewhere – it warns of a lack previously unknown to the infant. Lack and the desire this gives rise to emerges in the field of the (m)other, a finding encapsulated by Lacan in what has become one of his signature statements: 'Desire is the desire of the Other' (2004: 235). Something whole has been lost and the lack can be assuaged by seeking what it is that the other desires. The desire for what the other desires and the desire is to be desired by the other become the same. If what the other desires can be attained or reached then one can take its place and what needs to be unconditional and absolute will be restored. The Name-of-the-Father is not the intruder obtaining the mother's desire but a symptom of the need to symbolize and locate the mystery of the void that is now desire.

The other as alterity makes it part of the symbolic order and its signifiers. With language, one gathers for oneself an apparently inalienable identity that will serve as a way of coping with the impasse that is the Other's desire. The difficulty is that it leaves a space that cannot be filled and Lacan's 'symbolic castration' is the failure of one's mandated identity to explain who I am for the other and who I am to myself: '*I cannot ever truly communicate with myself*; the Other is originally the decentered Other Place of my own splitting' (TN 31). The plight of the hysteric is the traumatic awareness of being trapped in a symbolic order which itself lacks substantiality and cannot deliver what is desired. The trap is that everyone has to participate in language as a medium of the big Other, connecting us with others while simultaneously fencing us off; forever separate.

In a genuine encounter with the other, the Real of their being is fleetingly glimpsed when their *jouissance* shows itself. This does not usually occur as a heightened moment, a theatrical scene dramatizing its own importance, but as an incidental awareness of some otherwise insignificant detail – 'a compulsive gesture, an excessive facial expression' (TAF 25). Without details like these, the other remains a fiction and only accessible within the confines of the symbolic. The odd moments that kindle awareness of a *jouissance* that is not our own bring to the surface the other 'with whom no symmetrical dialogue, mediated by the symbolic Order, is possible' (DSS 163; IR 310).

At a wider sociopolitical level, multiculturalism can be adjudged a suspension of 'the traumatic kernel of the Other, reducing it to an aseptic folklorist entity' (TAF 26). Allowing oneself to be fascinated by the cultural 'diversity' of the other becomes a fetish that keeps at bay uncomfortable thoughts that might unsettle the ground of one's own self and question 'the unproblematic *identity* of our subjective position' (KNW 102).

My desire is to be desired by the other and establish what is in me that they want (*Che vuoi?*). An answer to the enigma of the other's desire – the angst-ridden puzzle that Kafka's fiction gives body to – is found in fantasy formations where the desire being staged is 'a way for the subject to answer the question of what object they are for the Other, in the eyes of the Other, for the Other's desire' (Žižek 1994b). The psychoanalytic cure involves giving up illusionary guarantees of what I am for the other. With 'subjective destitution', Lacan's term for a concluding moment in the psychoanalytic process, 'The Other is here reduced to a silent witness, to a mute presence that endorses the subject's *jouissance* by way of emitting a silent sign of acknowledgement, a "Yes!" to drive' (TAF 81).

A subject endeavours to express itself in a signifier, it fails, and the subject *is* this failure. This is what Lacan means by his deceptively simple claim that, ultimately, a subject is what is not an object – every hysteric knows this well, since the hysterical question is: What object am I for the Other? What does the Other desire in me?

(AR 150)

DSS 160–5; IR 307–11; L 42–4, 46–7; CA 70–1; AP 79–80; QH 3

Bailey 2009: 65–73

CONNECTIONS: big Other, hysteria, *jouissance*, neighbour, psychoanalysis, symbolic

P

Parallax

See *objet petit a*, ontology, real, transcendental.

Partial object

See the introduction and literary criticism, subject.

Perversion

> For psychoanalysis, the perversion of the human libidinal economy is what follows from the prohibition of some pleasurable activity: not a life led in strict obedience to the law and deprived of all pleasure but a life in which exercising the law provides a pleasure of its own, a life in which performance of the ritual destined to keep illicit temptation at bay becomes the source of libidinal satisfaction.
>
> (Žižek 1999c)

With perversion – not a term to be reduced by making it equivalent to sexual deviancy – the enigma of the Other is not questioned. There is the conviction that the Other's desire is assuredly known and contentment reposes in being positioned as the Other's means to enjoyment. Being a tool in this manner is bliss to the pervert, comparable to the sheer passivity of the bodies in *The Matrix* enclosed in slime (OWB 157).

Devotion to the *jouissance* of the Other entails embracing the superego's command to enjoy. Where the hysteric is within reach of going beyond the fantasy that they possess some *agalma* guaranteeing their worth in another's desire, the pervert accepts their fantasy of being the instrument of desire. In a jokey footnote that rephrases the dig at psychoanalysis ('Sometimes a phallus is just a phallus'), Žižek notes that 'the subject for whom a phallus is just a phallus has a precise name: the pervert' (LTN 592). The pervert 'offers himself loyally to the Other's *jouissance*' (Lacan 2014: 49), a severe desubjectivization that is shared by the Stalinist Communist and the Nazi SS (L 105–6), militaristic Zen (PD 29), Orpheus (TN 194) and the devout Christian runner in the film *Chariots of Fire* who says God 'made me fast. And when I run, I feel his pleasure' (TAF 103). The 2024 trial in France of Dominique Pelicot is seen to add a new dimension due to the perversion serving not just Pelicot and his associates but also the big Other's digitized territory where the films he made circulated (ZP 25–6).

Perversion's self-fuelling loop functions by producing what it needs to continue running. In *Tarrying with the Negative* its economy is distinguished from ideological self-legitimization by contrasting Lincoln's Gettysburg Address with a Patricia Highsmith short story where a character sets a house on fire to enable her saving of a child. Another given example is the apparatchiks under Stalin who framed the innocent, inventing their 'treason', in order to strengthen party unanimity. The pervert's object of desire is '*Law itself* – the Law is the Ideal he is longing for, he wants to be fully acknowledged by the Law, integrated into its functioning' (PF 17).

The pervert's insight is in knowing that the law requires transgression to maintain its rule. Unlike the hysteric's insubordinate challenge to social interpellation, there is nothing subversive in acting out repressed fantasies when the status quo is strengthened by transgressive gestures that function as the law's obscene supplement (DLC 29): 'The transgression which at first appeared to subvert the Law, turns out to pertain to the Law – the Law itself is the ultimate perversion' (Žižek 2010f). St Paul is appreciated because he struggles to 'avoid the trap of *perversion*' (TS 48), to break free of law that requires transgression in order for it to exist. This is borne out by the obscenities of Trump that serve no emancipatory purpose, serving instead to reinforce a reactionary agenda (ZP 9–10).

Perversion and hysteria, as terms employable within a broad range of situations and discourses, are relatable to race and capitalism. Those who suffer racial inequities are deemed right to respond to faux-radical, piecemeal reforms or assurances with the cry of 'that's not it' when they recognize them as facile ameliorations designed not to seriously change power relations; another case of changing things so that nothing really changes. Perversion, Zupančič explains, is the fending-off of desire, controlling it through the insistence of our world's social economy that enjoyment is all we desire. What is obfuscated is the lack that gives rise to desire and the falsity of forcing it onto putative objects of desire.

Capitalism's obsessional pursuit of surplus value assimilates desire's demand on the libido for a plethora of being, an excess that is surplus to the object. This might suggest that the consumer is a hysteric, always disappointed by the failure of the product to provide what is being sought ('that's not it'), but consumerism is seen to be more properly aligned with the libidinal economy of the pervert. The pervert realizes that desire cannot be satisfied and the consumerist, 'not haunted by questions' about desire, is 'a cynical pervert who knows' (SE 242). Capitalism is a system, trapped in its own perversion, 'that began with *counting* the pleasure (of gaining profit) and immediately reverts into the *pleasure of counting* (profit)' (CA 124).

TN 193–5; TS 148–51, 247–9; OWB 89–90; L 106–10; CA 36–9

Kaye 2023: 144–8; Kotsko 2008: 61–6; Kotsko 2015; Løland 2018: 122–5; Žižek 2010f; Zupančič 2023: 82–3, 86–9

CONNECTIONS: hysteria, superego

Plato

> **This is why Hitchcock's *Vertigo* is the ultimate anti-Platonic film, a systematic materialist undermining of the Platonic project … The shock here is not that the original turns out to be merely a copy – a standard deception against which Platonism continually warns us – but that (what we took to be) the copy turns out to be the original.**
>
> **(LTN 693)**

Part I of *Less Than Nothing*, setting out some themes that will be explored in the book has the title 'The Drink Before', and its inaugural chapter looks at Plato's Ideas/Forms. It pursues an impressively forensic analysis of his *Parmenides*, tunnels into that text's questions about being and not-being, about a whole and multiples.

A theory of Ideas is put forward by a young Socrates in the first one-third of *Parmenides*. Ideas stand as a bold response to the Sophists, contemporaries of Plato who, judging from the way they are described and quoted by other ancient Greek writers (there are no extant complete Sophist texts), are alert to relativism and, as paid teachers of rhetoric, to the role of discourse. Firmly rejecting their perspectivism, Plato argues for the existence of immutable Ideas, really existing but independent of the sensible world and its spatial-temporal fields. The concrete world is modelled as mere copies of immaterial but eternally presents Ideas. Plato's objection to art, that it delivers copies of these copies, is based on the logic of his premise.

Žižek's boldness equals Plato's by situating Ideas in accordance with a Hegelian sense of the inseparability of appearance and essence. What shows as phenomenal contains its essence in its appearance, essence is not something behind or beneath phenomena, and in this way Plato's Ideas 'are nothing but the form of appearance' (LTN 31). As form, they are virtual in Deleuze's sense of the term: not something identical to what is actual but something able to bring about an actualization without losing itself in the process. This is a way of characterizing the Lacanian real and Ideas belong to 'the Real that emerges in the guise of an illusory spectacle' (LTN 33). Various examples of ideas appearing in spectral states of the suprasensible, from the personal to the political and the artistic, are given in *Less Than Nothing*'s first chapter. To experience love is to partake in a fullness that abandons the quotidian; an authentic political act like the 2011 uprising that brought down Murbarak's regime in Egypt invested the idea of universal freedom with a numinous but bodily immediacy in Tahir Square; Picasso's *A Woman Throwing a Stone* painting is not a realistic representation yet it succeeds in realizing its title on another, aesthetic level.

Platonic ideas are returned to and reappropriated for the emancipatory value they give to what is non-physical, the sublime as an essential component to a full human existence. Without a metaphysical measure, life is reduced to the kind of cultural relativism and language games that were associated with the Sophists. The corporeal cannot account for what lies behind someone's willingness to give up their life for something held to be of a higher value. What is metaphysical is the Real, the gap that robs every position of its objectivity, the asymmetry between signifier and signified but which, for this very reason, is the space of inscription for subjective truths.

Plato is seen to argue for being's fullness by including in it a realm of Ideas that are above and beyond the material. Physical reality partakes in this higher realm, giving body to it but only imperfectly – in the way that a Notion for Hegel is '*what the thing should become in order to fully be what it is*' (LTN 398; AR 229). Eternal Ideas secure reality by saving it from reduction to an unstable multiplicity. Žižek's penetrating reading of *Parmenides* opens up a converse space which deepens the enigma surrounding the text's persistent questioning: 'The only result is that there is no consistent reality' (LTN 49). In the expositions that unfold in his later texts, Plato is seen to draw back from the ontological abyss as posited at the end of *Parmenides*: 'Then if we were to say, to sum up, "if one is not, nothing is", wouldn't we speak correctly?'(Plato 1997: 397). An alternative approach adopts this conclusion and, as developed in the other parts of *Less Than Nothing*, regards 'the problem as (containing) its own solution' (LTN 49). When this approach is adopted towards the two-thirds of *Parmenides* that more or less deconstruct Platonic Ideas, it yields a Hegelian infinite judgement. Instead of negating the statement 'in Plato, idealism is all there is' by a simple repudiation ('in Plato idealism is not all there is'), another mental chassis is expressed by saying 'in Plato, idealism is non-all'. The result, as Frank Ruda concludes, is a Žižekian idealist Platonism, 'an *idealism without idealism*, an incomplete idealism' (2015a: 54).

Cinematic representations of the logical disorder that haunts Platonic Ideas are drawn out in two films, Hitchcock's *Vertigo* and Robert Rossellini's lesser known *General Della Rovere*. The unsettling conclusion that Scottie experiences in the first movie is not that the original turns out to be a copy – often highlighted by Plato as a potential hazard – 'but that (what we took to be) *the copy turns out to be the original*' (OWB 157). The truth that emerges is that the Judy, whom Scottie thought he had crafted as a perfect facsimile of the original Madeline, was the original whose bodily presence has so besotted him. In Rossellini's film, the person charged by the Germans with impersonating a Resistance hero, so that his fellow prisoners will reveal to him vital secrets, fails utterly when he fully adopts the hero's identity and chooses to face death rather than use his fake persona to betray the Cause. Essence comes to reside in appearance as appearance.

DSS 150–1; OWB 157–60; PV 161–3; E 84–7; LTN 31–42, 48–55, 61–9; IV 7–8

Masarrat 2025; Ruda 2015a

CONNECTIONS: appearance and essence, infinite judgement, not-All/non-All, Real, *Vertigo*

Politics

Contestations from political history and interpretations of political events and figures feature throughout Žižek's work. In recent years, a pronounced tendency to publish on current political events finds his opinion pieces in newspapers, journals and online platforms. The primary online platform for bulletins and dispatches of a political kind is currently *Žižek's Goads and Prods* on Substack.

He has introduced and/or edited the writings of Mao Zedong, Robespierre and Lenin, plus a number of relatively philosophy-free books that have been prompted by contemporary events. *Welcome to the Desert of the Real!* is subtitled *Five Essays on September 11 and Related Dates*; the US invasion of Iraq is considered in *Iraq: The Borrowed Kettle*, published the year after the event; *The Year of Dreaming Dangerously* looks at uprisings and convulsive events around 2011, from the Arab Spring and Occupy Wall Street to Anders Behring Breivik's massacre in Norway; *Trouble in Paradise* (2014) considers, but by no means exclusively, the political situations in Egypt, Korea, China and Ukraine; the subtitle of *Against the Double Blackmail* (2016) – *Refugees, Terror and Other Troubles with the Neighbours* – makes clear its subject matter; *A Left that Dares to Speak Its Name* (2020) collects in one book rewritten versions of commentaries on public issues that were current at the time and *Heaven in Disorder* (2021) is made up of thirty-six fairly short pieces on international events and global crises from climate change to refugees; *Too Late to Awaken* (2023) also discusses emerging calamities and, in the same year, over a third of *Mad World* is devoted to Ukraine. *Zero Point*, published in the spring of 2025, is devoted to contemporary events and its second half focuses on Israel and its genocidal policies towards Palestinians. Published in autumn of the same year, the essays in *Against Progress* stare into the face of current catastrophes brought about by political failures and confronts them with a resilience that rejects passivity and resignation: 'We should act in all possible ways even without hope' (56) while not forgetting that nothing is written in stone (105). *Liberal Fascisms* (2026), a book whose working title was 'Donald Trump: A Fascist Libertarian', continues this conversation.

Žižek's political journalism sheds a lot of the left's baggage and inevitably invites criticism; his positions in the past regarding the Balkans have been adjudged conservative and he has been taxed over his stance on Ukraine, although his position on that issue may prove more justified than some previously thought. Political pessimism does not please everyone and vituperative comments emerge, from an element once associated with the kind of parties that had Marxist-Leninist in their names. The difficulty in following a party line arises from the scarcity of parties with a line worth following and this relates to his call for a new master. The reference here is to one of Lacan's four discourses – the Master, (the others being the University, the Analyst and the Hysteric) – and the concern it raises around questions of authority, knowledge and intersubjective relations. A true master for Žižek is not an authoritarian populist or fundamentalist but a figure who allows historical agents to pull themselves, like Baron Münchhausen, out of their political swamp – currently one of depression and despair – and, as at the end of a psychoanalytic analysis, surrender their subject-supposed-to-know status. The master enshrined by liberal democracy is 'a fetish created to prevent the possibility that individuals will themselves take care of themselves' (Žižek 2023j: 393).

The nature of a situation determines for Žižek at what level it could or should be dealt with or remedied. In the two *Pandemic!* books published in 2020, pragmatic responses have their place and the need for solidarity is emphasized but, it is also stressed, relying on a comforting rallying call to forget politics and for everyone – from beggars to bourgeois – to unite in facing the crisis ignores the way a call like this is itself political (P2 94). Solidarity has become one of those hegemonic signifiers effectively unable and unwilling to grasp class struggle as the basic division in society. The maxim about staying united should, in the spirit of forging new utterances, be reversed: *divided we stand, united we fall* (Žižek 2024g). In this respect, democracy as a signifier becomes questionable, an opinion he finds orchestrated by the actions in Gaza by an army purportedly representing the 'only democracy in the Middle East' (Žižek 2024g; QH 118).

The undertow of loyalties in much of the political commentary resonates with ideas and formulations from the work of Althusser, Rancière and Badiou. The importance of the *demos* in ancient Athens (Rancière 1997) reverberates in Žižek with the many citations of 'the part of no-part' and the crucial moment of politicization when the excluded insist on standing as a universality in opposition to all others who represent only their one-sided and privileged concerns. The conduct of conventional politics functions as a defence against the threat posed by the excluded; a 'post-political biopolitics' (R xxvi). The antagonism that defines any society creates a space for an element that stands for and materializes the pure difference. This element represents what comes to be treated as an intrusive presence and fascism operates by identifying it with a group of people (Jews, undocumented immigrants …) and seeking expurgation. Right-wing politics proceeds from seeing society as a Whole with a natural hierarchical disposition that needs preserving whereas for the Left the antagonism dividing society is the foundation for political action. This antagonism that divides is not about different cognitive maps but a 'real-impossible' difference that exceeds the symbolic (AR 369); if it did not, politics would not possess its explosive potential. The political in its philosophical expanse belongs with Hegel's absolute, the feminine logic of the 'non-all' and the non-existence of the big Other.

The merits of anarchism as a political doctrine are recognized but what works at a local level – from Barcelona in the Spanish Civil War to Rojava in Syria – does not obviate the need for coordinated action at national and international levels. In dispiriting times, a Bartleby-like refusal to be brought into the fold becomes the best option until another radical emancipatory event occurs with an opportunity to change the existing coordinates of the social and economic order. Part of the 'art of politics' becomes making an exacting demand which, though feasible, is ruled out as too destabilizing to warrant being implemented (like universal health care in the United States) – while bearing in mind that 'all we say now can be taken (recuperated) from us except our silence' (2013c: 199–200). In two more recent books, *Surplus Enjoyment* and *Christian Atheism*, a passage is repeated that looks back to the way Allende's Chile began with simple acts like providing free school meals and nationalizing copper mines. It failed in the face of armed resistance, with the support of the United States, and the lesson to be learned is that future revolutionaries should be more pragmatic but still begin with acts that are simple but subversive and sublime. Power takes its current forms because those being ruled accept their subordination; power's 'permanence' depends on acceptance and the question is how to combat this. Narcissism of the lost cause or of small differences is as much an escape from responsibility as the 'beautiful soul', described by Hegel as refraining from acting 'to preserve the purity of its heart' (2018: §6598). A way towards a politics of truth takes a theological turn in the concluding pages of *Living in the End Times* with a call for belief in the paradox of predestination. A retroactive determination of one's destiny becomes possible with the kind of divinity who emerges in a Bolshevik joke about a resolute Communist who convinces God of his own non-existence. No longer a big Other, God becomes a comrade 'who accepts his own erasure, passing over entirely into the love that binds all members of the "Holy Ghost", that is, of the Party or emancipatory collective' (LET 402). How a messianic theology like this unites with a recognition of the antagonism that splits the body politic is the subject matter of *Less Than Nothing*'s concluding chapter. It draws to an end with the situation in psychoanalysis where the analysand is cognisant of their symptoms as a response, an answer, to questions but remains in need of an analyst to articulate what is being asked. The vocabulary and grammar for formulating the questions are not those found in the politics of liberal democracy but the answers are visible in the chronicles of dissent and insurrection that makes up history. They may be records of failed attempts but a remark of G. K. Chesterton's is quoted to indicate how 'the lost causes are exactly those which might have saved the world' (LTN 1010). Politics should stand on the ground of events in the past and present that carry memories of what could be done in the future. Seminal figures as different St Paul, Lenin and Lacan worked within the scope of their teachers – Christ, Marx and Freud – repeating what they had learned but with a new accent and a neoteric vocabulary. Žižek's political acumen works in this tradition of formulating questions so that answers become more perspicuous.

Accompanying this is a facing up to the utopian thinking that often accompanies ideas about what an emancipated society might look like. A reckoning with the realities of maintaining effective political change, as addressed by Frederic Jameson in his essay 'An American Utopia', is the context for Žižek's editing of a book with this essay and a set of responses to it, including his own (2016h). The problem being confronted is summed up in the question about what might come after the insurrection that brings the movie *V for Vendetta* to its triumphant end: unarmed, Guy Fawkes-masked Londoners marching in their thousands to take power. 'OK, a nice ecstatic moment, but I was ready to sell my mother into slavery to see *V for Vendetta 2*. What would have happened the day after the victory of the people?' (2016h: 285). Political engagement can create intensive moments of commitment but, it is observed, they tend to be of limited duration and, moreover, a mass mobilization of protestors can be overcome by a silent majority who think otherwise.

The present ascendency of an emboldened Right and a militant fundamentalism – Christian, Jewish, Islamic and Hindu – impact on the public space of political discourse and the current political malaise reflects the absence of a language of the left and its replacement by the populism of the extreme right. In a similar kind of way, fundamentalism fills a gap created by the absence of a viable alternative and *Trouble in Paradise* (100–2) instances Afghanistan in this regard. The country enjoyed a secular tradition that brought a Communist party to power yet succumbed to extremism in the aftermath of invasions by Russia and then the United States.

The challenge in effecting radical political change, emerging explicitly in the second half of *Iraq: The Borrowed Kettle*, is the difficulty of formulating and implementing successful resistance. The ideology of liberal democracy, ushered in after the Second World War and maintaining its sway as 'one "truth" (or rather, one big Lie)' (2024i: 18), has considerably weakened its hegemonic grip. This weakening is a corollary of its evident failure to maintain the 'one big Lie' and the political consequences bear out the truth of Antonio Gramsci's remark about the old dying, the new prevented from being born and the morbid symptoms this occasions: 'The battles we are fighting today, from the populist Right to cancel culture, are mostly such morbid symptoms of the liberal centre' (AP 53). Žižek, bringing a Lacanian awareness to what needs to be a part of the political battles being fought in beleaguered times, calls for attending to 'the opaque *jouissance* of the symptom' and the 'shape of unsayability that sustains the subject's being' (2025i: 448).

> The most elementary feature of the political: the universe of politics is by definition ontologically open ... we always move in a minimal vicious cycle where a decision retroactively posits its own reasons. This is why political disputes can never be settled through rational debate ... There is no ultimate neutral Norm to which both sides could refer ('human rights', 'freedom' ...) because the struggle is precisely a struggle about what this Norm is.
>
> **(AR 197)**

TS 187–8; OB 1–5; RG; I; R vii–xxxix; M; LET 398–402; LTN 963–1010; AR 44–5, 369–71; YD; P; P2; TP 179–86; SE 183–4; MW; F 185–212, 276–8; TL; CA 199–201; ZP; AP; QH 116–22, 139–44, 149–56, 297–306, 356–62; LF

Homer 2016; Žižek 1998a, 2011a, 2016h, 2023i, 2024i, 2026

slavoj.substack.com

CONNECTIONS: absolute knowing, antagonism, Badiou, Bartleby's 'I would prefer not to', class struggle, communism, concrete universality, event/act, ideology, Lenin, not-All/non-All, predestination

Predestination

No old-school Marxist outlook, looking to the proletariat as the class destined to fulfil its historically determined role as the agent of revolution, underlies Žižek's deployment of the idea of predestination. There is no antecedent necessity and in the absence of a big Other, historical or divine, what is available is a radical opportunity: 'The freedom to retroactively determine (change) one's destiny itself' (Žižek 2010c: 197). An authentic act shreds the vector of an agent's current existence and, retroactively, creates out of the virtual past, a new projection. This, unlikely as it seems, chimes with the Protestant notion of predestination.

Predestination, in a way characteristic of Žižek's counterintuitive sagacity, can be employed to pose the shocking nature of the freedom that is available to us. We know we are predestined without knowing *how* and interpreting the past in a way opposed to the prevailing view of it allows for the possibility of a different kind of future. This is 'the unbearable burden of a really free choice – we know that what we will do is predestined, but we still have to take a risk and subjectively choose what is predestined' (F 60; SFA 392). An event/act is riddled with uncertainty, it is a 'step into the open, with no guarantee about the final outcome' (WD 152).

The story, from a play by Somerset Maugham, about a man meeting Death in the marketplace and fleeing in escape to Samarra only to find him waiting there, is first used in *The Sublime Object of Ideology*. It is taken to illustrate the temporal paradox of an intervention into the past, designed to alter its course of events, but having the effect of bringing about just what it hoped to avoid ever happening. The servant in the story misjudges the expression on Death's countenance when he is encountered in a marketplace, mistaking it as an interpellation when their meeting was never meant to occur in that place. Death was not hailing him but showing surprise, his appointment with the servant is to take place in Samarra and yet to come. The story is referenced to signpost the paradoxical association between truth and error but when the story is returned to in *Freedom* it is a paradox relating to predestination. The story at a surface level flags the ineluctable grip of fate but, Žižek speculates, the message could be that fate's grip can be loosened, not by trying to escape it but by accepting an apparent certainty and ignoring it. If the servant had responded to Death in the marketplace by questioning his presence and dismissing him, a discombobulated Death might have left in bewilderment, muttering an excuse before heading off to Samarra for an appointment that would not be met.

In line with Christian atheism, predestination is a theological notion speculatively brought into unholy alliance with Hegel's dialectical understanding of contingency and necessity. The refutation of an Aristotelian ontology privileges in its stead the changeability and *becoming* of being, a processual flow replete with open possibilities and alternative futures. The potential that Benjamin discerned in history's embodied memories, to redeem revolutionary failures of the past by releasing again their emancipatory promise, is the ground for political change: 'The burden of individuals' activities is not to performatively constitute their fate, but to discover (or guess) their pre-existing fate' (LTN 213). The historical agent becomes a genealogist, firmly situated in the present but finding there traces left from the past and 'unearthing, in the very heart of actuality, a secret striving towards potentiality' (LTN 464).

Predestination shares with retroactivity an openness of being that is interpretable with Deleuze's virtual/actuality axis in mind. The past which is open to change, in a virtual and not empirical one, is a past yet to be present in a future that cannot be predictable but which, when it comes about, will be as necessary as fate itself. Predestination also means it will be an ethical future, not one relying on the doing of good deeds because they bringing a return in the afterlife, but one brought about with 'no commerce, no tit-for, no exchange between man and God' (AR 67n22).

> That is to say, predestination does not mean that our fate is sealed in an actual text existing from eternity in the divine mind; the texture which predestines us belongs to the purely virtual eternal past which, as such, can be retrospectively rewritten by our acts.
>
> **(LTN 213)**

SO 60–1; DLC 314–16; LTN 213–19; AR 67–8; SE 246–8; F 31, 59–60

Žižek 2020g

CONNECTIONS: Aristotle, Benjamin, Christian atheism, contingency and
  necessity, event/act, freedom, retroactivity

Psychoanalysis

Freud (1981b: 284–5) famously compares psychoanalysis with the Copernican revolution, replacing the ego as the centre of our psychical universe with the unconscious. Lacan queries the implications of Freud's cosmological analogy and emphasizes not a change in the centre – from earth or ego to sun or unconscious – but a decentring: the subject is separated from a thinking self: 'I think where I am not, therefore I am where I do not think' (2001: 183). My existence no longer revolves around who I think I am because there is no open access to my inner 'self'. There is still a subject but one barred from directly assuming agency over its unconscious. Lacanian psychoanalysis and its political implications are what matter to Žižek.

Buddhism and psychoanalysis are alike in recognizing the illusory nature of the self, its emptiness as the kernel of subjectivity, but they diverge when it comes to recognising the space that is the source of desire. With Buddhist enlightenment, the craving for objects of desire dissipates but the nature of drive, as that which persists and cannot be eradicated, is not acknowledged. This failure becomes a blind spot that cannot see the home of the object, 'the place it occupies, the place of the Real' (LTN 133).

The psychoanalytic process does not conclude with the dissipation of an object of desire. It involves renunciation, but not elimination, of the role of fantasy in supporting my being: 'I have to renounce the fantasy-support of my being, my clinging to "my own private Idaho", to some hidden treasure in me, inaccessible to others' (TN 31). A position is reached where, says Lacan, the fantasy is 'traversed' (2004: 273). There is a travelling through or across the fantasy that enables the analysand to no longer rely on *objet a* and the fantasy that sustains it. The subject, perpetually puzzled by the desire of the Other, seeks to know what is in them that another person desires; nourishing this search is what impels the metonymical changing from one object to another. The actual objective is not to reach the end of the search and find nothing there; the quest ends with a reorientation, a full assumption of the impossibility behind our desire and the equal lack of ground in the Other's desire: 'The move accomplished by psychoanalysis is thus a Hegelian one: from external opposition to immanent impossibility' (Žižek 2021c), but this no more equates to abject submission than to seeing it as an instant passport to blissful enlightenment. A saying of Lacan's that Žižek refers to more than once – *les non-dupes errant* ('the unduped wander') – conveys the need to be first taken in by a fiction before progressing to a place beyond it. Those convinced of their ability to spot deception 'miss the truth concealed by this illusion' (LTN 102) and remain the ones most in error. The Real is there, unnegotiable, but as a fracture in the symbolic it is open to intervention through the symbolic (LTN 477, 971).

In a parodically macabre touch, Hannibal Lecter in the film *The Silence of the Lambs* serves to show 'a deep longing for a Lacanian psychoanalyst' (IR 147). He helps the character played by Jodie Foster to pass through her fantasy, maintain a distance from her mode of *jouissance*, and surrender that innermost part of her being to which she has been clinging.

Being able to dispossess oneself in this ground-clearing way is what Lacan calls 'subjective destitution'. The term is used by Žižek to describe the state when the analysand comes to 'accept that the traumatic encounters which traced out the itinerary of his life were utterly contingent and indifferent, that they bear no "deeper message"' (IRL 94); it is a moment of contact with the Real (Žižek 2024k: 7). Desire is not abolished and the dissatisfaction it entails remains as a fact of life but what comes to be admitted is drive as the inescapable motor of desire. Subjective destitution is constructed as a change of register from desire to drive because it 'involves a kind of inert satisfaction that always find its way' (TAF 80) by circling the void space that *objet a* occupies. As the concluding paragraph of *Surplus Enjoyment* puts it, seeking 'one's life in a spirit of furious indifference – this is how subjective destitution works' (SE 344). For Shakespeare's *Richard II*, it serves as a process of dehystericization and the means of a final settlement with his trauma (Žižek 2015a, D 213–16, 2017g: 294–9); for the Beckett of *Texts for Nothing* and *Not I*, it is the 'subject without subjectivization' (D 220, 2017g: 302).

What follows from subjective destitution is accepting responsibility for the *jouissance* that comes from drive and, in particular, from a *sinthome*. Lacan's neologism names a peculiar form of enjoyment that must be seen for what it is – a fixation on a symptom that cannot easily be removed: 'The aim of psychoanalysis is to get the subject to come to terms with the *sinthome*' (2005b: 175).

Psychoanalysis cannot hold out any promise of a nirvana, free of suffering and desire, but the condition of impossibility becomes a condition of possibility. Like predestination in this respect, the absence of free will is 'ultimately an appearance, not a fact waiting to be discovered by objective science' and 'this appearance itself has an efficiency of its own' (SE 147). What matters is not to use the absence of free will as a way to avoid being saddled with the responsibility that comes with existence. There is efficacy in coming to terms with existing as a decentred subject, at the mercy of the big Other and the unconscious – even if it increases the burden of responsibility by making us accountable for what evades our conscious awareness. It is not sufficient for the psychoanalyst to convince the patient about the truth behind their conscious symptom: 'The Unconscious itself must be brought to assume the truth' (D 276). One of those jokes that Žižek likes to recount, about the man who believes he is a grain of seed, encapsulates the point when the man, returning to his psychoanalyst, fully accepts he is not a grain of seed but remains anxious because the presence of a chicken outside the door alerts him to the possibility that maybe the chicken does not share his knowledge.

The condition of possibility that Lacanian psychoanalysis initiates is the bedrock for political involvement, its *sine qua non*. There is no big Other, no prescription, authority or agency that could ground political options, but the temptation is to succumb to false positions that shy away from recognising this. The gap, arising from the immanent antagonism that delimits any objectivity, can be filled in from various political standpoints. Chief among these are resigned acceptance of liberal democracy, with piecemeal solutions to flaws in the system, or the conservative position that seeks to batten down the hatches on what is regarded as an unruliness menacing every social order. The concluding chapter of *Less Than Nothing* begins by setting out these different possible positions and sees the only true one as a radical leftist perspective that accepts class struggle and the non-existence of the big Other.

> Traversing the fantasy does not mean simply going outside fantasy, but shattering its foundations, accepting its inconsistency ... To 'traverse the fantasy' therefore means, paradoxically, to *fully identify oneself with the fantasy*, to bring the fantasy out.
>
> (E 28–9)

IR 93–5, 148; LTN 131–3, 963–71; D 276–7; SE 247–8; ZP 19–21, 29–30; QH 69

Kotsko 2008: 65–7; Žižek 2006e

CONNECTIONS: big Other, Buddhism, drive, fantasy, *jouissance*, *objet petit a*, other, predestination, Real, the unconscious

Q

Quantum physics

An early and characteristic indication of why quantum physics – in particular, quantum mechanics – has become of abiding interest for Žižek comes in *The Indivisible Remainder* (TIR 208). Noting the self-reflectivity quantum physics introduces into the world of science, its approach to knowledge is seen to cohabit a conceptual space with Marxism and psychoanalysis. What they all have in common is a reluctance to place innocent trust in the availability of a neutral engagement with their subject matter. They claim, on the contrary, that a partial position is not only unavoidable but necessary. Moreover, the position from where knowing occurs affects what becomes known. Measuring a particle's position and its speed is not impossible, either or both is attainable to a calibrated degree, but making one of the measurements affects available information on the other and simultaneous measurements become impossible due to the involvement of the observer. This is the claim of what is called the 'Copenhagen interpretation' but it does not extend to declaring that thereby the nature of reality itself is changed. Žižek insists on this in order to avoid any idealist or mystical claim that observation creates reality.

Three decades after *The Indivisible Remainder*, in an article about non-commutativity for *The Philosophical Salon*, Heisenberg's uncertainty principle is again instanced in a thoughtful reflection on quantum physics. An observer's involvement in a situation – whether a quantum physicist conducting an experiment, Adam and Eve after the Fall or a political subject – denies them an epistemologically neutral role in their knowledge of the situation. There is no metalanguage and no access to an angelic position above and beyond the limitations posed by our involvement but it does not follow that relativism rules supreme, leaving only various and fleeting subjective perspectives. What is entailed is the necessary inclusion of the subject in the appearance of things as they are and the ontological implications of this continue to fascinate Žižek. There is agreement up to an extent with Karen Barad about the entanglement of matter and meaning in a phenomenon. Her argument in *Meeting the Universe Halfway* preserves Niels Bohr's insistence that we are embedded in the reality we observe but she does not absolutely rule out the possibility of objective access to it. The way phenomena are measured/recognized – whether via the physicist's apparatus or the use of a stick to orientate oneself in a darkened room – effects an 'agential cut' that 'enacts a resolution within the phenomenon of the inherent ontological (and semantic) indeterminacy' (Barad 2007: 140). One part of matter is given meaning by another part and this permits classical non-quantum norms to operate as a subordinate part of a larger and non-local quantum universe. The agential cut segregates 'the object as the "cause" and the mark in the measuring apparatus as the "effect", so that a change or difference in the object is entangled with a change or difference in the apparatus' – but Žižek adds his own crucial qualification: 'This cut is *inherent* to a phenomenon' (LTN 939). Barad is seen to rely and fall back on a view of nature as possessing a wholeness without a pure difference, without the short-circuit that an 'inherent' cut – the ontological cut in the phenomenon itself – has to occasion. This disallows any possible smooth and uniform correlation between matter and meaning. What is not ruled out, apropos Einstein's special theory of relativity and the proviso that observers in different frames of reference pinpoint an event using the same mathematics, is the determination of an absolute invariant for the interval between two events: 'the absolute observable' (AP 41).

The quantum world of physicists is not some guaranteed 'real' reality but experiments in this field serve as the currently best way of formulating what measuring equipment objectively indicates about our transcendentally constituted reality. The formulizations are highly mathematical but they express empirically contingent content (the course of a wave collapse cannot be predicted) and are not dependent on results of (unprovable) mathematical axioms. On this basis and seeking a more radical exposition than Barad's, the vacuum states of the Higgs field are taken to suggest an inherent ontological dissymmetry, an unceasing disturbance in the nature of the universe: negativity, to give it its Hegelian colouring. There is a quantum proto-reality and its stabilization within our quotidian reality is seen to require an equivalent to Lacan's 'quilting point' (*point de capiton*), the registering master signifier that gives the impression of totalizing a symbolic field of meaning. In a pre-ontological quantum universe of fluctuating pure potentiality, it is the collapse of the wave function in the act of perception that sutures the inconstant crypto-reality through the act of registration.

The deployment of a Lacanian term like *point de capiton* indicates similarities that can be drawn between the symbolic and the quantum orders. At a non-mathematical level, the collapse of the wave function is explained by physicists as a 'registration' by the experimental apparatus and this echoes the course of an event being actualized when inscribed into a symbolic system. A deeper equivalence also emerges between the symbolic order and quantum indeterminacy. The symbolic, as the human endeavour to cope with an ontological speechlessness, has an impossible task and the Real, a name for this lack that cannot be integrated, has its virtual home in the negativity that is the quantum vacuum: a state where momentary electromagnetic waves and particles are contingently present until they pop out of existence. The Real, here, is not the oscillation of waves itself but the movement of collapse that results in a constituted reality. In this proto-reality, a limbo state between cosmic nothingness and collapsible quantum waves, a particle is in a superposition of possible velocities and positions until one of these is registered by an observation and – a necessary corollary – the other one becomes unknowable. Out of the superposition that holds a multiplicity of quantum states, the act of perception (even if the measuring apparatus is not being used) occasions a differentiation that renders a result consonant with the minimum requirement of a self-identical entity: 'Our single reality emerges out of its own impossibility: single reality is impossible, it explodes into multiple superpositions, and these superpositions locally collapse into one reality' (IV 50).

Intellectual honesty compels Žižek to acknowledge perplexity over some of the enigmas and paradoxes of quantum physics. It is not obvious why or how the wave function collapses – physicists offer different accounts, including the Many Worlds interpretation where different probabilities are realized in different worlds. A world of superstrings and quantum vibrations indicates a micro-reality outside our direct experience but the wave function collapse that allows the emergence of a macro-reality from it is only describable from within this macro-reality and there is something wanting in the circularity of this. The intrarelationships between a quantum micro-reality, quotidian reality and the symbolic, virtual level of language that responds to this are grappled with in a section of *Sex and the Failed Absolute* and they are seen as pointing to a tension, or a gap within the wave oscillations that is part of material reality's ontological openness.

The problem, as Žižek puts it, is not posed by the classic question – why is there something rather than nothing – but how nothingness ('the void of pure potentiality') itself arises from a less-than-nothing and creates a space for something to exist. The model of the Klein bottle, the vacuums of the Higgs field, the death drive and the barred subject ($) are all called upon in order to make sense of this and avoid spiritualism or a return to pre-Kantian, naive realist claims that nature 'in-itself', as it really is, can be described.

As materialists, we should posit that there is nothing but quantum waves which form the 'basic grammar' of reality, no other reality, but this nothing is in itself a positive fact, which means that there must be some kind of a gap or cut in this 'basic grammar', a gap or cut which opens up space for the collapse of the wave function.

(SFA 281)

Žižek's conclusion is that a tension, 'some kind of a gap or cut', has to be presupposed in the grammar of proto-realty itself; what, in *Quantum History*, he calls 'primordial collapse' (QH 14). Any such gap, locatable precisely to a moment between the pre-ontological and the registering of the wave function's collapse, heralds an interstice, a moment in absentia, that breaches what could otherwise be imagined as a seamless flow from one order of reality to another. The significance attached to this accounts for a point of difference with Adrian Johnston, who thinks evolutionary biology provides a sounder materialist basis for mapping the emergence of different levels of existence. Johnson asks whether such an untotalized, One-less zero-level can be squared with the privileged role accorded to quantum physics. Any universal status for quantum physics as a worldview is refuted by Žižek but by allowing for a consonance, not a conflation, between the incompleteness of our symbolic/mediated reality and the presence of the Real, the irreducible contingency of wave collapse is invested with philosophical importance. 'Lack and absence must be here from the very beginning, already at the zero-level' (D 50) and in *Christian Atheism* this is reinforced apropos Bell's theorem, putative hidden variables and the theological implications of a non-All reality. Rather than bluntly querying Einstein's famous remark about God not playing dice by denying a hidden variable, divine or otherwise, it becomes more appropriate to postulate a God who is deceived, scammed by the paradoxes of quantum mechanics (QH 193–4; SFA 286–8).

When considering how time is to be figured in quantum physics, Žižek's elementary concern is to avoid a full-on determinism and avoid the 'block universe' view where time as we experience it is an illusion and temporal reality becomes an effect of our ignorance of the bigger system within which our quantum world is one small part. To keep alive the unexpected as immanent, to preserve mystery without mystification, requires a non-All world where negativity preserves an open ontology. Thus quantum holography, the idea of theoretical physicists that the universe is a hologram, is taken up with interest because of its implications for other areas of thought. A hologram as that which retains interference patterns of other possibilities before a quantum wave's collapse, serves to illuminate the role of retroactivity in Marx and Benjamin as well as offering a vertiginous scenario of existence: 'Is this the way we live now, in an unbearably prolonged burst of crackling static as different futures teeter on the brink of collapse and consolidation?' (AP 29).

Quantum History currently represents Žižek's most sustained engagement with the philosophical implications of quantum mechanics and particularly, in the wake of reconsiderations of the Copenhagen interpretation, the status of quantum waves and their collapse. The engagement is set out in the first of the book's three main sections, deploying the work of cosmologists and theoretical physicists like Thomas Hertog, Carlo Rovelli, Lee Smolin and Sean Carroll. The nature of the observer in Copenhagen interpretation orthodoxy gives way to the interactivity of what is known as relational quantum mechanics. The universalizing of relationality plus accounts of entangled particles interacting at speeds beyond the speed of light – allowing for time to non-metaphorically run from the future to the past – raise the possibility of some unknown reality that transcends observation. Žižek rebuffs this possibility, preferring to cast relationality as 'a limit beyond which is nothing' (QH 52). Onto-theological explanations are rejected as regression in the face of two levels of reality: our spatio-temporal one and a quantum one where 'the wave collapse happens because of the impossibility of a full description that would include the observer measuring a quantum state. So, in a properly-dialectical tension, waves collapse locally because they cannot collapse globally' (QH 55).

TIR 208–12, 220–31; LTN 917–24, 928–50; AR 223–6; D 48–53; IV 48–50; SFA 279–307; F 105–12; CA 91–118; AP 29–35, 37–42; QH

Johnston 2013; Žižek 2023h, 2024c, 2024h, 2025f

www.youtube.com/watch?v=735mYcl3Lrg

CONNECTIONS: Benjamin, Marx, negativity, Real, retroactivity, Schelling, symbolic

R

Race

The difference between enunciated content and position of enunciation helps elucidate an important aspect of Žižek's approach to racism and anti-racism. When a white racist sees and comments on a non-white refugee on the street, preconceptions give shape and meaning to the content of their enunciation and the position from where their enunciation takes place. The enunciated content of every anti-racist will oppose this but their positions of enunciation may vary. The possibility of there being different positions brings under critical scrutiny a strain of liberal thinking that is easily satisfied with preaching tolerance and diversity but not when its implications impact uncomfortably close to home. Buck-Morss's *Hegel, Haiti and Universal History* is praised for drawing attention to the silent reference in Hegel's dialectic of master-slave of the 1791 Revolution in Haiti, inspired by events in the country of its colonial rulers (FT 111).

A silence of the same order can be heard with failures in addressing racism in the context of capitalism and class struggle. Liberal anti-racism facilitates a disavowal of the socio-economic bodywork within which the history and practice of racism takes place. Globalized capitalism, the contemporary socio-economic order, tends no longer rely on colonization and nation states directly intervening in another country through a combination of military, political and economic force. Multinational corporations operate in a different way and multiculturalism is the ideology of choice for a system where everyone is a consumer waiting to be 'colonized' by the free market.

Multiculturalism is one of the molecules in the air that Afropessimism breathes. 'Blackness *is* social death', writes Wilderson uncompromisingly in *Afropessimism* (2020: 102), a violence beyond the carnage of capitalism and gender oppression, structurally excluding black people and making them 'the hosts of Human parasites' (16). The image of whiteness as a parasite is also employed by the psychoanalyst Donald Moss, as an organism that needs to be removed from

> Multiculturalism is a racism which empties its own position of all positive content (the multiculturalist is not a direct racist, he doesn't oppose to the Other the particular values of his own culture), but nonetheless retains this position as the privileged empty point of universality from which one is able to appreciate (and depreciate) properly other particular cultures – the multiculturalist respect for the Other's specificity is the very form of asserting one's own superiority.
>
> (TS 216; LTN 389–90)

the body and mind of those infected with it. In *Freedom*, discussing this in the racial context of South Africa, Žižek lines up a white academic's proposal for people of his colour in the country to 'commit suicide as an ethical act' (80) with Afropessimism's insistence that the grammar of hurt for black people is *sui generis* and demanding of a truly radical agenda for change. Whatever this might mean for white people, such a change is seen to involve the need for symbolic suicide by blacks in South Africa, one that will wipe out their identity as something moulded by white rule. It requires the resolve shown by Malcolm X in making X his family name as a signifier for a possible future arising from the erasure of a past identity.

Žižek discerns the void that is the nucleus of subjectivity being imbued with a political gravity by Afropessimism and thereby brings it down to earth and keeps it there. It does so when the masculine logic of liberal humanism is disassembled and the exception that it requires to fashion itself is isolated in a clear space. This exception, the excluded element, is the category of blackness as not human. Brown people, Latinos and others have their place in the subaltern order but blackness occupies the ground-zero space for the exception that proves the rule of humanism. Zahi Zalloua looks to similarities between the anti-colonial theorist Frantz Fanon and Žižek in the way they see Blackness as affected by an ontology that 'operates in a racial mix' to deem some human bodies 'not-quite human or nonhuman' (2025a: 1). This makes Slavery an ontological condition that outlives its historical moment, a question not of deprivation or servitude but of being. There is a dialectic at work in slavery's impact on the interactions of white and black people which is prised open by Louisa Yousfi in *In Defence of Barbarism*. She does so by way of Toni Morrison's *Beloved* (a novel which Žižek looks at *The Fragile Absolute*) and other texts.

Afropessimism is not self-defeatism, mourning does not exclude agency, but its defiance provokes asking how an authentic anti-racism should be constructed. Afropessimism is correct in trenchantly confronting the pathological nature of anti-black racism and insisting that the singularity of this racism cannot be flattened out in the language of multiculturalism. Arising from this, Afropessimism runs the risk of isolating itself from other struggles. Wilderson rules out any correspondence between American blacks and Palestinians, viewing it as a distraction, but a cross-racial similarity can be built out of their shared status as 'the part of no-part' (Rancière's term for those in a community without a proper place). Existing in opposition to the prevailing logic of universality, 'the part of no-part' as an emancipatory force becomes the form and the ground of universality itself.

Hegel's delineation of concrete universality is of relevance here. A particular, for Hegel, differentiates itself from another particular not by possession of some intrinsic quality but through and in opposition to the universal. Particulars are alike in being particulars but the 'universal determines *itself*, and so is itself the particular; the determinateness is *its* difference; it is only differentiated from itself' (Hegel 2010a: 535). Todd McGowan finds this illuminating Nazism where German as one particular defines itself in opposition to Jew which, ironically, becomes the universal. Not surprisingly, the ideologue Alfred Rosenberg – the only philosopher of Nazism executed at Nuremburg – classifies Jewishness an 'anti-race' and Žižek (LD 176–84) extends McGowan's insight to the irony of Zionist anti-Semitism.

In *Žižek on Race* and *Fanon, Žižek, and the Violence of Resistance*, Zalloua situates Palestinians within the field of anti-black racism and looks towards a shared resolve 'to breach the racial script' (2020: 124) and create a concerted arsenal of resistance. A shared vocation would possess a militant, political valency if Afropessimism's ontologizing of black experience became a springboard for allying itself with other movements. It depends, as Cadava and Nadal-Melsió pose it in *Politically Red*, 'on whether one understands Afropessimism as a point of departure or a point of arrival' (2023: 370).

Returning to the position of enunciation, there is a disavowal when the racist knows that race is not about biological difference but acts as if it is. The discrepancy comes from the unconscious and the engendering of enjoyment through the racializing of otherness. This is difficult to moderate when the wellspring is also the failure of capitalism to deliver contentment, a failure that finds expression in a redoubling, a return of the repressed. Gratification 'in the obscenity of the populist discourse permeated by racist and sexist enjoyment' (F 272) comes from tapping into affective attractors that the Left currently finds difficulty in combatting.

FA 142–3; F 79–83; CA 27–35

McGowan 2019: 192–5; Wilderson 2020: 14–17, 225–9; Zalloua 2020,
     2025a: 42–54, 171–6, 183–4; Zalloua, 2025b; Yousfi 2025: 23–4

CONNECTIONS: concrete universality, enunciated and enunciation, fantasy,
     hysteria, *jouissance*, not-All/non-All, perversion

Rancière, Jacques

See communism, politics, race.

Real

The Real, a Lacanian term for a non-topographical, unanalysable register of formless being, is elaborated by Žižek into a mega concept bearing different modalities and intonations. It would be misleading to think of it as an axis, being neither imaginary or a line in space, and the 'quasi-transcendental' early Lacan suggestion of the Real as 'the impossible Thing-in-itself' (KNW xii) is acknowledged as an approach needing to be moved beyond. Refined as primordial, proto-ontological and unrepresentable in symbolic schemas, the Real is what emerges 'when meaning is evacuated from reality' (LTN 697). Reality does not add up to a consistent whole and, like the Kantian antimonies of thought that arise when trying to represent all of reality, the Real *is* the inconsistency. It is not a material phenomenon in the form of a vortex or 'black hole' but the complete absence of any central, fixed location. The Real is like the theoretical physicist's hologram where every state shares its existential space with interference patterns of other possibilities that could have existed (AP 29). It does not easily lend itself to a cartographical representation.

If the Real eludes the symbolic as an external reality beyond our ken, the limitation would be merely epistemological in nature. The impossibility that divides the real from the symbolic pertains to an impossibility that defines the real: its status resides in its absence of any 'substantial density in itself; it is just a gap between two points of perspective, perceptible only in the shift from one to the other' (SE 131). It is both what is necessarily inaccessible and the obstacle preventing access to it.

The Real has a peculiar standing in relation to material reality; being empirically unavailable in itself, it can be said to lack an ontology. It cannot act as a signifier for a positive and consistent order of being – there not being one in the first place – but as the untranscendable horizon of existence it cannot be dismissed: 'The order of Being and the Real are mutually exclusive: the Real is the immanent blockage or impediment of the order of Being, what makes the order of Being inconsistent' (LTN 958). It cannot ever be the Kantian noumenal, reality 'in itself' outside transcendental frames of reference. The 'existence' of the Real, when the symbolic becomes inadequate to the task of making ontological sense of the world, can only be felt through its ability to perturb and this allows for talk of its noumenal presence. This presence, not indicative of any lumpy reality, can only be rendered in the non-linguistic formulas of quantum physics and is a symptom of the convergence of contraries that is the Real: the symbolic always distorts its representation but at the same time the Real is the force that accounts for the distortion (IV 243); it is a word for the fact that shifts in perspectives, anamorphosis, are possible.

By its necessary foreclosure from the mortifying nature of the symbolic order, the void of the Real shows what cannot be integrated with that order: it is the black nothingness in Magritte's *La lunette d'approche*, glimpsed through the narrow space revealed by a half-opened window pane that itself looks out to an external reality of blue sky with clouds (1993b: 219–20, [2005] 2013b: 135).

The Real … although nowhere present, curves/distorts any space of symbolic representation and condemns it to ultimate failure.

(PF 124)

One modality of the Real refers to the sense, disconcerting enough to border on the monstrous, of an indefinable life force. It is understandable but misleading to conceive of this as a raw and brutal amorphous materiality (a sense like this is found in early Lacan). No such substance, however inchoate, lies behind the anxiety that can result from the symbolic order being disturbed by the pre-ontological Real. Contrariwise, reality may serve as a safeguard to thwart and keep the Real at bay and this is seen to be illustrated in a dream, reported by Freud, of a father who is watching over his son's coffin but falls asleep; awakened, he finds that the cloth over the coffin has accidentally caught fire by a falling candle. Following Lacan's interpretation, Žižek reads the sleeping father as being disturbed by the smoking cloth and incorporating it into his dream so as to prolong his sleep but waking up when it becomes an unbearable reminder of guilt over his son's death. The dream and its recriminating appeal – 'Father, can't you see that I am burning' – is the Real of trauma and waking up is a way of not confronting this.

The Real also makes itself felt in other ways: in the antagonism of class struggle and, in sexual difference, the impossibility of satisfactorily accommodating the discord at the heart of sexual relationships. It is not some hidden X, or a clandestine, mystical kernel that cannot be properly articulated. The status of the Real as 'impossible' is not because the right words cannot be found to express it. In the case of class struggle, the Real arises from there being no metalanguage, no neutral language or perspective capable of avoiding an engagement that reveals a particular position or attitude towards it (including attempts to deny or diminish its cogency). This failure to approach the topic impartially does nothing to weaken the actuality of class struggle; on the contrary, it confirms its grip on social reality.

> **The Real is not a transcendent thing-in-itself at which we arrive when we abstract from all our perceptual distortions but the fluid 'unorientable' space in which, through reflexive turns-into-oneself, multiple realities can emerge.**
>
> **(HWB 36)**

The failure to be non-discriminatory about class struggle, the incommensurability of different perspectives entailed in it, bears testimony to the presence of that which the symbolic cannot represent. The parallax Real 'accounts for the very *multiplicity* of appearances of the same underlying Real' and it is 'the hard bone of contention which pulverises the sameness into the multitude of appearances' (SE 131). It is this pure 'sameness' that cannot be sheltered within the failed homeostasis of the symbolic order. It steers towards the philosophical demarcation between Kant's 'thing-in-itself', what for him is the hard core of indefinable materiality that lies inaccessibly behind reality's fabric, and the insubstantial but certain Real that uncannily stages itself in tiny but absolute differences in appearance. In Hitchcock's *Vertigo*, Judy and Madeleine turn out to be the same person but the unaccountable difference between them lies in a tangible ethereal otherness that Scottie attaches to the fake Madeleine (really Judy) and which he hopes to find in Judy when she recreates herself as Madeleine. The Real, says Žižek in *On Belief*, 'not only appears WITHIN appearances, but it is NOTHING BUT its own appearance ... [the] ultimately illusory feature that accounts for the absolute difference within the identity'.

It is important to stress that the Real of pure appearance or the inherent inability of being neutral about class struggle do not validate post-modern doxa about cultural relativism, multiple realities and the reduction of truth to particular perspectives and narratives that generate their own perceptions. Class struggle is the dominant form of an objective social antagonism and, though biologically the same person, Judy and Madeleine are different because of the actual trauma around which sexual difference is structured.

The Real, preventing direct access to a reality where there is no full identity of anything with itself, is 'a formal category ... nothing in itself' (Žižek 2022c). Nonetheless, there remains a nagging need to ask what, if any, *material* level relates to the Real. It is not matter as a substantial entity, nor even bits of matter so tiny as not to count as such but, nevertheless, something in the world of quantum physics is being registered by scientists in that field. This remains true even if quantum waves and their indeterminacy are more virtual than real and best expressed in mathematical formalizations outside the reach of most people. Žižek's ontology locates the Real in the substanceless quantum void, where nothing can become itself (IV 46), and the Real 'in itself' is the very gap that we experience as our separation from it (SE 274).

SO 44–5 (and L 57–8); ME 30; IR 150; TN 35–6; PF 112–14, 276–80, 958–9; OB 79–83; PD 64–80; OWB 101–3; LTN 958–61; AR 72–3, 380–1; SE 130–1

Freud 2006: 526–7; Žižek 2004e, 2022c

CONNECTIONS: antagonism, class struggle, Hegel, Kant, ontology, real, sexual difference, symbolic

Reflection

Reflection, as Hegel states in the *Encyclopaedia Logic*, is commonly used for the phenomenon of light bouncing back from a surface and in this way it serves as trope for the process of thinking about something (1991: 176). This is how it is used in his Doctrine of Essence in *The Science of Logic*, as the structure of movement between thought and what is taken to be outside of it, the independent immediacy of being. Three moments in the structure of reflection are given – positing, external and determining – and in the final chapter of *The Sublime Object of Ideology*, where Žižek first introduces these moments, literary criticism is used to model them. Given a particular text, say *Hamlet*, it is assumed that when Shakespeare wrote it a warranted meaning was directly embodied in the drama. Such a 'positing' is a presupposing of what is deemed necessary, some substantial truth now inaccessible by the passage of time. Positing has to give ground when it is faced with a plurality of convincing but not always compatible readings that come later: *Hamlet* as detective story, a political thriller, a revenge study, a Freudian and then Lacanian psycho drama and so on. These are all 'external' reflections that arise in retrospect, free of presuppositions. 'Determining' reflection is achieved when any putative 'essence' of *Hamlet* is recognized as a chimera, the attributes ascribed to it being those put there by the movement of thought in response to the indeterminateness of Shakespeare's text. Determining reflection, not adding anything to external reflection, reveals the lack of any substantial core, any supposed transcendent in-itself or essence.

Subjectivism is not being taken to an extreme here and reality per se is not presented as something solipsistically created. 'Positing' reflection is a presupposing of an immediacy which in fact is mediated and this is spelt out by Hegel: 'There is nothing to which only the determination of immediacy is applicable to the exclusion of mediation, and immediacy itself is essentially mediated' (1988: 157).

This does not mean there is absolutely nothing there to be transformed. Absolute recoil is Hegel's term for a process of transformation; being itself is not treated as a postulate of thought but 'the unfathomable X of the immediate life-experience reflection is after' is 'its own tail' (TIR 51).

The movement that is reflection signals Hegel's departure from the presumption of the transcendental circle where everything we bear witness to is mediated by pre-given categories. These categories may be ones embedded in the mind, linguistically determined or historically conceptualized and formed as a social praxis. Regardless of their source, within the transcendental circle there is presumed to be a 'real' reality that remains outside/beyond/behind the horizon of meaning. Reflection is the mobile process of thought that finds its own content which is then posited as always and already existing but what exists is not true to itself; appearance and essence as an opposition collapses.

> **Determinate reflection enacts an even stronger negation of the In-itself than external reflection. External reflection merely posits the In-itself as an inaccessible transcendence, while determinate reflection empties the In-itself of all presupposed substantial content, reducing it to a void.**
>
> **(D 132)**

In chapter four of *Tarrying with the Negative*, the sphere of reflection is looked at as the requirement of thought when considering contradiction and contingency and necessity. By the time of *Absolute Recoil*, two decades later, the moments of reflection imprint what is missing from traditional descriptions of the dialectic by underscoring how its process does not start with a positive.

SO 241–4; KNW 167–8; ME 38–9; TIR 50–2; TN 130; LTN 378–9; AR 4, 154, 338; D 130–4; SFA 239–40

Hegel 2010a: 346–53; Houlgate 2011; Longuenesse [1981] 2007: 30–6, 51–4

CONNECTIONS: absolute recoil, appearance and essence, contingency and necessity, dialectic, ontology, transcendental

Retroactivity

Retroactivity's purview is a surprising and momentously wide one. After the owl of Minerva has flapped its wings and flown on its unmapped course, 'there always is a story to be told at the end which ("retroactively" and "contingently" as much as one wants) reconstitutes the Sense of the preceding process' (LTN 224). A narrative shapes the past and, at a deeper level, retroactivity is a part of the dialectical movement characterizing our construction of reality. There can never be a straight line connecting moments and our comprehension of them (LET 28) and, as Rosa Luxemburg clearly discerned, a temporal distortion accompanies the spatial deformation (AR 190–1).

In psychoanalysis, the memory of something in the past that was not shattering at the time can retrospectively become a libidinally invested event as a way of coping with a current perplexity about sexuality. This is how retroactivity is first introduced in *The Sublime Object of Ideology*, illustrating how a psychoanalytic meaning, given to behaviour of a compulsive kind, comes from the future. Although a symptom seems to announce itself before its attributed meaning, something not registered as such when it occurred only becomes a symptom afterwards. Freud's analysis of the 'Wolf Man' is taken as illustrative of this temporal displacement (AR 381).

In the theology of Žižek's Christian atheism, the fall of man from god in Eden is mirrored in the fall of god from himself on Calvary when Christ utters his cry of abandonment. His human call is an act of self-disbelief, a separation of god from himself, and this separation from what was never there in the first place is the moment when god is created: 'There is nothing that precedes this fall: "god" is the retroactive effect of its own fall' (SE 275). The paradisal harmony that Adam and Eve lost when expelled from Eden, 'the Fall itself', never existed; it was '*just a retroactive illusion*' (E 49–50).

The same movement is applicable to Samuel Beckett's apercu about every word being an unnecessary stain on silence and nothingness. The silence is created when language is seen as its blemish: 'Yes, words are by definition inadequate, but they retroactively create the very standard with regard to which they appear as inadequate' (HWB 112).

Retroactivity, as a mode of imputing meaning to the past, hermeneutically gathers what has happened into a symbolic order and then, after the event, comes into operation. As an intervention into the past, a paradox emerges when an intervention creates what emerges as that past, a structure represented in the myth of Oedipus who kills his father and marries his mother only because he tried to prevent this occurring. Retroactivity's political aspect is seen at work in Benjamin's *Theses on the Philosophy of History/On the Concept of History* when a revolutionary moment from the past is redeemed by bringing it into a future not yet realized.

In *Less Than Nothing*, the difference in Deleuze's ontology between the 'actual' as an existing state of affairs, and the 'virtual' as a field of openness or tendencies able to provide for different actualities, is read in terms of retroaction. Deleuze refers to a 'pure' past, a virtual realm of unrealized but conserved tendencies that disrupt discrete temporal divisions. A past that is not fixed allows interpretation to be figured as something decided on retroactively and Hegel's image of the owl of Minerva indicates how meaning unfolds from a position of looking backwards. The past that existed before something new occurs is subject to change and T. S. Eliot's account of how literary tradition, seemingly inscribed in history, is modified and subject to rearrangement by the work of a new writer is recalled to illustrate this. There is no way of being sure how the present will be interpreted in the future; the present is indebted to the future. Nothing at a strictly factual level can be retroactively changed – this is not the world of Ursula Le Guin's *The Lathe of Heaven* – but it can be viewed and figured in different ways.

Given the past's openness to being reconfigured and mediated, the distinction drawn by Meillassoux between potentiality and virtuality is deployed in support of a radical contingency. Pre-existing possibilities are subject to chance, they may or may not be realized, but they are indexable; with virtuality, there is no computable set of possibilities. When something new arises that could not have been previously allowed for, its existence retroactively creates a potentiality *ex nihilo*. Such an emergence adverts to a lack of completeness in reality and Hegel's dialectic, classically presented in terms of a potentiality coming into existence, becomes a process of groundless becoming that involves a retroactive movement from contingency to necessity. Retroactivity as the temporal mode of the dialectic is a part of absolute recoil.

Retroactivity – and the unpredictability of the future it entails – haunts teleology and produces a version of it in a reverse gear. It discredits the notion of progress driving history and in a way that is not unlike Darwin's removal of it from biology. Something from an earlier time may be best understood only when looking back at it from a later stage of development. Marx provides a case when, referring to capitalist society as the most highly developed historical form of production, he observes how its complexity gives insight into pre-bourgeois forms that came to be incorporated within it. Žižek quotes Marx's analogy for this – 'Human anatomy contains a key to the anatomy of the ape' – and provides his own example by seeing the French Revolution as only acquiring its universal significance when, in Haiti, it was repeated with the successful revolt of black slaves demanding their own enfranchisement and a like-minded republic. The act of the Haitian revolt lays bare the electrifying impact of the French Revolution and what it represents. In the sciences, regarding current difficulties in integrating relativity theory and quantum physics are resolved: 'All we can do is wait for a contingent scientific breakthrough – only then will it be possible to retroactively reconstruct the logic of the process' (LTN 909).

> **If the anatomy of man offers the key to the anatomy of the ape this doesn't mean that, if humans were not to evolve accidentally out of apes the anatomy of apes would be missing its key – more precisely, this key would be different, it would emerge retroactively out of a different process of evolutionary change.**
>
> (F 152–3)

Retroactivity, playing paradoxically with a linear sense of time and cause and effect, displays itself in the reasons that can be given for determining why we did or decided on something. The reasons do not axiomatically pertain to a time preceding the action or the decision; the reasons may be retroactively recognized by us. The Bolshevik who situates October 1917 as the continuation of what began with Spartacus and continued with the French Revolution is not tracing a factual line of descent but retrospectively constructing a narrative. What happened in the past cannot be changed but how it appears to us is determined by what happens afterwards. An example provided is the contouring through Stalinism of Lenin's rule. The show trials and gulags can be traced back to Lenin's response to Kronstadt, the development of an intolerant and ruthless mindset laid down in 1921. On the other hand, Stalinism can be viewed as an aberration that Lenin recognized in its incipience and tried to warn others about before his untimely death (F 47).

A similar after-the-event logic may be seen operating in the metapsychological territory of desire and the deep impulse to find something which is felt to have been lost but which if found will restore a fulfilling consistency and wholeness to one's being. The search for a substantial completeness is fruitless because it does not exist but a sense of loss, elicited from a felt absence of what should be there, can take the form of a wished-for presence. Like the woman preoccupying the narrative voice in Bob Dylan's 'Visions of Johanna', what cannot be materially manifested allows for a form of *jouissance* and one's own private *sinthome*. In this way, the *objet petit a* is retroactively produced and becomes the cause of the effect that is experienced as the yearning for a lost object of desire.

Two different states used to illustrate a causal logic of retroversion whereby a cause comes to be grounded *after* its effect are those of the Christian and the person experiencing love. The causality in service in both the belief and the feeling is circular in nature and involves an element of delay: the Christian's faith does not arise as the result of being convinced by reasons for belief and nor is love dependent on a beloved's particular features. The reasons for believing in Christ come to be appreciated after believing; the lips or smile of a loved one become charming after knowing one is in love; the causal logic is one of retroversion.

MSH 29–31; SO 57–61, 114–16, 151–8; LA 12; TN 37; 126–7; OB 12; LTN 207–13, 221, 229–31; AR 73–5, 188–92; E 2–3; D 280; AP 33–5

Hegel 1975: 13; Marx 1973: 50

CONNECTIONS: absolute recoil, Christian atheism, contingency and necessity, Deleuze, desire, dialectic, love, spirit, subject

Robespierre, Maximilien

See politics.

Russian (October) Revolution

See cinema, communism, event/act, Lenin, Marx, retroactivity.

S

Schelling, F. W. J.

Schelling, highly valued by Žižek as one of the key figures of German Idealism, is the subject of *The Indivisible Remainder: On Schelling and Related Matters* (1986). The following year *The Abyss of Freedom/Ages of the World* was published: half of the book is an essay devoted to Schelling and an English translation of the second draft (1813) of his *Die Weltalter* ('Ages of the World') makes up the rest of the book. Schelling's philosophical territory, the archaeology of being and its beginnings, overlaps with Žižek's and the two thinkers trace equally radical patterns of thought in the course of their ontological inquiries.

After Kant's philosophical revolution – reality's mediation by categories of thought – Fichte was the first to question the idea of things-in-themselves as what can be thought about but never directly known. He advanced instead a free-ranging subjectivity, a self-positing I, but this was rejected by the philosophically inclined poet Hölderlin (a close friend of Schelling and Hegel when they all attended the same university). Hölderlin maintains a division between subject and object, keeping the subject always on the other side of substance. There is a gap that cannot be crossed by the subject yearning for a lost unity and this presupposes a substantial realm that must remain beyond reach.

Schelling's response proposes, in *Philosophical Inquiries into the Essence of Human Freedom*, known as his *Freiheitsschrift* ('freedom essay'), a temporal beginning that effects a necessary division. Ground (*Grund*), an eternally past divine vortex of blind drives in rotary motion, is separated from fully constituted experiential reality. The division forms an antagonism that see-saws between an unintegrated, pre-ontological state and moments of potential expansion that threaten a fragile balance of forces. In a beginning before the beginning of time, being contracts out of its own predicament, a resolution imagined as Baron Münchhausen lifting himself by pulling his hair upwards; the philosophical equivalent of the biblical inauguration, 'In the beginning was the Word.' It erupts for Schelling from an abyss of pure, primordial freedom (*Ungrund*) and is read as emergence into a symbolic existence and the 'symbolic castration' that comes from the divorce between the verbal signifier for the subject and its inadequacy as a representation in a system of signifiers where the original has been irrecoverably lost.

What makes *The Indivisible Remainder* a richly rewarding text is the weight of Lacanian interpretations brought by Žižek to a reading of Schelling. He formulates Schelling's thinking as a prescient dialectical materialism that accounts for the emergence of the subject from the Real, the birth of freedom and the symbolic order from the rotary drives of unrealized matter. The agitated driving of the bus in the movie *Speed* serves as an image for the unruly activity of Ground and its less-than-total containment by a mortifying symbolic order that is never fully secure (TIR 27–8). *Die Weltalter* offers an original account of the genesis of *logos* out of the dissonance that haunts Ground and of that which it cannot keep in check: the 'indivisible remainder', the left over that remains outside the symbolic, the drive's circling around *objet a*.

The drafts of Schelling's *Die Weltalter*, grappling with formulating the transition from the spectral real of the pre-ontological to transcendently constituted reality, relate the Baron Münchhausen-moment to a primordial decision that marks 'the very founding gesture of consciousness' (LTN 274). Philosophy is rescued from collapsing into pre-Kantian, proto-cosmic metaphysics by pinpointing a subtraction from the undifferentiated 'horrible vortex of the Real' (LTN 275) to a state hyphenated between self-dispossession and self-actualization. The moment of decision itself, Schelling insists at the end of his second draft, must recede into the background after it has been made: 'That primordial deed which makes a man genuinely himself precedes all individual actions; but immediately after it is put into exuberant freedom, this deed sinks into the night of unconsciousness' (TAF 181). This is registered as a supreme moment in German Idealism, foreseeing psychoanalysis by locating the unconscious as the site of the subject's choice of their character, the subject's assumption of who they will be. The choice appears to be a forced one, as in the fable of the scorpion that stings the frog carrying it across a river, dooming them both ('I am sorry, but I couldn't help myself. It's my character'), but at a transcendental level it is a free choice for which the subject holds responsibility. It only seems as if we are forced to choose our unconscious.

In the third draft of his *Die Weltalter*, Schelling provides an algebraic 'Formula of the Whole' (reproduced, SFA 345) abridging the activity that begins with material brute reality and its contractive constitution and which over time raises itself to higher levels of life. There is a tension in the processual course of development, writes Schelling, that 'is decided by the exuberant deed similar to the one in which a person decides to be utterly one thing or another' (2000: 83–4).

The Indivisible Remainder concludes by sketching a homology between Schelling's account of the 'primordial deed', arising out of the abyss of freedom, and the universe of quantum physics. Science reveals that what lies beneath seemingly solid, observable reality is a quantum uncertainty, a realm of potentialities and fluctuations. This state of pure becoming 'collapses' into self-identical, highly elementary entities when the incompatibility of wave–particle duality passes to a consistent actuality. An affiliation is found between this and Schelling's moment of *creatio ex nihilo*, the act/decision that emerges from the void before ineluctably receding into the unconscious. In both cases, there is no straightforward movement from a site of production (the undifferentiated drives of Ground or the oscillations of the quantum world) to a coherent and fixed order. Schelling never satisfactorily explained the transition and, in its sphere, quantum physics remains undecided about the nature of the 'collapse' of wave fluctuations. Žižek's conclusion is that a tensional constitution must inhere in both Ground and wave oscillations and, in the parlance of Schelling, this means that Ground is not primordial: it 'already presupposes the Void it envelops, and it is this (primordially repressed) Void that "returns" in human freedom' (F 105).

One is tempted to claim that Schelling's freedom ... which of itself, by its own power, actualizes itself and acquires existence (this highest enigma which Schelling failed to explain again and again) is prefigured and/or concretized (here also, linear temporal succession is suspended) in quantum physics' notion of the emergence of 'something' (a particle) out of the 'nothingness' of a vacuum fluctuation.

(TIR 230–1; LTN 389–90)

TIR; TAF; OWB 74–7; PV 64–5, 157–8; LTN 11–16, 273–5; AR 256–9; F 71–3, 103–5; QH 261–5

Carew 2014: 193–222; Johnston 2008: 69–122; Johnston 2023; Kaye 2023: 43–6

CONNECTIONS: drive, German Idealism, *objet petit a*, ontology, quantum physics, the unconscious

Sexuality

The emergence of the human from an earlier animal stage turns sexuality into something new, imbuing it with a metaphysical aspect that takes it beyond the instinct to reproduce, beyond nature's logistics. The process of this change could be considered a derailment but, in the absence of any overall linearity in the development of life, the image of a short circuit serves better by making the arrival of human sexuality a rupture in the natural order: 'We become human exactly when sex leaves behind its "natural" of procreation and turns into an end in itself' (CA 63). Being an end in itself, human sexuality is neither instrumental nor a supine surrender to sensuality but a transubstantial intimacy that goes beyond carnality and into a stretch of being that for the theologically minded could be labelled the spiritual.

What confounds Catholic Church orthodoxy on the subject of sexuality is that humans invest the erotic with a passion rivalling the Church's own brand of ecstatic spirituality. It introduces an exalted quality by transcending the indifference of quotidian life and bringing into it not just something sublime but, bound up with the uplifting, a lasting disequilibrium. Zupančič summarizes the import of this in *What Is Sex?*: 'In psychoanalysis sex is above all a concept that formulates a persisting contradiction of reality. And, second, that this contradiction cannot be circumscribed or reduced to a secondary level (as a contradiction between already well-established entities/beings), but is – *as a contradiction* – involved in the very structuring of these entities, in their very being. In this precise sense, sex is of ontological relevance: not as an ultimate reality, but as an inherent twist, or stumbling block, of reality' (2017: 3). Arising from this, Žižek asks why sexuality, at most levels from the vegetal to the human, depends on a contingent coming together of two parts and not one or three or more parts (SFA 154–5).

It is tempting to evoke an uncomplicated variance between nature and culture, between instinct and drive, but the idea of a stable instinctual sexuality may reside in the all-too-human longing to belatedly create a state that never actually existed. Television programmes about the animal kingdom and their mating rituals are seen to fascinate audiences because they depict sexuality without complication. Humans, on the other hand, have to contend with sexual difference.

> **Human sexuality is thus not an exception with regard to nature, a pathological dislocation of natural instinctual sexuality, but *the point at which the dislocation/impossibility that pertains to sexual copulation appears as such*.**
>
> **(AR 204)**

The level of difference indicates that, while animals are not by instinct cognisant of the dislocation at the heart of sexuality, humans are unconsciously aware of it and they register its troubling presence within themselves: sexuality 'cannot find satisfaction in itself, because it never attains its goal' (OWB 89). This failure opens the ground for the role of fantasy, a role that compensates for the lack of harmony inherent to sexual relationships.

In *Lacan*, Žižek instances scenes from two movies to show how fantasy conspires with sexuality to reduce the impact of the unacknowledged awareness that there is no sexual relationship: in *Ryan's Daughter*, sound effects in the forest love scene are a conventional index of sexual passion but here they also detract attention from an act of copulation in all its discomforting bluntness; in *Reds*, scenes of historic revolutionary fervour are intercut with one of lovemaking to proclaim the exquisite ecstasy of the characters' sexual rapport. In the two cases, a construction of fantasy becomes a necessary background to embellish an unalloyed coupling of two bodies that is both inherently traumatic and crudely physical. In courtly love, the noble knight's forlorn quest that he must fulfil is a scheme of fantasy that allows the knight to always postpone an untimely confrontation with the troubling puzzle of human sexuality.

Lacan's maxim – 'there is no sexual relationship' ('il n'y a pas de rapport sexuel') – has become a *locus classicus* for Žižek when contextualizing the human sexual act within a framework where such physical proximity between two bodies is fraught with uncertainties surrounding the Other. Fantasy plays a primary role in helping to manage the doubts and angsts that accompany a relationship with an Other. A humorous dialogue from the movie *Brassed Off* occurs when a young woman invites a man in for a coffee and when he artlessly admits to not drinking that particular beverage she replies that it's not a problem because she doesn't have any in her home. This is seen to illustrate the need for a fantasmatic complement to sex, compensating for a difficulty in dealing with it. A sexual relationship brings to the fore unavoidable anxiety about the exposure of oneself to the other, a vulnerability missing in animal coupling, and the impossibility of comprehending sexual difference. The obverse of this role for fantasy is the kind of outright ban that prohibits women from revealing their hair or bare neck or walking with metal heels in case the clicking of their heels provoke male desire (CH 128).

Sexuality is a complex mess, and attempts to corral it with deliberations around political correctness and wokeness fall prey to inherent pressures and conflicts that reflect 'antagonisms which traverse the entire social body' (TL 111). Sexual identity, it follows, is 'full of inconsistencies and unconscious features' (CA 220) and, ultimately, sexuality as a whole lies beyond our knowledge. Infantile sexuality, expressive of the need to try and comprehend what sexuality is about, cannot be encompassed by seeing it as part of 'polymorphously perverse drives which are then totalized by the Oedipal genital norm' (AR 198). Given that the act of copulation never presents the desired satisfaction only partial drives – which for Lacan are the oral, scopic, anal and auditory – deliver pleasures of an unadorned kind.

> This role of fantasy hinges on the fact that 'there is no sexual relationship', no universal formula or matrix guaranteeing harmonious sexual relations with one's partner: every subject has to invent a fantasy of his own, a 'private' formula for the sexual relationship – for a man, his relationship with a woman is possible only insofar as she fits his formula.
>
> (AR 199)

PF 82–3; OWB 89–94; L 49–51; LET 83–4; AR 196–206; CH 215–24; SFA 115–17, 152–3; TL 109–11; QH 335–51

CONNECTIONS: drive, fantasy, other, sexual difference, wokeness

Sexual difference

Lacan's formulas of sexual difference are not about male and female as biological determinants or culturally constructed gender identities. Male and female are positions taken up in response to the failure, the impossibility, of speaking beings achieving a full sense of identity. The positions are not reducible to a traditional binary order of opposites, a *yin*-and-*yang* duality that ideally is held together in a harmonious balance.

There is a sense of loss, signified as castration, which is inseparable from the infant's entry into language – where words are substituted for things – and the symbolic order as a whole. The entry into language is a trauma that is played out in relation to the phallus: 'The signifier elevated into the stand-in for the lack is precisely the phallus' (ME 202). The physical organ becomes not the penis but the signifier of a lack of a signifier for a harrowing loss of wholeness – '(it does not tell us "what mother really wants"), it just designates the impenetrable space of her desire' (AR 124) – and the demarcation of men and women is formulated as contending libidinal responses to the phallus: 'Sexual difference is not binary/differential, it is an antagonism that binary symbolic difference tries to "normalize" by translating it into symbolic oppositions' (IV 16). The difference has its own positive actuality in the trans-subject who, as the subject who does not fit into the binary categories, is a representation of the antagonism that imbues sexual difference with a potency cannot be corralled into fixed identities.

> ***Trans-subjects**: they are not external to sexual difference, a reminder of some primordial polymorphous-perverse multiplicity; they are constitutive of sexual difference as such, the privileged point of its positive existence.*
>
> (F 100)

Woman, relating to *jouissance* in a different way to man, is not so willing to believe in the possibility of its full attainment; man is more subordinated to the symbolic order: 'A woman's identity cannot be fixed into a signifier' and patriarchy, the history of this failure, seeks to gentrify the 'hysterical core of (feminine) subjectivity' which questions the imposition of an ill-fitting identity: 'So it's not women who are deficient (fallen) men, men are women who "fell" into determinate positive identity' (CA 75).

The difference is not an essentialist, biological classification but relates to structural positions straddling an undefined, asymmetric ground between the natural and the cultural. It is out of this asymmetric ground that a lacuna forms at the heart of any sexual relationship. There is an irreconcilable space, filled by contending notions about whose lack is looking for what kind of enjoyment, and it throws up impasses difficult to surmount.

Articulating the mirroring of dissonance within the field of sexual difference, principally in chapter eleven of *Less Than Nothing* and returned to in a less dense way in *Sex and the Failed Absolute*, is a way of standing up to contemporary and competing accounts of what reality is by insisting on the abyssal depth of its ontological inadequacy. The feminine 'not-all' provides a point of contact with the 'not-One' of absolute knowing and the elaboration of this involves tracing an intricate convergence between philosophy and sexual difference. It requires a relocation of the difference abiding within every sexual identity into the meta-difference that divides everything from itself: 'the difference that splits from within the very universality of sex' (SFA 117). The trans-subject as the third element representing the impossibility of a simple duality shaping the universality of sex is akin to the figure of the Jew as the supplement giving body to the impossibility of a harmonious social order. In their mismatched ways, both of them transform 'clear symbolic difference into the impossible/Real of an antagonism' (SFA 134).

ME 201–2; LTN 739–802; AR 197–9, 406–7; IV 87–9; SFA 107–19, 132–6; CA 87–8; 227–8; QH 329

Homer 2005: 95–109; Kotsko 2008: 48–50; McGowan 2025: 136–43; Neill 2023: 78–81; Penny 2023; Rose 2005: 49–81

CONNECTIONS: anti-Semitism, big Other, hysteria and perversion, not-All/not-All, symbolic

Shakespeare

Only one thing is sure: the only way to be faithful to a classic work is to take such a risk. Avoiding it, sticking to the traditional letter, is the safest way to betray the spirit of the classic. In other words, the only way to keep a classical work alive is to treat it as 'open', pointing towards the future, or, to use the metaphor evoked by Walter Benjamin, to act as if the classic work is a film for which the appropriate chemical liquid to develop it was invented only later, so that it is only today that we can get the full picture. And this is also how Travelling Symphony [in *Station Eleven*] treats Shakespeare.

(Žižek 2025c)

A trope that Benjamin evokes – images of the past being left in literary texts like photographic negatives, waiting for a future when means become available to develop them – is used more than once by Žižek (2013e: xv, E 116, YD 128, A xii) and on occasion (2017g: 290) with reference to Shakespeare's perspicuity in prefiguring notions that emerge more legibly only in later times.

Passages from *Richard II* are looked at, sometimes in detail, for the way they uncannily anticipate psychoanalytic concerns (Žižek 2015a: 271–6, D 211–16, 2017g: 294–9). *Looking Awry*'s title comes from dialogue in the play, between Bushy and the Queen in Act 2, Scene 2, and Bushy's lines (beginning 'Each substance of a grief hath twenty shadows') receive close reading in the book (LA 9–12).

Troilus and Cressida is of interest not only for Cressida's convoluted sense of herself but also for the ideological import in the logic of Ulysses's words to Achilles about time and fame (DLC 26–9, 81–2; AR 1–3). Time, argues Ulysses, in the nature of its inexorable passing enacts an inflexible rule that sees worthy values, like love and friendship, sacrificed by being eventually forgotten. While claiming to want to maintain what is innately worthy, he resorts to violating these virtues to manipulate Achilles by exploiting the warrior's hurt pride. Truth and appearance, like rules and their transgression, are cynically played with as if upholding a value depends on secreting cheating to disrupt what ought to be at peace with itself.

In the comic drama *As You Like It*, deception is again resorted to in order to establish what ought to take place without the need for underhand duplicity. In order for Rosalind to test Orlando's love for her she first disguises herself as a male called Ganymede and then redoubles the subterfuge by persuading Orlando to let Ganymede pretend to be Rosalind and practise wooing her before they marry in a mock ceremony: 'In this ceremony, Rosalind literally feigns to feign to be what she is: truth itself, in order to win, has to be *staged* in a redoubled deception' (Žižek 2009g: 115).

Law is like time as described by Ulysses in *Troilus and Cressida*: strictly ruled but with necessary transgressions for its operation. In another comedy, *All's Well that Ends Well*, this fuels the outrageous plotting announced by one of its instigators – which, if it speed, Is wicked meaning in a lawful deed, And lawful meaning in a lawful act, Where both not sin, and yet a sinful fact. But let's about it (Act 3, Scene 7) – lines quoted by Žižek to imply, as borne out by his summary of how the scheme is carried out, that the operation of law requires acts that undermine its claim to legitimacy (2009g: 135–6).

Not surprisingly, *Hamlet*, the subject of exhaustive Shakespeare scholarship and intellectual curiosity, stimulates interpretations by Žižek of a psychoanalytic and Hegelian kind. Mythic versions of a murdered father with his son feigning madness while planning revenge against his uncle for committing the deed predate the Oedipus story As a sign of an unconscious thought common to all the variations, an unspoken thought, a forbidden awareness of something obscene in the father's desire, is discerned. What differentiates Hamlet from Oedipus is his knowledge of the suppressed secret. It is a knowledge shared by his own dead father who dramatically brings it to consciousness and this melodramatic touch becomes part of the tragedy's special quality (DSS 9–12).

Earlier mythic versions resolve the difficulty of the hero's predicament by achieving a restoration of the disharmony created by a transgressive murder. Hamlet cannot manage this because 'the element "out of joint" in his world is ultimately himself, the negativity that defines his status as a subject' (HWB 117). Unable to find a symbolic mandate for himself, unable to complete 'to be or not to be …' with an assigned term for his identity, he has to return, tautologically, to the beginning (AR 240–1) but 'the second "to be" is not the same as the first one since it includes negation, negativity that forms the core of a subject' (2025b).

This interpretive move away from classic Freudian readings goes back to Lacan's use of the play to probe the nature of desire. What is revealed is not the importance of turbulent Oedipal undercurrents but the eternal question ('What do you want?') asked to the Other. The libidinal root of Hamlet's anguish is the failure of interpellation in the face of the mystery of the Other's desire (SO 135). There is a bare 'minimum of idealization' necessary to sustain relations with another person and it decomposes when Ophelia no longer holds the place of the object of his desire (PF 83–4).

The role of *Hamlet* in the television mini-series created by Patrick Somerville, *Station Eleven*, is discussed for the way it adjusts a thematically crucial part of Shakespeare's story. In the final episode of the series, a line is added to the Travelling Symphony's production of the play to effect a key moment of reconciliation The resolution attained in the original text is very different – coming in the graveyard scene when Yorick's skull reveals for Hamlet a sheer materiality that enables him to finally escape the 'pseudo-materiality' of a ghost (AR 332–3) – and while the change brought to the play by the Travelling Symphony indicates how 'we are already in the space of modernity, that we have lost our immediate contact with tradition' (2025c) this is not judged a heinous literary crime.

Sinthome

See cinema, *jouissance*, psychoanalysis, unconscious.

Speculative reason

Speculation as a conjecture or a risky investment is referred to by Hegel in *The Encyclopaedia Logic* but only to bracket these ordinary senses of the word. What is retained is the idea of a going beyond, a bold venturing that surpasses what at first appears to be indisputably the case. Speculative reason does this, he explains in *The Science of Logic*, by keeping opposites together. This is possible because the dialectic is the business of the speculative. Philosophically, speculative thinking follows the kind of unexpected logic that allows for the coalescence of a determination that is objective but also the result of subjective mediations.

The negative and the positive are held together in the dialectic as a performative contradiction – like an oxymoron, it contains opposites – and the speculative 'apprehends the unity of the determinations in their opposition, the *affirmative* that is contained in their dissolution and in their transition' (Hegel 1991: 131). Not surprisingly then, Hegel is fond of instances in language which reflect this, as with the word *Aufhebung* (sublation) which can mean both to preserve, to elevate to a higher level, but also to cancel. Wordplay is also found with *Grund* (ground/reason) and *zu Grunde gehen* (perish/fall apart) and is likely to be lost in translation. It occurs again when Hegel expounds a difficulty in the relationship between representational form as a 'picture' – what he calls *Vorstellung* – and the unalloyed concept it draws upon. To explain how the two levels are related, 'the same kind of connection of higher and lower' is found in nature where the penis is the organ of both insemination and urination (2018: §346). Knowing something (*Wissen*), in this case the generative power of insemination can get ignored and become mere urination (*pissen*). Behind the wordplay is a speculative reading that does not rely on one function of the penis being 'higher' than the other but on their propinquity. The 'lower' has to be chosen first, an error has to be made, before the right choice is arrived at (TS 93; LTN 205).

What is unstable needs holding onto firmly and a judgement in an ordinary proposition cannot do this. In 'the sky is blue', the identity of the subject, the sky, is confirmed as an unequivocal given and the predicate adds something to this. Hegel is not satisfied with this, finding it an abstract and illusory kind of identity. As Scott's pathetic fallacy nicely puts it: 'The copula "is", taken as the marker of identity, is in fact a metaphor which has forgotten that it is one' (35). What is non-metaphorical is that 'the mark of identity between its subject and predicate designates only and precisely the specific modality of their *lack of identity*' (KNW 103). The insufficiency and inadequacy of the 'the mark of identity' to indicate a full identity is the paradox of Hegel's term 'speculative identity' (KNW 103). The Real validates speculative reasoning by allowing for the possibility, in the words of Stephen Dedalus in Joyce's *Ulysses*, that 'God becomes man becomes fish becomes barnacle goose becomes featherbed mountain' (3:377–9). A speculative proposition is not, as Malabou puts it, 'an instrument of ontological capture' (182), but nor is it deliriously subjective.

A speculative proposition uses the grammatical form of an ordinary proposition but destabilizes the supposedly fixed identity of the subject and unsettles the status of the copula. It does so – Hegel's remark about spirit being a bone (or Proudhon's about property being theft) is exemplary in this regard – by linking the subject with a predicate that may seem incongruous. Only in this way can the subject of a speculative sentence be properly expressed and identified. The predicate does not merely add something but becomes essential to grasping the nature of the subject;

A speculative approach is what allows Žižek to refine the philosophical movement from Kant to Hegel. An explanation that relies on a straightforward contrast between epistemology (a gap between our understanding and knowing things-in-themselves) and ontology (the gap is always there, defining reality) dilutes an appreciation of a radicality in Kant that he himself did not take on board. The self-limiting function of distinguishing phenomena from an unknown noumenal, Kant acknowledges, cannot be given a positive sense and, if so, a speculative reading allows the self-limiting to belong entirely to phenomena and its negativity. The unknown becomes not something that could in principle be known but a state of utter indifference to being known (LTN 280–3).

Speculative reasoning is applied in overturning the usual reading of Freud's statement that 'anatomy is destiny'. A reductive picturing of sexual difference depends on anatomical distinctions being the basis for differentiating societal roles for men and women. Freud's statement could be taken as an endorsement of such an approach. An opposite meaning emerges when anatomy is viewed as less than a simple given, an immutable fact, and more as something relied on to warrant unequal socio-symbolic 'destinies' for men and women. The fact that someone may or may not physically possess a penis is used to narrow the choices available for one's symbolic identity and consequently accept a given identity as natural. When biology is used in this way to determine one's symbolic identity, anatomy does become destiny but a speculative reading destabilizes the assumed meaning attached to anatomy. What a speculative reading articulates in this case is a truth about the way biology is used to brace symbolic roles.

> 'Anatomy is destiny' … should be read as a Hegelian 'speculative judgement' in which the predicate 'passes over' into the subject … an anatomical difference is 'sublated', turned into the medium of appearance/expression – more precisely into the material support – of a certain symbolic formation.
>
> **(IV 88; AR 150)**

A speculative attitude is needed to release a creative way of reading what on the face of it has an obvious meaning and, as with the case where the organ of urination is also the organ of insemination, it 'arises from the very failure of the first, "immediate" reading' (SO 235). Thinking, says Hegel, is loosened when subject and object speculatively interfere with each other and 'achieve the goal of plasticity' (2018: §45). When 'anatomy is destiny' is read speculatively, in the light of Lacan's logic of sexual difference, biological differences become unimportant and destiny becomes something freely chosen. The choice of a sexual identity appears to be a forced one, dictated by biology but, in the way Schelling locates a primordial decision receding into the unconscious after it has been made, our destiny is decided upon in our unconscious when we choose our character and the kind of person we will become. Transcendentally, it is a free choice: 'We choose our destiny in a forced choice and this choice underlies the everyday perception of our sexual identity being based on anatomy' (SE 257).

The process of breaking the grammatical mould that informs non-speculative propositions finds consonance and amplitude in Hegel's absolute recoil. The paradox of absolute recoil, whereby something comes into existence as the result of being presupposed, is part of a logic of becoming that accounts for an ontology of 'plasticity', one not premised on an objectively existing and fixed reality external to the mind but on the dialectic of identity and difference. Coming to see the subject itself as emerging through its loss is a 'speculative insight' (AR 151). The transition from external to determining reflection is speculative and absolute knowing is 'speculative cognition' (SO xv). What is often registered as counterintuitive in Žižek's thinking is speculative reasoning at work and it is integral to much of his writing.

KNW 103–9, 117–21; AR 313–14; D 73–4, 76–7; IV 88

Comay and Ruda 2018: 55–9; Daly 2019: xii–xv; Hegel 2010a: 35, 121–2, 382–3; Hegel 2018: §§43–5; Malabou 2005: 176–83; Ng 2020: 95–122; Ruda 2018: 22–33; Scott 2025: 35–41, 44–6; Taheri 2021: 1–7

CONNECTIONS: absolute recoil, Christian atheism, dialectic, identity and difference, infinity, predestination, Schelling, sexual difference, 'spirit is a bone'

Spirit

The term *Geist* is usually translated as spirit and in English its nebulous association with ghosts, the supernatural, the cosmic or the divine (the Holy Spirit) has helped create misunderstandings about how Hegel uses the word.

Spirit is not an otherworldly power or presence and older translations of *Geist* as 'mind' are more useful in directing attention to human consciousness and a level of self-awareness that distinguishes it from other forms of life. It is not obviously tangible although it can be spoken of as something to be seen or touched – a way of thinking, says Hegel, that 'may be expressed in this way: The *being of spirit is a bone*' (2018: §343).

Commentaries on Hegel tend to explain his use of spirit in terms of structures or processes of sociality whereby humans explain themselves; less a private introspective act and more a group mindedness that accounts for itself at the level of norms and agreed expectations. Žižek's problem with confining spirit to a heightened self-consciousness, albeit it a decentred one within a context of collective practices, is that it allows for or presupposes a stability that is unwarranted in the face of Hegel's insistence that 'substance is also subject'. Spirit is normalized, neutered to an extent when just a form of life able to reflect on its own ground rules, facilitating self-reflection and the affirmation of an identity. Žižek wants to retain its teeth and make it consistent with Hegel's insistence in *The Phenomenology of Spirit* that *Geist* only finds itself in 'absolute disruption', powered by 'looking the negative in the face' and lingering with it and which, as subject, 'is itself the true substance' (§32).

The subject as foreign to itself, the result of the antagonism that robs substance of any unity, is an ontological wound that can be healed by the dialectical process operating without the need for any illusionary substantiality: 'Spirit heals its wound not directly, but by getting rid of the full and sane Body into which the wound was cut … the wound itself is its own healing when seen from another standpoint' (D 118; AR 141; HWB 85). From this other standpoint, in 'a negation of the negation', the subject is not robbed of its intrinsic identity, having never possessed one to begin with; dispossession is a way of describing the void and the subject is a name for the absence of identity. The 'wounds' are imagined, presupposed, markers for losses that were never really lost and the healing comes when the presupposition is acknowledged. This is Žižek's reading of Hegel's claim that the 'wounds of the spirit heal and leave no scars behind' (2018: §669). There are no scars when the wounds are no longer posited as something that need treatment.

Far from making it a gesture of unification, spirit at its most fundamental level arises from the 'wound' that is the break in nature. There is a self-severing from a pre-human brute immediacy but not as a substantial, thinking thing. In the movement that is absolute recoil, the subject's alienation from itself is what creates the space in which the subject exists as a substantial whole.

To this extent, there is agreement with Pippin that spirit becomes itself through a process where agency is only an entity at a virtual level. Disagreement appears when spirit is taken further and situated as a self-developing circularity that brings into existence what was earlier only a presupposition. Outlandish at first, it might seem a verbal sleight of hand to say something is the result of itself, that it does not exist until it finds itself. It becomes a sensible notion when applied to the way something like communism can exist because people believe in it and act towards helping bring it about. Another example provided is a nation, something which also has no substantiality unless or until a group of people consistently embody it through their self-reflective endeavours. Spirit effectuates itself: 'It is in this way, in the restlessness of immanence, that the spirit of the world becomes' (Nancy 2002: 5). When Hegel writes of spirit as 'shapes of the world' (2018: §440), the indefinite article is indicative of a historically and culturally determined world and not something permanently universal.

Spirit as a collective mindedness within which people recognize themselves and constitute what unites them has an important place in Žižek's Christian atheism. The Incarnation, God sublating himself as Christ, gives body to spirit as a mortal event and not a mega-spiritual agency directing the course of affairs. Some grandiose lines from Hegel's *Lectures on the Philosophy of Religion* (2008: 233) are quoted to this effect: 'It is in the finite consciousness that the process of knowing spirit's essence takes place and that the divine self-consciousness thus arises. Out of the foaming ferment of finitude, spirit rises up fragrantly' (PV 65; Žižek 2009c: 60). The theology bespeaks God's actuality arising through his believers, 'posited through our activity as its presupposition … impotent in himself' (Žižek 2009c: 61).

The mention of 'our activity' in a theological context serves as a reminder that spirit, though immaterial and self-posited, has a material basis: 'If we destroy the body, spirit vanishes' (HWB 79). In possession of its own actuality and potency, spirit is not an illusion. Žižek's praise for the films of Andrei Tarkovsky is tracked to the way he avoids religious obscurantism by, as in *Solaris*, associating the spiritual with earthly physicality. His achievement is seen as the development of a most singular '*materialist theology*, of a deep spiritual stance which draws its strength from its very abandonment of intellect and its immersion into material reality' (FRT 103).

Spirit is not a positive counter-force to nature, a different substance which gradually breaks and shines through the inert natural stuff; it is *nothing but* this process of freeing-itself-from … this means that the standard talk about the Hegelian spirit which alienates itself to itself and then recognises itself in its otherness and thus reappropriates its content is deeply misleading: the Self to which Spirit returns is produced in the very movement of this return.

(PV 46; LTN 186; LET 230)

The third Person in the Christian Trinity, the Holy Spirit, is conceived in a similarly atheistic manner: with the death of Christ, forsaken by a god who collapses into his own inexistence, the spirit that returns is a truly universal community of believers. Emancipatory political movements do likewise, epitomized in the 'Joe Hill' ballad about the trade unionist whose judicial murder keeps him alive in the minds of those who continue the struggle (2009d). *Geist* as spirit comes down to earth and makes itself what it is when the narrator of the song is told by Joe Hill that he always there at the side of striking workers.

FRT 102–7; PV 46–7; LTN 186, 520; AR 17–18, 140, 192–3; E 114–15; D 117–18; HWB 79, 84–5; SFA 421–2

Comay 2011: 129–31; Nancy 2002: 5–6, 19–21, 29–31; Žižek 2009f: 116–17

CONNECTIONS: absolute recoil, antagonism, Christian atheism, *'spirit is a bone'*, subject, substance as also subject

'Spirit is a bone'

> However much of it is otherwise said of spirit that it *is*, it has a *being*, it is a *thing*, a singular *actuality*, still it is not thereby *meant* that it is something we can see, or take in our hands, or push around and so forth, but that is what is *said* of it, and what in truth the forgoing has been saying may be expressed in this way: *The being of spirit is a bone.*
>
> (Hegel 2018: §343)

Hegel's statement that the *'being of spirit is a bone'*, on the face of it a silly remark, is referred to often by Žižek as a speculative truth where the inadequacy of its subject–predicate relationship *is* its meaning. A bone, inert and unresponsive, is the predicate assigned to the subject as active and vital spirit. The incongruity is startling and more than anticlimactic in the conjoining of the highest with the lowest, destabilizing what spirit is for-itself, something of its own. To reach the speculative truth displayed by the statement entails incorporating within it the position from which it is viewed as discrepant: the first reading, registering the obvious incompatibility of spirit and bone, gives way to comprehending the incompatibility as that which defines spirit.

The official in the sardonic Rabinovitch joke reacts to the Jew's wish to leave the Soviet Union with the kind of baffled astonishment that thinking of the spirit as a bone occasions and, as with the two reasons for the Jew's request, it is the failure of a first reading that provides the true reading. In the joke, the first reason given for wanting to emigrate is that Jews will be blamed if the Soviet Union were to collapse. This is easily dealt with by the official's confident assurance that the power of the regime will last for ever. The Jew's disarming reply is that this *is* his second reason. The true result, the precisely real reason why someone would wish to escape Soviet rule, can only be reached via a false step.

In *The Most Sublime Hysteric*, the '*spirit is a bone*' statement is explained as a Hegelian version of the subject's emptiness and its failure to find proper representation within a signifying system: a bone, the skull, 'is not a sign, not an expression of an internality, it does not represent anything' (MSH 93). This is how it is introduced in *The Sublime Object of Ideology*, as that which objectifies the lack that is the subject, testimony to the negativity of the subject in the form of an infinite judgement.

It is also glossed in *The Most Sublime Hysteric* as a version of Lacan's matheme, *$ <> a* (*$* as the barred subject of desire, *a* standing for *objet petit a* and the lozenge symbol for their interrelationship) – where fantasy fills out the empty space that is the subject. In *Tarrying with the Negative*, this is returned to, via a publicity poster for *Alien* depicting Sigourney Weaver's terrified avoidance of the gaze of the monster. The inadequacy exposed by equating the spirit with a bone becomes a version of the failure of Descartes's 'I think therefore I am', the thing that doubts and thinks. The I of the *cogito* cannot be anything but what comes from the void shrinking away from the horror of its own vacuity and 'via the fantasy-being, the being of a "person", the being in "reality" whose frame is structured by fantasy' (TN 61).

A not dissimilar understanding is applied to breakthroughs in biogenetics, mapping the human psyche as genomes accessible to manipulation, and the resulting ethical issues about threats to our autonomy. What is revealed in reading Hegel's proposition as an infinite judgement, the nothingness that is the subject, finds a parallel in the scientific discoveries capable of reducing the wealth of a person's self-being to the contingency and meaninglessness of the genome. Sigourney Weaver's gesture of foreclosure in the film poster, averting her eyes from the skull of the monster, is no longer possible: with the advances in biogenetics, 'I am compelled to directly access the Real' (OB 133).

A further application of the subject–predicate disparity in Hegel's statement is made when it is aligned with the movement of reversal in the dialectical process. The *Aufhebung* that occurs in the dialectic, the perspectival shift that turns a failure into success, an obstacle into an opening, is mirrored in the sublation that resolves the incongruity of animate spirit and passive bone into a condition of possibility for discerning the negativity of pure subjectivity. In *Hamlet*, the tragic hero resolves the false world of seeming when, in the graveyard scene, he finds a truth in the 'non-spectral, inert, and vulgar materiality' (AR 332) of the skull-bone belonging to someone of 'infinite jest' who once gave him piggybacks. Working along a similar line in *The Phenomenology of Spirit*, Hegel has the scene in mind when he contrasts the universe of meaning, where 'even a post hammered onto a desert island' signifies something, with the 'indifferent, unencumbered thing … nothing else immediately to be seen in it' of Yorick's skull (Hegel 2018: §333).

The dramatic impetus of Shakespeare's scene captures and disturbs the imagination and perhaps this partly underlies Žižek's repeated references to Hegel's remark (made only once) about spirit being a bone. The discord it arouses is mined in a variety of ways and extends to serving as a succinct summation of Marx's account of capital in the *Grundrisse*. Marx writes of the product of labour as capital acquiring 'its own soul from living labour', making labour power 'merely an entity for others' and objectively, 'the being of its non-being' (Marx 1973: 119); Žižek writes of Lacan's formula, $\$ <> a$, as 'the junction of the empty, barred subjectivity and money (the object-cause of desire in capitalism)', the 'point of pure negativity' when the spirit of the proletariat becomes a matter of mere money, something as inert in itself as a bone (KNW 57).

MSH 92–3; SO 196–201, 234; KNW 119, 139; TN 61–2, 269n43; TS 88, 92–3; PD 82–3; PV 84; AR 32–3, 332–3; D 73, 76–7; QH 12

CONNECTIONS: dialectic, infinite judgement, speculative reason, spirit, subject

Stalinism

See Badiou, Lenin, Marx, retroactivity.

Subject

The subject is to be distinguished from selfhood, commonly understood as possession of a self-awareness that grows from introspection. The subject, put simply, 'is not its own origin' (LET 229). There is no core from which the subject can develop when substance, lacking the fullness that would endow it with a full identity, is insufficient to itself; it 'is in no way the *self all to itself*' (Nancy 2002: 5). Instead of wholeness, there is the negativity of self-alienated being. The incompleteness is always already there – 'there is no actual life external to alienation which serves as its positive foundation' (SE 39) – and the subject is a response to this failure, the immanent inability to access itself. The only sense of a core, that which could be said to be always there, is the trauma of a being's disconnectedness at seeing substance as also subject.

While subjectivization is a process of acquiring a sense of wholeness, what the subject cannot help but lack makes it more of a partial object. As 'an organ without a body', subject is divorced from 'the topic of the personality, a soul-body unity', suffering in its alienation (OWB 175). An appealing but impossible vision from utopian communism conjures up a community free of alienation but the subject that abides has no 'true', organic self waiting to be released; the reality may be Norman Bates at the end of *Pyscho* speaking with the voice of his mother: 'The price he has to pay in order to become "really himself", undivided subject, is total alienation, becoming an Other with regard to himself: the obstacle to full self-identity is the very condition of selfhood' (ES 241). What is emancipatory is the subject figured as an object before subjectivization, a way of reckoning the revolutionary agent as s/he who assumes their action on behalf of freedom; not as a subjectivized person but as an epitome giving (partial) body to a Cause.

Like being banned from a club one would very much like to join, the subject is represented by Lacan as barred: $\$$. Not being a substantial entity, the subject cannot be fully assimilated by the symbolic order and 'this impossibility of the big Other to integrate me IS myself' (SE 201). The subject as $\$$ 'is divided between its appearance and the void in the core of its being, not between appearance and its hidden substantial ground' (Žižek 2016f: 188). Žižek's texts are peppered with reminders that '$\$$ is nothing but its own inaccessibility, its own failure to be substance' (SFA 366) and this inability to represent itself has a Hegelian and Lacanian weight. It is the speculative truth of Hegel's statement that '*spirit is a bone*' and it is also found in Lacan's concept of separation. For Lacan, separation is what gives rise to the subject: the infant's distance from the (m)Other marks a going beyond born out of desire and an essential lack, 'a nothing where there should have been something' (AR 331).

The subject, lacking self-identity, is unpreventably foreign to itself and has no 'inner' self. It is a 'fantasmatic wealth' that fills the void of the subject turns what is a zero self into a person (CA 121). There is a line from Mozart's *Parsifal*, about the wound being healed only by the spear that smote it, that Žižek paraphrases by describing the subject as being itself the wound it tries to heal (2016f: 190). The 'wound' is the cut in the Real, a traumatic injury, and in this sense the creation of a world of self-experience and fantasy is a self-administered medicine that comprises the process of subjectivity.

The subject, a result of the failure to be something more than a void, necessarily lacks accessibility to itself. As an emergence from failure, it is not an agency but the cause '(presup)posed by its effect' (ME 32–3). The meaning of this baffling condensation of meaning is that, as being, the subject surfaces from the split between its self-appearance as something apparently substantial and the abyssal void that is its home. Disconnected being, wanting to be and supposing a substantiality (the 'effect'), fronts what must be deemed a 'cause' of this substantiality and the subject *is* the assumption of there being such a cause.

The shadow of this diremption is *objet petit a* as that which cannot be given positive embodiment but, by standing in for what is missing, becomes 'the subject itself in the mode of objectivity' (ME 32–3). As 'the self-appearance of nothing' (D 43), the subject is a virtual object that requires something to represent its own impossibility as a positive substance and *objet petit a* is this something. In *Absolute Recoil*, by way of analogy, the subject is said to be like an empty frame missing its object while *objet petit a* is compared to an object lacking a frame that would give it a meaningful place (79).

To render the subject in philosophy as something virtual is a radical move but is seen to follow from a logic that admittedly defies common sense: the subject defines itself negatively as an inherent inability to actualize itself, to be anything but its own lack. This emergence from its own loss is what makes it a case of absolute recoil. The formal nature of the logic should not obscure the traumatic movement that accounts for the emergence of a subject. Hegel's describes this movement as a mad 'night-of-the-world' moment of withdrawal from immersion in complete naturalization, and for Žižek it opens a space to be filled by the symbolic.

> **The subject is not just thwarted, blocked, impeded, stigmatized by a constitutive impossibility; the subject is the result of its own failure, of the failure of its symbolic representation – a subject endeavors to express itself in a signifier; it fails, and the subject is this failure.**
>
> **(AR 150)**

The pure subject is an empty shell that the process of subjectivization provides with content – a person's symbolic identity, their fantasies, an interiority to which they alone have direct access – but this largeness of subjecthood at a formal level is processual at a dialectical level. The self looks for a representation, a staging, felt to be adequate to the supposition that it possesses an undispersed distinctiveness, and, by way of a reversal, actualizes itself retrospectively as this search.

At the same time and equally dialectically, the tendency to reduce the Lacanian subject to a state of endless privation is redressed by also finding there an excess as the other side of lack. The + in terms like LGBT+ is used by way of illustration to indicate how the subject, 'inscribed into a series of its possible identities' (SFA 159) is this very +. This bears only a surface resemblance to the way postmodernism places the subject in a space conditioned by discursive practices that provide various positions. The difference looms large when the Lacanian subject is freighted with Hegel's remark about the importance of seeing substance as also subject.

The self of subjecthood as an emergence from a failure to find a harmony in being brings a problematic to any Marxist understanding of alienation that ignores the subject's self-alienation. Such an ignoring works against Marxist veins in the Lukács of *History and Class Consciousness* and aspects of early Marx in *The*

German Ideology and *Economic and Philosophic Manuscripts of 1844*. What is found there is a reading of the subject as unpaired from a substantial social integrity but capable of reappropriating it as the proletariat of history. What is not accounted for is the subject's constitutive alienation and its need to confront the big Other's lack of cohesion and stability (D 36–7). Most unexpectedly, self-alienation proffers a way out of picturing the individual as solipsistically trapped, unable to communicate with others in society. The barred subject cannot access the truth of its own being and its desire and this keeps alive the hope that the other will provide what cannot be found within itself.

ME 32–3; TN 30–1; TS 158–60; OWB 174–6; AR 28–9, 78–80, 150–1, 403–5; D 43, 133–4; IV 232; SE 39–40, 200–1; F 159

McGowan 2014: 10–38; Sbriglia and Žižek 2020: 12–15; Taheri 2021: 49–58

CONNECTIONS: absolute recoil, negativity, 'night of the world', *objet petit a*, other, '*spirit is a bone*', substance as also subject

'Subjective destitution'

See Christian atheism, cinema, other, psychoanalysis.

Substance as also subject

The everyday sense of substance as 'stuff' is not wildly off the mark from its philosophical use as a term for what has being in its own right, a sense going back to Aristotle whose word for it, *ousia*, comes from the Greek 'to be'. In his preface to *The Phenomenology of Spirit*, Hegel states how 'everything hangs on grasping and expressing the true not just as *substance* but just as much as *subject*' (2018: §17). This has been interpreted with varying degrees of misapprehension, many of which arise from caricatures of Hegel's philosophy as a behemoth where subject subordinates all substance. There is also Lukács's projection, via early Marx, of the proletariat as the subject of history overcoming alienation and reclaiming its true substance through revolution.

In place of such one-directional movements, Hegel's dialectical approach establishes mutuality in what might appear to be a straightforward separation between subject and substance. After all, we are subjects, as agents with our experiences, but we also know that, as little physical bits of matter that do not exists in that form for very long, we are also objects. Instead of a severance, the lack that is the subject mirrors a disjunction in substance itself so that both terms, sharing a basic limitation, are foundationless: the subject looks for a content that is whole and the failure that results is a function of substance's own inability to attain full identity with itself. Subject and substance are not the same but the non-identity between them correlates with the non-identity that defines substance. It is in that sense that subject 'is ultimately nothing but a name for the externality of the Substance to itself' (TN 30) and why 'in the Hegelian passage from substance to subject, subject is the truth of substance' (SE 39).

Subject as the truth of substance can be understood in different ways. The sense of us as subjects conscious of ourselves in the universe, does not make it crazily pantheistic to say 'in some very minimal and restricted sense' that through the subject the universe becomes conscious of itself, that '*being* becomes aware of itself through *human* beings' (Bunyard 2020: 58–90). Another way of getting under the bonnet of Hegel's gnarled prose about substance and subject is via his notion of the absolute and absolute knowing. A subtraction from the multitude of moments that make up reality's shifting appearance leads not to substance's kernel, the source of an ontological completion, but to subject's (mis)representations of reality. The distortions of appearance are the appearance of substance's incompletion as registered by the perceiving subject inscribed into substance.

> The inequality which takes place in consciousness between the I and the substance which is its object is their difference, the *negative* itself. It can be viewed as the *defect* of the two, but it is their very soul or is what moves them … However much this negative now initially appears as the inequality between the I and the object, still it is just as much the inequality of the substance with itself. What seems to take place outside of the substance, to be an activity directed against it, is its own doing, and substance shows that it is essentially subject.
>
> (Hegel 2018: §37)

An analogy that Žižek likes to use is a theologically scandalous parallel between the existentialist individual isolated from a transcendent God and the self-alienation of God who in his own solitariness is wrested from himself (2009c: 59). The human plight comes from within the imperfection of the divine just as Hegel links the source of the subject's sense of 'inequality' to the 'inequality of the substance with itself'.

In *Less Than Nothing*, *objet petit a* is designated as that which gives body to the failure that is the subject. Žižek uses Hegelian language to capture the imbrication of substance with subject: 'It [*objet petit a*] is the substantial remainder of the process of the subjectivization of substance, of the latter's *Aufhebung* in a subjective order.' Denoting a resolution between apparent opposites, *Aufhebung* is being used here to mark a confluence of substance and subject. There is unrest in being and the subject effectuates this as one of the two dimensions of the same disharmony. Substance, Žižek accentuates in italics, *'is nothing but the subject at work'* (LTN 379) but absolutely not in the sense that subject generates or posits substance but in the way that both display the gap in reality that prevents it being comprehended as a consistent totality.

KNW 105–6; LET 228; LTN 258–9, 379–80, 707–8, 750; AR 29 (and D 133); QH 91–2

CONNECTIONS: absolute knowing, Christian atheism, identity and difference, subject

Superego

In his original delineation of id, ego and superego, Freud discerned less-than-straightforward relations between his triad of terms. Analysing the superego, he saw it as libidinally charged from the depths of the id and Žižek deepens and complicates this involvedness: 'It is not that Superego is the agent of morality and Id the reservoir of dark "evil" drives, but it is also not that Superego stands for internalized social oppression and Id for drives that should be liberated' (SE 204).

Commands of the superego have a paradoxical effect of increasing the demand they purport to control; akin to consumerism's dictate that 'the more you buy, the more you have to spend' (FA 21) and, the capitalist's credo, 'the more profit you amass, the more you need' (LET 239). The libidinal dynamics of the superego belong with those of the *objet petit a*, as both the cause and non-erotic object of desire, and surplus enjoyment as the overflow that accrues from the failure of the symbolic to renounce *jouissance*. Death drive and superego run along the same loop, repetitively enacting a failure while obfuscating 'the cause of the terror constitutive of our being-human, the inhuman core of being-human' (LTN 830).

For Lacan, the superego has less to do with moral conscience than with a vindictive, unremunerative injunction to enjoy: 'Nothing forces anyone to enjoy (*jouir*) except the superego. The superego is the imperative of jouissance – Enjoy!' (Lacan 1999: 3). The demand to enjoy then becomes punishable for not being fulfilled and consequently (as Freud noted of the superego) a source of guilt. This evolution from the Freudian to the Lacanian superego is bizarrely dramatized in the scene from *The Sound of Music* when Maria, unable to deal with her sexual feelings for Baron von Trapp, returns to the nunnery out of a sense of guilt. The Mother Superior, an archetypal figure of the disciplining superego, instead of preaching renunciation celebrates fidelity to desire in her song 'Climb Every Mountain' and advises Maria to return to the von Trapp family (LET 320; TP 77). She must follow the injunction to 'Enjoy!' Elizabeth in Coralie Fargeat's *The*

Substance is under a similar compunction, injecting herself with the eponymous substance to restore her youthful beauty and show business fame, but with a less-than-happy ending (Žižek 2025c).

The insistence on enjoyment reverses Kant's unconditional ethical imperative and turns 'You can because you must' into 'You should [you must], because you can' (FA 124). The superego has a complicit, conspiratorial role in the functioning of the law which operates at two levels: it represents an internalization of law as an external authority but it also takes the form of an obscene supplement that incites the enjoyment that comes from transgression. Hence the way too much permissiveness does not inevitably deliver emancipation but can have the opposite effect of diminishing desire and enabling oppressive guilt through the inability to thoroughly enjoy the permissiveness. The origins of law lay in arbitrary acts of hegemonic violence and the enjoyment of unofficially permitted acts of undermining the law sustains its shaky foundations. Enjoyment as a political factor is on show in contemporary nationalism – attitudes and behaviour in Israel and its Occupied Territories provides blatant examples – when a passionate allegiance serves to tolerate transgressions of an otherwise rule-governed existence.

For Žižek, there is an ideological plane of operation to the immoderate imperative of the superego, inducing guilt at an individual level that deflects attention from more pertinent political approaches (ZP 15). The environmental crisis provides one example in the way it makes us feel guilty at an individual level – worrying if we have repaid our debt to Mother Nature by using the correct recycling bin – so 'I get lost in my own self-examination instead of raising much more pertinent global questions about our entire industrial civilization' (SE 249). Another field that is referenced in this way, political correctness, is cogently taken up by Zahi Zalloua in *Žižek on Race*. The superego's complicity with liberalism interrogates citizens – 'Did you check your privilege before speaking? Did you dutifully scrutinize and call out the behavior of others?' (Zalloua 2020: 35) – but such self-policing can remain superficial and conveniently avoid political questioning about the causes of social exclusion.

> **Does the predominant ecological discourse not address us as a priori guilty, indebted to Mother Nature, under the constant pressure of the ecological superego-agency which addresses us in our individuality: 'What did you do today to repay your debt to nature? Did you put all newspapers into a proper recycling bin? And all the bottles of beer or cans of Coke ...' This is why it is in a way quite justified that I feel guilty: following the injunction to recycle etc. ultimately means that I follow rituals which allow me to postpone doing something that would really address the causes of ecological crisis.**
>
> **(SE 249)**

ME 54–62; L 79–84; DLC 89–90; TP 78–89; SE 203–6, 248–50

Homer 2005: 57–9; Žižek 1999c, 2021c

CONNECTIONS: drive, *jouissance*

The symbolic

As the network of signs and meanings, conducted principally as language, the symbolic order does not create reality in the ontic sense but it does structure our sense of being and belonging in everyday reality. As a structure, there can be a place in it which waits to be filled, as with the father whose ideal role is impossible to fulfil but who can be imagined and filled in by a father figure.

At least as equally interesting as what the symbolic succeeds in achieving is what it fails to do. It serves as scaffolding for making sense of and ordering our lives but, like scaffolding, is not designed to be permanent; it is self-enclosed but temporary. We are born into the symbolic and it endows us with a subjecthood that holds out the promise of a unified identity but the appearance of durability is deceptive.

Language as the symbolic cannot help but reflect an unavoidable impasse. Word as the murder of what it seeks to represent (ES 59; Lacan 2001: 114) gives vivid expression to the contrast between the lived, experiential presence of something and the 'dead' nature of the linguistic classification within which it must needs be represented. Utterance is diminished, becoming the struggle for articulation so memorably realized in the fourth episode in the first season of *The Wire* when the two detectives visit a crime scene (YD 92; AP 80–1; QH 197–8).

The phallus is the signifier for the gap that arises between a person's felt selfhood and the mandates conferred on them by the symbolic order. What is meant by symbolic castration is 'the very fact of being caught in the symbolic order' (OWB 87). While managing our enjoyment, attempts by the symbolic to renounce *jouissance* produce a leftover, a surplus enjoyment, which is also indicative of the symbolic order's limitations and inadequacy.

Working with and through the big Other, the symbolic authorizes our expectations but depends on shared agreements to keep its fabric stable and when these break down or are missing the result can be uncomfortable; the person next door becomes the monstrous Neighbour. There is, moreover, something the symbolic cannot negotiate and, using Sarah Kay's image of the Real as the hole in the doughnut (2005: 4), the symbolic is the dough around it, its shape dependent on the absence at its centre. The image perfectly captures the impossibility that pertains to the symbolic for, in a way analogous to the curving of space by matter and energy, the Real curves the space of the symbolic and thwarts it from within.

In an intricate entanglement, *objet petit a* is both the virtual complement to the impossibility existing at the heart of the symbolic and its internal impediment. Lacanian topology meshes with the Hegelian when the empty hole is the negativity, the 'night of the world' that pre-exists the symbolic. There is a complex mediation at work which can also be drawn in terms of a frame and its unstable contents being contained but tensed in a fragile and contradictory alliance. Seeking a cinematic analogy, Žižek turns to Hitchcock: the birds in *The Birds* are the obstacle, an intrusive presence so disturbingly felt, but the film also allows them to become the frame though which the story is told.

> **Complete symbolization would have realized a structure without subject, a structure that would no longer be symbolic. The key to this paradox is that symbolization is as such, in its very notion, incomplete, non-all, failed; it is a structure of its own failure.**
>
> **(IV 17)**

OWB 87–8; L 29–34; LTN 958–61; IV 17–19, 113–14; AP 79–80; QH 195–8

McGowan 2025: 48–55

CONNECTIONS: big Other, *jouissance*, neighbour, 'night of the world', *objet petit a*, subject

T

The transcendental

'It all begins with Kant, with his idea of the *transcendental constitution of reality*' (LTN 9). Kant's seminal argument is that some concepts are not empirically derived but are already there in us, planted and organized in our minds. They are transcendental, coming before experience, concepts of an a priori kind. Labelled 'categories' by Kant, they serve as necessary conditions for making sense of what we encounter. Without them, it would not be possible to explain how objects come to be represented in our minds in the ways they do. Categories do not create our reality but this reality only appears to us in the way it does because there is a transcendental horizon.

The mind intellects order out of sensuous intuition – it assumes, for instance, that every event has a cause – but it cannot directly access the object that causes us to experience it in the first place. A distinction is made between the phenomenal and the noumenal thing-in-itself: the difference between an object's properties that depend for their existence on the perceiver's categories and the properties, outside any hermeneutic circle, that inhere in the object itself. This distinction is the gap between the empirical and the transcendental and neither level can be reduced to the other (OWB xi).

The Kantian transcendental approach separates objects from their subjective conditions of possibility. This is very much at odds with Hegelian reflection and absolute recoil as an immanent movement arising from the inherent impossibility of an object to be a fully constituted, positive entity. The difference is stark.

For Kant, transcendental movement arises from the impossibility of the subject, given its limited constitution, to apprehend the object's fully constituted positiveness. It indicates a limitation of our knowledge; the thing-in-itself cannot be accessed and we are reduced to the phenomenal which is not the same as things-in-themselves and our notions of them. For Žižek, the transcendental is not so purely Kantian but it does indicate, as the scope of meaning that frames the coordinates of our reality, a limitation: what we feel or know has to appear 'within a horizon of meaning or symbolic space' (ZR 86). This 'transcendental turn' signals an irreversible revolution: Spinoza tends to be used as shorthand for pre-Kantian philosophy where ontology is global in its positivity, a 'knowledge about All', and lacking 'the notion of the transcendental-hermeneutic horizon of the World' (Žižek 2020c: 107).

The departure from Kant comes when the makeup of an always-present horizon is subject to alteration, when significant changes are coterminous with transcendental shifts. An example given is the change in understanding motion from the concept of impetus in medieval physics to inertia in post-Copernicus physics (AR 91–2); a change of this order of magnitude is an event. A more comprehensive paradigm shift catalogues the change from pre-modern worldviews, happily accommodating spirits and divine manifestations, to contemporary scientific naturalism (P2 126–7).

> **The transcendental standpoint is in a sense irreducible, for one cannot look 'objectively' at oneself and locate oneself in reality; and the task is to *think this impossibility itself as an ontological fact*, not only as an epistemological limitation.**
>
> **(LTN 239)**

While philosophers and theorists as varied as Heidegger and Habermas adopt a transcendental understanding, Žižek complicates the relationship between transcendental signifying structures and empirical events. The parallax effect in Lévi-Strauss's analysis of how villagers describe the layout of their buildings in one of the Great Lakes tribes (Žižek 1994a; PV 25–6; DLC 287; IV 113–14; AR 104; PD 74–5; QH 21–2) reveals what is non-integrable, a Real that cuts across a transcendental construal of reality As an alternative to representing form as structure, and content as the material it works with, the transcendental is traversed when form is reflected back into content. The villagers draw incommensurable maps of their community's ground space – one group pictures a circular arrangement of houses, the other a vertical arrangement by separating the circle with a dividing line – and they cannot have a form in common because any content is riven by incompatible social relations that shape the form. There is a core antagonism that the villagers cannot stabilize into an agreed symbolic form and this antagonism is a constant that rules out slippage into talk of cultural relativism. The solution is not drone photography showing the village's 'real' layout when every view of reality arises from a particular standpoint. What occurs in quantum physics –when it is the act of perception that collapses the quantum waves into a single figure of reality – can be extended and universalized.

Different animals, including ourselves, see their own reality, as it is for them, transcendentally constituted. They are not distorting a fully realized reality that it out there, contiguous, regardless of the observer: 'The path to the In-itself leads through the subjective gap, since the gap between For-us and In-itself is immanent to the In-itself' (LTN 906).

In a similar vein, with the Hegelian scholar Pippin in mind, the transcendentalism that governs universalist readings of Hegel is also questioned. The creating of coherence by the human subject's self-consciousness, Kant's apperception, is seen to be elevated by Pippin into a primary Hegelian principle and this is hotly disputed by Adrian Johnston.

Žižek refines and elaborates Kant's notion of the transcendental in various and valuable ways. In *The Sublime Object of Ideology*, the form of consciousness that Hegel calls the beautiful soul (Hegel 2018: §658) is discussed. For Hegel, it is an empty gesture of withdrawal from the wicked world in order to preserve a purity and for Žižek this gesture operates within a background or framing that is transcendental. A beautiful soul has its set of coordinates ready, in advance of a particular encounter with the world, so as to readily provide it with the role of the sensitive victim recoiling from what would taint its innocence. What Hegel is seen to be drawing out as important is not the enunciated content, the empirical activity or in this case the non-activity, but the position of enunciation that is the frame within which something is or is not done: 'The real act thus *precedes* the (particular-factual) activity; it consists in the previous restructuring of our symbolic universe into which our (factual, particular) act will be inscribed' (SO 245).

In *Revolution at the Gates*, 'a kind of socio-transcendental a priori' accounts for the way so many contemporary philosophers devalue a political awareness of the sphere of economics (RG 271).

SO 244–7; KNW 216–19; TN 84–5; LTN 237–9, 906–10; AR 98–103; D 24–7; SFA 237–8; SE 263–70; F 53–4

Johnston 2018: 43–53; Gardner 2015

CONNECTIONS: absolute recoil, enunciated and enunciation, event/act, Hegel, Heidegger, In-itself/For-itself, Kant, reflection, subject, transcendental

Truth

See the introduction and absolute knowing, appearance and essence, Badiou, communism, dialectical materialism, Lenin, love, negation of negation, psychoanalysis, '*spirit is a bone*'

U

Unconscious

> As Lacan clearly saw, the Freudian Unconscious is not the substantial domain of Jungian archetypes as the ultimate psychic reality of the subject being … but the virtual point of reference that exists (or, rather insists) only as the absent point of reference of its effects, the Unconscious as the cause which doesn't precede its effects but is only actualized in its effects.
>
> (HWB 97–8)

That there are things we do not know that we know, the self's unknowing of its own self-awareness, points to the unconscious as the 'unknown knowns' singularly missing from Donald Rumsfeld's pitch about relations between the known and the unknown (I 9–10; AR 204–5). Lacan's notion of the Freudian unconscious, unlike Jung's, does not situate it as a place subject to mistreatment by the ego and, through psychoanalysis, open to healthy readjustments and rebalancing. Jung's concept of compensation, with its 'elevation of the Unconscious into the hidden substantial Truth of the human subject' (LTN 300), is not the unconscious for Žižek.

Self-consciousness exists at different levels and below the level of conscious awareness there is another elusive and more fundamental plane of self-consciousness. Žižek regards this as a framework for making sense of Lacan's seemingly outré claim that 'the Cartesian *cogito* (or, rather, the Kantian Self-Consciousness) is the very subject of the Unconscious' (HWB 178). Self-consciousness as its most fundamental level is aware of what comes to it as content of a conscious kind and responds towards it reflexively but not in a form that is transparent. *The Sublime Object of Ideology* sets out this form with the homology between Freud's dreamwork and Marx's analysis of the commodity. In both cases, a conscious latent content is masked and it is the process of distortion – through substitution, displacement, distortion, condensation – and not the content that makes the unconscious what it is: not a depository of repressed wishes but something virtual, insubstantial, outside of cognitive sciences.

The mode of the unconscious as something virtual is not as readily assimilable as thinking of it as the mind's hidden cellar, especially when it upsets the usual sense of cause and effect. With the homology between Freud and Marx in mind, a quirk of behaviour which an individual cannot account for, or social activity displaying how an attitude towards a commodity, can be regarded as an effect. The cause could then be traced to a traumatic childhood event or the relations between people under capitalism. For Lacan and Žižek, the Freudian unconscious does not precede its effect but is actualized in its effect. The accomplishment of the unconscious lies between the effect and its cause. What is unconscious is denied a topological status because, residing only at a virtual level, it is only present when it is transcribed as the distortion of a disavowed lack: 'Here, we cannot but repeat after Lacan: there is no repression previous to the return of the repressed; the repressed content does not precede its return in symptoms' (ES 17).

On three occasions in *Disparities* (44–5, 82, 135), Lacan's key achievement is given as his de-substantializing of the unconscious. 'What is "deep in me" is not the Unconscious proper', Žižek goes on to say, 'but a mess of the real' (139). Some contingent event in childhood, a chance encounter in adult life, becomes freighted with a libidinal force arising from a part of the 'mess of the real' (ES 13–14). The mistaking of Thornhill for a CIA spy in Hitchcock's *North by Northwest* is proffered as an example of how a contingent happening might have aroused in the character dormant desires and wishes. The crucial point is not the possible state of dormancy but how something accidental – in Thornhill's case his acquisition of a new name – 'performatively forms out of this mess in me a set of desires, fears and passions' (D 139). There is reason but no causality at work in the unconscious; there is passage but no determinate chain of events in the face of 'a mad dance of distortions' (LTN 456; AR 163) and 'the radical discontinuity that threatens the consistency of every symbolic formation' (AR 408).

Alenka Zupančič (2024) describes the unconscious and its 'radical discontinuity' in language with a Žižekian resonance: 'The unconscious is a gap in being, and this gap in being has a certain positive, albeit "spectral" consistency: it is, as it were, a non-being that is. It *ex-sists*, it insists in the *with* of the without. The unconscious is not simply that which is not there: it is there precisely as a gap, a gap in being that affects, animates being and its modes of being. It is not simply nothing, but it is not being either.' As 'a thinking outside what I am, a thinking in which I cannot recognise myself' (QH 71), the task of psychoanalysis is for the patient to come to realize this.

Žižek illuminates the nature of the unconscious by contrasting it with the formal role that Hegel allows for it in the edifice of his thought. Hegel cannot formulate a negation which, failing to negate itself, remains hidden in the background. Yet this is what distinguishes the unconscious for Freud and Lacan, 'a contingent knot – *sinthome* holding together the subject's universe' (LTN 484) but remaining unresolved, a disunity of opposites. The negation of negation in Hegel's dialectic cannot accommodate what characterizes Freud's analyses of his patients' dreams: overdetermination, overlays of association that disguise meaning through condensation.

In the 'Reflexivity of the Unconscious' chapter in *Hegel in a Wired Brain*, it is this way of understanding the unconscious that underscores what it is about being human that complicates the notion of a direct link between a digital machine and mental processes. Examples from movies and – used from *The Parallax View* (365–6) to *Quantum History* (275) – the written score of a Schumann's piano piece are called upon to elucidate what Žižek calls a 'virtual point of reference', something not three-dimensionally real but not ineffable either, existing immanently in a way that accounts for the retrospectively created cause of visible effects. One of the examples, the diner who orders a coffee without cream but can only be offered a coffee without milk, has already been referred to (in the context of *objet petit a*) to show how an object as trivial as a cup of coffee can be invested with sublimity when it is placed in the space of reflexive desire, a space that is the unconscious. The unconscious 'is not the content of my desire but my reflexive stance towards it' (HWB 106). In the field of sexuality, the reactive stance is one of puzzlement at the instability of sexuality's foundation; the human animal is not unaware of this lack of knowledge but is 'unconscious' of it (AR 204–5).

The unconscious as the site of decisions about ourselves is seen to be what distinguishes the Joker in Christopher Nolan's *The Dark Knight* from his portrayal in Todd Phillip's *Joker* (HWB 94–5). What the first movie intimates is an approach to the unconscious that views its effect – the Joker is who he has decided to be– and mocks the idea of a background trauma as the cause of his choice. Schelling is read as anticipating this approach to the unconscious, identifying it with a primordial decision-making act, a self-positing choice which then has to recede, encrypted and never-ending, into the background. Žižek relates this to the way in which a person who acts as if driven by an evil force, beyond their control, is nonetheless held responsible for their deeds (HWB 178).

SO 4–9; TS 247–8; IR 33–4; PV 64–5; LTN 274–5, 300–2, 484–8; AR 184–5; 407–8; D 134–9; HWB 97–107, 178–81; SFA 147–8; QH 92–5

Lacan 1997; Zupančič 2024

CONNECTIONS: Badiou, Lacan, negation of negation, psychoanalysis, Schelling, sexuality, *Vertigo*

V

Vertigo

The abyss Scottie is finally able to look into is the very abyss of the hole in the Other … This abyss is figured in the shots accompanying the titles of *Vertigo*, the closeups of a woman's eyes out of which swirls a nightmarish partial object. We could say that at the end of the film, Scottie is finally able to 'look a woman in the eye', i.e. to bear the view shown during the film's titles.

(LA 86–7)

Alfred Hitchcock's films are championed by Žižek for their cinematic dramatizations of key ideas of psychoanalytic interest. *Vertigo* (1958), one of the Hitchcock films looked at in *The Pervert's Guide to the Cinema*, is repeatedly returned to as 'the film which stands for cinema as such, *tout court*' (OWB 151).

The scene from the film in Ernie's restaurant, where Madeline is seen by Scottie for the first time, receives a close analysis of two of its shots in particular. The first is of Madeline seated at a table, with the camera gradually approaching her naked back and the second is a mysteriously partial profile shot of Madeline while she is waiting for her husband before they leave the restaurant. The two shots are conventionally read by film theorists as point-of-view shots but Žižek regards them as subjectivized ones but uncanny in being unattributable to Scottie's subjective point of view. They are invested with an exorbitance, 'a kind of acephalous passion' (OWB 154) where the gaze becomes an object divorced from the subject. The theoretical context is Lacan's Seminar XI and an understanding of the gaze that is different to the way it was used in film theory as a controlling look from a position of power. Gaze becomes an object bearing witness to a subject's unconscious desire which is drawn into and thereby disturbing a visual field. There can be no neutral perspective when the subject's desire distorts what is seen. Lacan distinguishes between the eye of a conscious, knowledge-aware subject and the gaze that is unconscious desire. The Madeline that fascinates Scottie and exists as a staging for his gaze is like the door that the man from the country thinks will access Law in the 'Before the Law' parable in Kafka's *The Trial*. The door, he finds out just before he dies, could never have been entered by anyone else because it was only ever there for him; similarly Madeline was only ever there for Scottie.

The more general interest aroused by *Vertigo* for Žižek is traced to its anti-Platonic orbit around questions of appearance and reality. The physical reality of Judy as Madeline cannot satisfy Scottie's inordinate dreams until he curates her elevation to the ethereal level which will grant access to a sublime encounter with a Platonic originary Idea. The untwisting of this comes with the realization that Judy was a fake of the original Madeline: 'The *objet a* disintegrates, the very loss is lost, we get a negation of negation' (LTN 479).

LA 83–7; PF 89, 232; OWB 151–5, 157–63; PC; LET 29–30; LTN 478–9, 708–9; IV 67–8; QH 69

Lacan 2014: 67–119; McGowan 2024; Shaul 2022

CONNECTIONS: love, Plato, Real

W

Wokeness

Articles, interviews and op-eds in print and online media are ongoing testimony to Žižek's provocative engagements with current affairs and to an iconoclasm that does not exempt the liberal left from critical fire. His disesteem for wokeness, aligning it with populism and religious fundamentalism, targets dogmatism and the simplification of complex issues. He cites in an article the way a private London clinic used puberty blockers as evidence of an unholy alliance between a pushy trans lobby and the profit motive, calling it 'woke capitalism' (2023e). Also referred to is the way an 'awokened black elite' stifled freedom of thought in a prestigious US university. Elsewhere, a case from academia in the United States is referenced to show how political correctness depends on a figure of the big Other (CA 216–17) while at *École Normale Supérieure* a woke stance is seen transforming permissiveness into prohibition (F 219).

As with Žižek's talks about the demands of political correctness (readily available on YouTube), the superego is seen to facilitate social domination by, on this occasion, demanding submission to woke mandates.

Instead of facing up to the challenge of dealing with issues, wokeness is an escape into controlling how they are spoken about and a parallel is sketched with Lacan's interpretation of the 'Father, can't you see that I am burning' dream reported by Freud. The son's reproach in the dream is too traumatic for the father to bear and he escapes from the reality of his feeling of guilt by waking up into the wide-awake world where he can avoid having to confront his sense of responsibility for his son's death. The reversal by Lacan of the familiar idea that dreaming is an escape from reality allegorizes the way wokeness comes to represent its opposite.

> The woke awaken us – to racism and sexism – precisely to enable us to go on sleeping. They show us certain realities so that we can go on ignoring the true roots and depth of our racial and sexual traumas.
>
> (Žižek 2023e)

Wokeness as a cloaking device for a liberal elite comes to mirror anti-woke populists presenting themselves as champions of common-sense. Neither party wants to destabilize the existing order; both are complicit in maintaining social injustice, and culture wars become a convenient way of masking class struggle. There is a space here for purportedly radical intellectuals of the Left who happily write and read about insurgents but are reluctant to engage in real political struggle. This is made clear in a '(not too) vulgar' joke retold by Žižek (CA 82).

TN 213–14; TL 105–21; F 218–19; CA 41–2

Žižek 2023e

CONNECTIONS: big Other, class struggle, Lacan, sexual difference, superego

Z

Zupančîč, Alenka

See Antigone, desire, sexuality.

References

Žižek

Žižek. ([1989] 2008). *The Sublime Object of Ideology*. London: Verso.

Žižek. (1991). *Looking Awry: An Introduction to Jacques Lacan through Popular Culture*. Cambridge, MA: MIT Press.

Žižek. (1993a). *Tarrying with the Negative: Kant, Hegel, and the Critique of Ideology*. Durham, NC: Duke University Press.

Žižek. (1993b). ' "The Thing that Thinks": The Kantian Background to the *Noir* Subject'. In J. Copjec (ed.), *Shades of Noir: A Reader*, 199–226. London: Verso.

Žižek. (1994a). 'Introduction: The Spectre of Ideology'. In S. Žižek (ed.), *Mapping Ideology*, 1–33. London: Verso. Also in *The Žižek Reader*, ed. W. and E. Wright, 55–86. Oxford: Blackwell, 1999.

Žižek. (1994b). 'Connections of the Freudian Field to Philosophy and Popular Culture'. *Analysis* 6, 54. www.lacan.com/zizlacan3.htm (accessed 19 October 2025).

Žižek. ([1996] 2007). *The Indivisible Remainder: An Essay on Schelling and Related Matters*. London: Verso.

Žižek. (1996). ' "In Hear You with My Eyes", or, The Invisible Master'. In R. Salecl and S. Žižek (eds), *Gaze and Voice as Love Objects*, 90–128. Durham, NC: Duke University Press.

Žižek. (1997). *The Abyss of Freedom/Ages of the World*. Ann Arbor: University of Michigan Press.

Žižek. (1998a). 'A Leftist Plea for "Eurocentrism" '. *Critical Inquiry* 24, 4: 988–1009.

Žižek. (1998b). 'Psychoanalysis in Post-Marxism: The Case of Alain Badiou'. In R. Miklitsch (ed.), Special issue: Psycho-Marxism: Marxism and Psychoanalysis Late in the Twentieth Century. *South Atlantic Quarterly* 97, 2: 235–62.

Žižek. (1998c). 'The Cartesian Subject versus the Cartesian Theatre'. In S. Žižek (ed.), *Cogito and the Unconscious*, 247–74. Durham, NC: Duke University Press.

Žižek. (1999a). 'Preface: Burning the Bridges'. In W. and E. Wright (eds), *The Žižek Reader*, vii–xx. Oxford: Blackwell.

Žižek. (1999b). 'The Matrix, or Malebranche in Hollywood'. *Philosophy Today* 43, supplement: 11–26.

Žižek. (1999c). 'You May!' *London Review of Books* 21, 6. www.lrb.co.uk/the-paper/v21/n06/slavoj-zizek/you-may! (accessed 19 October 2025).

Žižek. (2000a). *The Art of the Ridiculous Sublime: On David Lynch's Lost Highway*. Seattle: University of Washington Press.

Žižek. (2000b). 'Repeating Lenin'. www.lacan.com/replenin.htm (accessed 19 October 2025).

Žižek. (2000c). 'Class Struggle or Postmodernism? Yes, Please!'. In J. Butler, E. Laclau and S. Žižek (eds), *Contingency, Hegemony, Universality: Contemporary Dialogues on the Left*, 90–135. London: Verso.

Žižek. (2000d). 'The Thing from Inner Space'. In R. Salecl (ed.), *Sexuation*, 216–59. Durham, NC: Duke University Press.

Žižek. (2001). *On Belief*. New York: Routledge.

Žižek, S. ([2001] 2002a). *Did Somebody Say Totalitarianism: Five Interventions in the (Mis)use of a Notion*. London: Verso.

Žižek, S. (2002b). *Welcome to the Desert of the Real! Five Essays on September 11 and Related Dates*. London: Verso.

Žižek, S. (2002c). 'I Do Not Order My Dreams'. In S. Žižek and M. Dolar (eds), *Opera's Second Death*, 103–225. London: Routledge.

Žižek, S. (2003a). *The Puppet and the Dwarf: The Perverse Core of Christianity*. Cambridge, MA: MIT Press.

Žižek, S. (2003b). 'The Violence of the Fantasy'. *Communication Review* 6, 4: 275–87. www.scribd.com/doc/67555391/Zizek-Slavoj-The-Violence-of-the-Fantasy (accessed 19 October 2025).

Žižek, S. (2004a). *Iraq: The Borrowed Kettle*. London: Verso.

Žižek, S. (2004b). *Organs without Bodies*: *On Deleuze and Consequences*. London: Routledge.

Žižek, S., ed. ([2002] 2004c). *Revolution at the Gates: A Selection of Writings from February to October 1917, V. I. Lenin*. London: Verso.

Žižek, S. (2004d). 'From Purification to Subtraction: Badiou and the Real'. In P. Hallward (ed.), *Think Again: Alain Badiou and the Future of Philosophy*, 165–81. London: Continuum.

Žižek, S. (2004e). *The Reality of the Virtual*, dir. Ben Wright. www.youtube.com/watch?v=gBRToxGyKZo (accessed 19 October 2025).

Žižek, S. ([1994] 2005a). *The Metastases of Enjoyment*. London: Verso.

Žižek, S. (2005b). 'Neighbors and Other Monsters: A Plea for Ethical Violence'. In S. Žižek, E. L. Santner and K. Reinhard (eds), *The Neighbor*, 134–90. Chicago: University of Chicago Press.

Žižek, S. (2006a). *The Parallax View*. Cambridge, MA: MIT Press.

Žižek, S. (2006b). *How to Read Lacan*. London: Granta.

Žižek, S. (2006c). *A Pervert's Guide to the Cinema*, dir. Sophie Fiennes. www.theperver tsguide.com (accessed 19 October 2025).

Žižek, S. ([2005] 2006d). *Demanding the Impossible*. London: Continuum.

Žižek, S. (2006e). 'Freud Lives!'. *London Review of Books* 28, 10. www.lrb.co.uk/the-paper/v28/n10/slavoj-zizek/freud-lives (accessed 19 October 2025).

Žižek, S. (2006f). 'Zizek on Commodity Fetishism, Ideology and Belief'. www.youtube.com/watch?v=SsFC3FuuRVw (accessed 19 October 2025).

Žižek, S. (2007a). *Mao on Practice and Contradiction*. London: Verso.

Žižek, S. (2007b). 'Robespierre, OR, The Divine Violence of Terror'. In *Virtue and Terror: Maximilien Robespierre*, vii–xxxix. London: Verso

Žižek, S. (2007c). 'Afterword: With Defenders Like These, Who Needs Attackers?'. In P. Bowman and R. Stamp (eds), *The Truth of Žižek*, 197–255. New York: Continuum.

Žižek, S. (2007d). 'Badiou: Notes from an Ongoing Debate'. *International Journal of Žižek Studies* 1, 2. https://zizekstudies.org/index.php/IJZS/article/view/37 (accessed 30 July 2013).

Žižek, S. ([1991] 2008a). *For They Know Not What They Do: Enjoyment as a Political Factor*. London: Verso.

Žižek, S. ([1992] 2008b). *Enjoy Your Symptom! Jacques Lacan in Hollywood and Out*. London: Roudedge.

Žižek, S. ([1997] 2008c). *The Plague of Fantasies*. London: Verso.

Žižek, S. (2008d). *In Defense of Lost Causes*. London: Verso.

Žižek, S. (2008e). *Violence: Six Sideways Reflections*. London: Profile.

Žižek, S. ([2000] 2008f). *The Fragile Absolute, or Why Is the Christian Legacy Worth Fighting For?* London: Verso.

Žižek, S. ([1999] 2008g). *The Ticklish Subject*. London: Verso.

Žižek, S. ([2001] 2009a). *The Fright of Real Tears: Krzysztof Kieślowski between Theory and Post-Theory*. London: British Film Institute and Palgrave Macmillan.

Žižek, S. (2009b). *First as Tragedy, Then as Farce*. London: Verso.

Žižek, S. (2009c). 'The Fear of Four Words: A Modest Plea for the Hegelian Reading of Christianity'. In C. Davis (ed.), *The Monstrosity of Christ: Paradox or Dialectic?*, 24–109. Cambridge, MA: MIT Press.

Žižek, S. (2009d). 'Dialectical Clarity versus the Misty Conceit of Paradox'. In C. Davis (ed.), *The Monstrosity of Christ: Paradox or Dialectic?*, 234–306. Cambridge, MA: MIT Press.

Žižek, S. (2009e). 'Forward: The Camera's Posthuman Eye'. In H. Bond (ed.), *Lacan at the Scene*. Cambridge, MA: MIT Press.

Žižek, S. (2009f). 'Discipline between Two Freedoms: Madness and Habit in German Idealism'. In M. Gabriel and S. Žižek (eds), *Mythology, Madness and Laughter: Subjectivity in German Idealism*, 95–121. London: Continuum.

Žižek, S. (2009g). 'Fichte's Laughter'. In M. Gabriel and S. Žižek (eds), *Mythology, Madness and Laughter: Subjectivity in German Idealism*, 122–67. London: Continuum.

Žižek, S. (2010a). *Living in the End Times*. London: Verso.

Žižek, S. (2010b). 'To Begin from the Beginning'. In C. Douzinos and S. Žižek (eds), *The Idea of Communism*, 209–26. London: Verso.

Žižek, S. (2010c). 'Thinking Backward: Predestination and Apocalypse'. In J. Milbank, S. Žižek and C. Davis (eds), *Paul's New Moment: Continental Philosophy and the Future of Christian Theology*, 185–210. Grand Rapids, MI: Brazos Press.

Žižek, S. (2010d). 'A Meditation on Michangelo's *Christ on the Cross*'. In J. Milbank, S. Žižek and C. Davis (eds), *Paul's New Moment: Continental Philosophy and the Future of Christian Theology*, 169–81. Grand Rapids, MI: Brazos Press.

Žižek, S. (2010e). 'Afterword'. In *Five Lessons on Wagner*, 169–81. Grand Rapids, MI: Brazos Press.

Žižek, S. ([1992] 2010f). 'In His Bold Gaze My Ruin Is Writ Large'. In *Everything You Always Wanted to Know about Lacan (But Were Afraid to Ask Hitchcock)*, 211–72. London: Verso.

Žižek, S. ([2004] 2011a). 'The Lesson of Rancière'. In J. Rancière, *The Politics of Aesthetics: The Distribution of the Sensible*, ed. and trans. G. Rockhill, 65–76. London: Bloomsbury.

Žižek, S. (2011b). 'Preface: Hegel's Century'. In S. Žižek, C. Crockett and C. Davis (eds), *Hegel and the Infinite: Religion, Politics and Dialectic*, ix–xi. New York: Columbia University Press.

Žižek, S. (2011c). 'Hegel and Shitting: The Idea's Constipation'. In S. Žižek, C. Crockett and C. Davis (eds), *Hegel and the Infinite: Religion, Politics, and Dialectic*, 221–32. New York: Columbia University Press.

Žižek, S. (2011d). 'The Politics of Negativity'. In F. Ruda (ed.), *Hegel's Rabble: An Investigation into Hegel's Philosophy of Right*, x–xviii. London: Continuum.

Žižek, S. (2012a). *The Year of Dreaming Dangerously*. London: Verso.

Žižek, S. (2012b). *A Pervert's Guide to Ideology*, dir. Sophie Fiennes. www.youtube.com/watch?v=oBcFLmu_tlc (accessed 19 October 2025).

Žižek, S. (2013a). *Demanding the Impossible*, ed. Yong-june Park. Cambridge, MA: Polity.

Žižek, S. ([2005] 2013b). *Interrogating the Real*, ed. R. Butler and S. Stephens. London: Bloomsbury.

Žižek, S. (2013c). 'Answers without Questions'. In S. Žižek (ed.), *The Idea of Communism, Vol. 2*, 177–205. London: Verso.

Žižek, S. (2013d). 'The Simple Courage of Decision: A Leftist Tribute to Thatcher'. *Blog Boitempo*, 18 April. https://blogdaboitempo.com.br/2013/04/18/the-simple-cour age-of-decision-a-leftist-tribute-to-thatcher-by-slavoj-zizek/ (accessed 30 July 2013).

Žižek, S. (2013e). 'Preface: Bloch's Ontology of Not-Yet-Being'. In P. Thompson and S. Žižek (eds), *The Privatization of Hope: Ernst Bloch and the Future of Utopia*, xv–xx. Durham, NC: Duke University Press.

Žižek, S. (2014a). *Absolute Recoil: Towards a New Foundation of Dialectical Materialism*. London: Verso.

Žižek, S. (2014b). *Event: Philosophy in Transit*. London: Penguin.

Žižek, S. ([2006] 2014c). *The Universal Exception*. London: Bloomsbury.

Žižek, S. (2014d). *Trouble in Paradise: From the End of History to the End of Capitalism*. London: Allen Lane.

Žižek, S. ([2011] 2014e). *The Most Sublime Hysteric: Hegel with Lacan*. London: Polity.

Žižek, S. (2014f). 'Anti-Semitism and Its Transformations'. In G. Vattimo and M. Marder (eds), *Deconstructing Zionism: A Critique of Political Metaphysics*, 1–14. London: Bloomsbury.

Žižek, S. (2014g). 'The Hegelian Wound', a talk at New York University, 26 September. www.youtube.com/watch?v=DRsrYi-wXro (accessed 30 July 2013).

Žižek, S. (2015a). 'Afterword. The Minimal Event: From Hystericization to Subjective Destitution'. In A. Hamza (ed.), *Repeating Žižek*, 269–85. Durham, NC: Duke University Press.

Žižek, S. (2015b). 'Postscript: The Rule of Law between Obscenity and the Right to Distress'. In L. De Sutter (ed.), *Žižek and Law*, 220–47. London: Routledge.

Žižek, S. (2015c). 'Why Heidegger Should Not Be Criminalized'. *New Statesman*, 13 May. www.newstatesman.com/culture/2015/05/slavoj-zizek-why-heidegger-sho uld-not-be-criminalised (accessed 19 October 2025).

Žižek, S. (2016a). *Disparities*. London: Bloomsbury.

Žižek, S. (2016b). *Against the Double Blackmail: Refugees, Terror and Other Troubles with the Neighbours*. London: Bloomsbury.

Žižek, S. (2016c). *Antigone*. London: Bloomsbury.

Žižek, S. (2016d). 'Christ, Hegel, Wagner'. *International Journal of Žižek Studies* 2, 2. https://zizekstudies.org/index.php/IJZS/article/view/38 (accessed 19 October 2013).

Žižek, S. (2016e). 'No Way Out: Communism in the New Century'. In A. Taek-Gwang Lee and S. Žižek (eds), *The Idea of Communism, Vol. 3*, 240–57. London: Verso.

Žižek, S. (2016f). 'Afterword'. In A. Hamza and F. Ruda (eds), *Slavoj Žižek and Dialectical Materialism*, 177–92. London: Palgrave Macmillan.

Žižek, S. (2016g). 'Slavoj Žižek: We Are All Basically Evil, Egotistical, Disgusting'. *The Guardian*, 10 December. www.theguardian.com/lifeandstyle/2016/dec/10/sla voj-zizek-we-are-all-basically-evil-egotistical-disgusting (accessed 30 July 2013).

Žižek, S. (2016h). 'The Seeds of Imagination'. In S. Žižek (ed.), *An American Utopia, Dual Power and the Universal Army: Frederic Jameson*, 267–308. London: Verso.

Žižek, S. (2016i). 'The Three Events of Philosophy'. *International Journal of Žižek Studies*. https://zizekstudies.org/index.php/IJZS/article/view/697/703 (accessed 19 October 2013).

Žižek, S. (2016j). 'Events through Imaginary, Symbolic, and Real'. In A. Ceerda-Rueda (ed.), *Sex and Nothing: Bridges from Psychoanalysis to Philosophy*, 37–56. London: Karnac.

Žižek, S. (2017a). *Incontinence of the Void*. Cambridge, MA: MIT Press.

Žižek, S. ([2007] 2017b). *Mao: On Practice and Contradiction*. London: Verso.

Žižek, S. (2017c). *The Courage of Hopelessness: Chronicles of a Year of Acting Dangerously*. London: Allen Lane.

Žižek, S. (2017d). *Lenin 2017: Remembering, Repeating, and Working through V.I. Lenin* (later published as *Lenin: The Day after the Revolution*). London: Verso.

Žižek, S. (2017e). 'Terrorists with a Human Face'. In J. Krečič (ed.), *The Final Countdown: Europe, Refugees and the Left*, 187–201. Ljubljana: IRWIN.

Žižek, S. (2017f). 'Religion and Commodity Fetishism'. www.youtube.com/watch?v=Vcrh jDm4mcQ (accessed 19 October 2025).

Žižek, S. (2017g). 'The Minimal Event: Subjective Destitution in Shakespeare and Beckett'. In R. Sbriglia (ed.), *Everything You Always Wanted to Know about Literature but Were Afraid to Ask Žižek*, 290–315. Durham, NC: Duke University Press.

Žižek, S. (2017h). 'Blade Runner 2049: A View of Post-Human Capitalism'. *Philosophical Salon*, 30 October. https://thephilosophicalsalon.com/blade-run ner-2049-a-view-of-post-human-capitalism/#_ednref3 (accessed 19 October 2025).

Žižek, S. (2018). 'The Dash:' A Discussion with Slavoj Žižek, Rebecca Comay, and Frank Ruda'. www.youtube.com/watch?v=SoRIMXFy5Mw (accessed 19 October 2025).

Žižek, S. (2020a). *Sex and the Failed Absolute*. London: Bloomsbury.

Žižek, S. (2020b). *A Left That Dares Speak Its Name*. Cambridge, MA: Polity.

Žižek, S. (2020c). 'Intellectual Intuition and *Intellectus Archetypus*: Reflexivity from Kant to Hegel'. In R. Sbriglia and S. Žižek (eds), *Subject Lessons: Hegel, Lacan, and the Future of Materialism,* 102–21. Evanston, IL: Northwestern University Press.

Žižek, S. (2020d). *Pandemic! COVID-19 Shakes the World*. London: OR Books.

Žižek, S. (2020e). *Pandemic! 2: Chronicles of a Time Lost*. London: OR Books.

Žižek, S. (2020f). 'Forward: The Importance of Theory'. In Z. Zalloua (ed.), *Žižek and Race: Towards an Anti-Racist Future*, x–xiii. London: Bloomsbury.

Žižek, S. (2020g). 'The Appointment in Samarra: A New Use for Some Old Jokes'. *International Journal of Žižek Studies* 14, 2. https://zizekstudies.org/index.php/IJZS/article/view/1178 (accessed 19 October 2025).

Žižek, S. (2021a). *Heaven in Disorder*. London: OR Books.

Žižek, S. (2021b). 'Lenin: Which Lenin?' In H. J. Joffre-Eichhorn (ed.), *Lenin 150,* 291–3. Wakefield: Dajara Press.

Žižek, S. (2021c). 'The Vagaries of the Superego'. *Elementa* 1, 1–2. www.ledonline.it/index.php/Elementa/article/view/2814 (accessed 19 October 2025).

Žižek, S. (2021d). 'The Two Ends of Philosophy'. *Philosophy World Democracy*, 15 September. www.philosophy-world-democracy.org/articles-1/the-two-ends-of-phi losophy (accessed 19 October 2025).

Žižek, S. (2021e). 'A Short Note on Hegel and the Exemplum of Christ'. *Crisis & Critique* 8, 2: 433–41. www.crisiscritique.org/storage/app/media/2021-12-13/cc82sla voj-zizek.pdf (accessed 19 October 2025).

Žižek, S. (2021f). 'The Parallax of Ontology. Reality and Its Transcendental Supplement'. In D. Finkelde, S. Žižek and C. Menke (eds), *Parallax: The Dialectics of Mind and World*, 107–17. London: Bloomsbury.

Žižek, S. (2022a). 'Hegel: The Spirit of Distrust'. In S. Žižek, F. Ruda and A. Hamza (eds), *Reading Hegel*, 13–100. Cambridge, MA: Polity.

Žižek, S. (2022b). 'Marx's Theory of Fictions'. In A. Johnston, B. Nedoh and A. Zupančič (eds), *Objective Fictions*, 13–23. Edinburgh: Edinburgh University Press.

Žižek, S. (2022c). 'Žižek on the Lacanian Real'. www.youtube.com/watch?v=InZUkhk4 heg (accessed 19 October 2025).

Žižek, S. (2022d). 'Slavoj Žižek, Todd McGowan, and Russ Sbriglia Discuss Jacques Lacan'. www.youtube.com/watch?v=gRQduUvaSVkInZUkhk4heg (accessed 19 October 2025).

Žižek, S. (2022e). 'A Muddle Instead of a Move'. *Philosophical Salon*, 10 January. https://thephilosophicalsalon.com/a-muddle-instead-of-a-movie/ (accessed 19 October 2025).

Žižek, S. (2023a). *Too Late to Awaken: What Lies Ahead When There Is No Future?* London: Allen Lane.

Žižek, S. (2023b). *Surplus Enjoyment: A Guide for the Non-Perplexed*. London: Bloomsbury.

Žižek, S. (2023c). *Freedom: A Disease without a Cure*. London: Bloomsbury.

Žižek, S. (2023d). *Mad World: War, Movies, Sex*. New York: OR Books.

Žižek, S. (2023e). 'Wokeness Is Here to Stay'. https://compactmag.com/article/woken ess-is-here-to-stay (accessed 19 October 2025).

Žižek, S. (2023f). 'Response to Ruti'. In D. Finkelde and T. McGowan (eds), *Žižek Responds*, 281–5. London: Bloomsbury.

Žižek, S. (2023g). 'Anti-Semitism and Its Vagaries'. *Žižek Goads and Prods*, 5 December. https://slavoj.substack.com/p/anti-semitism-and-its-vagaries (accessed 19 October 2025).

Žižek, S. (2023h). 'Slavoj Žižek and Sean Carroll: Quantum Physics and Time Travel'. www.youtube.com/watch?v=735mYcl3Lrg (accessed 19 October 2025).

Žižek, S. (2023i). 'Class Struggle: Antagonism beyond Fighting an Enemy'. *Crisis & Critique* 10, 1: 349–59. www.crisiscritique.org/storage/app/media/2023-05-18/sla voj-ziiziek.pdf (accessed 19 October 2025).

Žižek, S. (2023j). 'Whose Servant Is a Master'. *Problemi International* 6: 385–96. https:// problemi.si/issues/p2023-6/15_Zizek_p2023_international6.pdf (accessed 19 October 2025).

Žižek, S. (2024a). *Christian Atheism: How to Be a Real Materialist*. London: Bloomsbury.

Žižek, S. (2024b). 'Larger Than Life'. https://slavoj.substack.com/p/larger-than-life?utm _source=publication-search (accessed 19 October 2025).

Žižek, S. (2024c). 'Some Remarks on the Ontological Implications of Quantum Mechanics'. *Philosophical Salon*, 29 April. https://thephilosophicalsalon.com/nonco mmutativity-in-the-symbolic-and-in-the-quantum-real/ (accessed 19 October 2025).

Žižek, S. (2024d). 'After Trump's Victory: From MAGA to MEGA'. *e-flux*, 13 November. www.e-flux.com/notes/641013/after-trump-s-victory-from-maga-to-mega (accessed 19 October 2025).

Žižek, S. (2024e). 'Change Things So That Nothing Will Really Change!' *Žižek Goads and Prods*, 6 July. https://slavoj.substack.com/p/change-things-so-that-nothing-will (accessed 19 October 2025).

Žižek, S. (2024f). 'Lacan's Lesson for Philosophy: Why True Atheism Has to Be Indirect'. In A. Taheri, C. Vanderwees and R. Naderi (eds), *Philosophy after Lacan: Politics, Science, Art*, 7–26. London: Routledge.

Žižek, S. (2024g). 'Divided We Stand, United We Fall'. *Žižek Goads and Prods*, 14 September. https://slavoj.substack.com/p/divided-we-stand-united-we-fall (accessed 19 October 2025).

Žižek, S. (2024h). 'Noncommutativity in the Symbolic and in the (Quantum) Real'. *Philosophical Salon*, 17 June. https://thephilosophicalsalon.com/noncommutativity-in-the-symbolic-and-in-the-quantum-real/ (accessed 19 October 2025).

Žižek, S. (2024i). 'On the Material Existence of Ideology'. In N. A. Barria-Asenjo and S. Žižek (eds), *Political Jouissance*, 9–22. London: Bloomsbury.

Žižek, S. (2024j). 'Reconciliation, from Wagner to Rammstein'. *Philosophical Salon*, 2 January. https://thephilosophicalsalon.com/reconciliation-from-wagner-to-rammstein/ (accessed 19 October 2025).

Žižek, S. (2024k). 'Kant, Mysticism and the Pre-Ontological Real'. *Problemi International* 7: 7–21. https://problemi.si/issues/p2024-7/01_Zizek_p2024_international7.pdf (accessed 19 October 2025).

Žižek, S. (2024l). 'Lacan's Lesson for Philosophy: Why True Atheism Has to Be Indirect'. In A. Taheri, C. Vanderwees and R. Naderi (eds), *Philosophy after Lacan*, 7–26. London: Routledge.

Žižek, S. (2025a). *Against Progress*. London: Bloomsbury.

Žižek, S. (2025b). 'When God Cries: Hamlet and the Art of World-Shattering Change'. *Žižek Goads and Prods*, 15 February. https://slavoj.substack.com/p/when-god-cries-hamlet-and-the-art (accessed 19 October 2025).

Žižek, S. (2025c). 'Station Eleven: Ophelia in War Communism'. *Philosophical Salon*, 3 March. www.thephilosophicalsalon.com/station-eleven-ophelia-in-war-communism/ (accessed 19 October 2025).

Žižek, S. (2025d). 'Forward'. In M. Marder, *Pyropolitics: Fire and the Political*, 11–19. Stuttgart: Ibidem Press.

Žižek, S. (2025e). *Zero Point*. London: Bloomsbury.

Žižek, S. (2025f). *Quantum History: A New Materialist Philosophy*. London: Bloomsbury.

Žižek, S. (2025g). 'The Parallax of Lack and Surplus in Politics'. LACKv, 15 March. www.youtube.com/watch?v=zHmsqEMRf54 (accessed 19 October 2025).

Žižek, S. (2025h). 'A Hegelian Reading of the New Science of Consciousness'. *Crisis & Critique* 12, 1: 366–92. www.crisiscritique.org/storage/app/media/2025-08-25/slavoj-zizek.pdf (accessed 19 October 2025).

Žižek, S. (2025i). 'A Love-and-Hate Letter to Crisis and Critique'. *Crisis & Critique* 12, 1: 444–9. www.crisiscritique.org/storage/app/media/a-love-and-hate-le (accessed 19 October 2025).

Žižek, S. (2025j). 'David Lynch as a Pre-Raphaelite'. 17 January. www.e-flux.com/notes/650324/david-lynch-as-a-pre-raphaelite (accessed 15 October, 2025).

Žižek, S. (2026). *Liberal Fascisms*. London: Bloomsbury.

Žižek, S. and Daly, G. (2004). *Conversations with Žižek*. London: Polity.

Žižek, S. and Gunjević, B. (2012). *God in Pain: Inversions of Apocalypse*. New York: Seven Stories Press.

Žižek, S. and Hanlon, C. (2001). 'Psychoanalysis and the Post-political: An Interview with Slavoj Žižek'. *New Literary History* 32, 1: 1–21.

Other works cited

Adorno, T. W. (1993). 'Skoteinos, or How to Read Hegel'. In S. W. Nicholsen (trans.), *Hegel: Three Studies*, 39–148. Cambridge, MA: MIT Press.

Althusser, L. ([1971] 2001). 'Ideology and Ideological State Apparatuses (Notes towards an Investigation)'. In B. Brewster (trans.), *Lenin and Philosophy*, 127–86. New York: Monthly Review Press. www.marxists.org/reference/archive/althus ser/1970/ideology.htm (accessed 19 October 2025).

Aristotle. (1998). *Metaphysics*, trans. H. Lawson-Tancred. London: Penguin.

Badiou, A. (2007). *Being and Event*, trans. O. Feltham. London: Continuum.

Badiou, A. (2009). *Logics of Worlds*: *Being and Event, 2*, trans. A. Toscano. London: Continuum.

Badiou, A. and Žižek, S. (2009). *Philosophy in the Present*, ed. P. Engelmann, trans. P. Thomas and A. Toscano. Cambridge, MA: Polity.

Bailly, L. (2009). *Lacan*. Oxford: Oneworld.

Ballard, J. G. (2023). *Selected Nonfiction, 1962–2007*, ed. M. Blacklock. Cambridge, MA: MIT Press.

Barad, K. (2007). *Meeting the Universe Halfway: Quantum Physics and the Entanglement of Matter and Meaning*. Durham, NC: Duke University Press.

Bar-El, E. (2025). *How Slavoj Became Žižek*: *The Digital Making of a Public Intellectual*: *revised edition*. Chicago: University of Chicago Press.

Bar-El, E. and Baert, P. (2021). 'The Fool Revisited: The Making of Žižek as Sacrificial Public Intellectual'. *Cultural Sociology* 15, 4: 539–57. https://eprints.whiterose. ac.uk/206614/1/bar-el-baert-2021-the-fool-revisited-the-making-of-zizek-as-sacrific ial-public-intellectual.pdf (accessed 19 October 2025).

Bates, J. A. (2010). *Hegel and Shakespeare on Moral Imagination*. Albany: SUNY Press.

Benjamin, W. (1996a). 'The Task of the Translator'. In M. Bullock and M. W. Jenkins (eds), *Walter Benjamin Selected Writings, Vol. 1, 1913–26*, 253–63. Cambridge, MA: Harvard University Press.

Benjamin, W. (1996b). 'One-Way Street'. In M. Bullock and M. W. Jenkins (eds), *Walter Benjamin Selected Writings, Vol. 1, 1913–26*, 444–88. Cambridge, MA: Harvard University Press.

Benjamin, W. (1999). *The Arcades Project*, trans. H. Eiland and K. McLauglin. Cambridge, MA: Harvard University Press.

Benjamin, W. (2003). 'On the Concept of History'. In M. W. Jenkins, H. Eiland and G. Smith (eds), *Walter Benjamin Selected Writings, Vol. 4, 1938–40*, 389–400. Cambridge, MA: Harvard University Press.

Benjamin, W. (2005). 'The Crisis of the Novel'. In M. W. Jenkins and H. Eiland (eds), *Walter Benjamin Selected Writings, Vol. 2, Part 1, 1927–30*, 299–304. Cambridge, MA: Harvard University Press.

Benjamin, W. (2021). *Towards the Critique of Violence: A Critical Edition*, ed. P. Fenves and J. Ng. Stanford: Stanford University Press.

Beverungen, A. and Dunne, S. (2007). '"I'd Prefer Not To". Bartleby and the Excesses of Interpretation'. *Culture and Organization* 13: 171–83. www.researchgate.net/publ ication/27247478_'I'd_Prefer_Not_To'_Bartleby_and_the_Excesses_of_Interpretation (accessed 19 October 2025).

Bosteels, B. (2011). *The Actuality of Communism*. London: Verso.

Bosteels, B. (2013). 'Žižek and Christianity: Or the Critique of Religion after Marx and Freud'. In J. Khader and M. A. Rothenberg (eds), *Žižek Now: Current Perspectives in Žižek Studies*, 54–83. London: Polity.

Bou Ali, N. and Singh, S., eds (2025). *Extimacy*. Evanston, IL: Northwestern University Press.

Buck-Morss, S. (2009). *Hegel, Haiti, and Universal History*. Pittsburgh, PA: University of Pittsburgh Press.

Budgen, S., Kouvelakis, S. and Žižek, S., eds (2007). *Lenin Reloaded: Towards a Politics of Truth*. Durham, NC: Duke University Press.

Bunyard, T. (2020). 'The Situationists, Hegel and Hegelian Marxism in France'. In A. Hemmens and G. Zacarias (eds), *The Situationist International: A Critical Handbook*, 51–70. London: Pluto Press.

Burnham, C. (2018). *Does the Internet Have an Unconscious? Slavoj Žižek and Digital Culture*. London: Bloomsbury.

Butler, J. (2000). *Antigone's Claim: Kinship between Life & Death*. New York: Columbia University Press.

Butler, R., ed. (2014). *The Žižek Dictionary*. London: Routledge.

Cadava, E. and Nadal-Melsió, S. (2023). *Politically Red*. Cambridge, MA: MIT Press.

Carew, J. (2014). *Ontological Catastrophe: Žižek and the Paradoxical Metaphysics of German Idealism*. http://openhumanitiespress.org/books/download/Carew_2014_ Ontological-Catastrophe.pdf (accessed 19 October 2025).

Chiesa, L. (2007). *Subjectivity and Otherness: A Philosophical Reading of Lacan*. Cambridge, MA: MIT Press.

Chiesa, L. and Johnston, A. (2025). *God Is Undead*. London: Bloomsbury.

Cixous, H. and Clément, C. ([1986] 1996). *The Newly Born Woman*, trans. B. Wing. Minneapolis: University of Minnesota Press.

Cole, A. (2014). *The Birth of Theory*. Chicago: University of Chicago Press.

Comay, R. (2011). *Mourning Sickness: Hegel and the French Revolution*. Stanford: Stanford University Press.

Comay, R. and Ruda, F. (2018). *The Dash: The Other Side of Absolute Knowing*. Cambridge, MA: MIT Press.

Copjec, J. (2025). 'Reading Awry'. *Crisis & Critique* 12, 1: 394–401. www.crisiscritique. org/storage/app/media/2025-08-25/joan-copjec.pdf (accessed 19 October 2025).

Daly, G. (2014). 'Enjoyment/Jouissance'. In R. Butler (ed.), *The Žižek Dictionary*, 80–3. London: Routledge.

Daly, G. (2019). *Speculation: Politics, Ideology, Event*. Evanston, IL: Northwestern University Press.

De Boer, K. (2010). 'Hegel's Account of Contradiction in the Science of Logic Reconsidered'. *Journal of the History of Philosophy* 48, 30. https://philarchive.org/ rec/DEBHAO-2 (accessed 19 October 2015).

Eagleton, T. (2024). *The Real Thing: Reflections on a Literary Form*. New Haven, CT: Yale University Press.

Eliot, T. S. (2015). *The Poems of T. S. Eliot, Vol. 1*, ed. C. Ricks and J. McCue . London: Faber & Faber.

Finkelde, D., ed. (2026). *The Bloomsbury Handbook to Slavoj Žižek*. London: Bloomsbury.

Finkelde, D. and McGowan, T. (2023). 'Introduction'. In D. Finkelde and T. McGowan (eds), *Žižek Responds*, 2–24. London: Bloomsbury.

Flisfeder, M. (2012). *The Symbolic, The Sublime, and Slavoj Žižek's Theory of Film*. London: Palgrave Macmillan.

Flisfeder, M. (2014). 'Communism'. In R. Butler (ed.), *The Žižek Dictionary*, 40–3. London: Routledge.

Freud, S. (1981a). *The Standard Edition of the Complete Psychological Works of Sigmund Freud, Vol. VII*, trans. J. Strachey. London: Hogarth Press.

Freud, S. (1981b). *The Standard Edition of the Complete Psychological Works of Sigmund Freud, Vol. XVI*, Introductory Lectures on Psycho-Analysis (Part III), trans. J. Strachey. London: Hogarth Press.

Freud, S. ([1899] 2006). *Interpreting Dreams*. London: Penguin.

Gabriel, M. and Žižek, S. (2009). *Mythology, Madness and Laughter: Subjectivity in German Idealism*. London: Continuum.

Gardner, S. (2015). 'Introduction: The Transcendental Turn'. In S. Gardner and M. Grist (eds), *The Transcendental Turn*, 1–19. Oxford: Oxford University Press.

Hamza, A. (2016). 'Going to One's Ground: Žižek's Dialectical Materialism'. In A. Hamza and F. Ruda (eds), *Slavoj Žižek and Dialectical Materialism*, 163–75. London: Palgrave Macmillan.

Hamza, A. (2022). 'The Future of the Absolute'. In S. Žižek, F. Ruda and A. Hamza (eds), *Reading Hegel*, 158–208. Cambridge, MA: Polity.

Hamza, A. and Rouda, F., eds (2016). *Slavoj Žižek and Dialectical Materialism*, 43–55. London: Palgrave Macmillan.

Hardwick, E. (2022). *The Uncollected Essays*. New York: New York Review of Books.

Harpham, G. (2003). 'Doing the Impossible: Slavoj Žiżek and the End of Knowledge'. *Critical Inquiry* 29, 3: 453–85.

Hegel, G. W. F. (1975). *Philosophy of Right*. Oxford: Oxford University Press.

Hegel, G. W. F. (1977). *The Difference between Fichte's and Schelling's System of Philosophy*, trans. H. S. Harris and W. Cerf. New York: SUNY Press.

Hegel, G. W. F. (1979). *System of Ethical Life (1802–3) and First Philosophy of Spirit Part III of the System of Speculative Philosophy 1803/4*, ed. and trans. H. S. Harris and T. M. Knox. New York: SUNY Press.

Hegel, G. W. F. (1988). *Lectures on the Philosophy of Religion: One-Volume Edition*, *The Lectures of 1827*, ed. P. C. Hodgson, trans. R. F. Brown, P. C. Hodgson and J. M. Stewart. Los Angeles: University of California Press.

Hegel, G. W. F. (1991). *The Encyclopaedia Logic: Part 1 of the Encyclopedia of the Philosophical Sciences with the Zusätze*, trans. T. F. Geraets, W. A. Suchting and H. S. Harris. Indianapolis, IN: Hackett.

Hegel, G. W. F. (1995). *Lectures on the History of Philosophy: Medieval and Modern Philosophy*, trans. E. S. Haldane and F. H. Simson. Lincoln: University of Nebraska Press.

Hegel, G. W. F. (2006). *Lectures on the History of Philosophy: 1825–6, Vol. II, Greek Philosophy*, trans. R. F. Brown and J. M. Stewart. Oxford: Clarendon Press.

Hegel, G. W. F. (2008). *Lectures on the Philosophy of Religion, Vol. 111: The Consummate Religion*, ed. P. C. Hodgson. Oxford: Clarendon Press.

Hegel, G. W. F. (2010a). *The Science of Logic*, ed. and trans. D. Di Giovanni. Cambridge: Cambridge University Press.

Hegel, G. W. F. (2010b). *Philosophy of Mind*, trans. W. Wallace and A. V. Miller. Oxford: Clarendon Press.

Hegel, G. W. F. ([1969] 2010c). *Science of Logic*, trans. W. Wallace and A. V. Miller. Cambridge: Cambridge University Press.

Hegel, G. W. F. (2010d). *Encyclopedia of the Philosophical Sciences in Basic Outline, Part 1: Science of Logic*, trans. K. Brinkmann and D. O. Dahlstrom. Cambridge: Cambridge University Press.

Hegel, G. W. F. (2018). *The Phenomenology of Spirit*, trans. T. Pinkard. Cambridge: Cambridge University Press.

Heidegger, M. (1978] 1993). *Basic Writings*, rev. and expanded ed., ed. D. F. Krell. London: Routledge.

Heinrich, M. (2021). *How to Read Marx's Capital: Commentary and Explanations on the Beginning Chapters*, trans. A. Locascio. New York: Monthly Review Press.

Homer, S. (2005). *Jacques Lacan*. London: Routledge.

Homer, S. (2016). *Slavoj Žižek and Radical Politics*. London: Routledge.

Homer, S. (2017). 'The Persistence of Theoretical Anti-humanism, or, The Politics of the Subject in Alain Badiou and Slavoj Žižek'. *Annual Review of Critical Psychology*. https://discourseunit.com/wp-content/uploads/2017/08/arcpseanh.pdf (accessed 19 October 2025).

Houlgate, S. (2006). *The Opening of Hegel's Logic*. West Lafayette: Purdue University Press.

Houlgate, S. (2011). 'Essence, Reflexion, and Immediacy in Hegel's *Science of Logic*'. In S. Houlgate and M. Baur (eds), *A Companion to Hegel*, 139–58. Oxford: Blackwell.

Jameson, F. (2010). *The Hegel Variations: On the Phenomenology of Spirit*. London: Verso.

Jameson, F. (2016). 'An American Utopia'. In S. Žižek (ed.), *An American Utopia, Dual Power and the Universal Army: Frederic Jameson*, 1–96. London: Verso.

Johnston, A. (2008). *Žižek's Ontology*. Evanston, IL: Northwestern University Press.

Johnston, A. (2009). *Badiou, Žižek, and Political Transformations*. Evanston, IL: Northwestern University Press.

Johnston, A. (2013). 'A Critique of Natural Economy'. In J. Khader and M. A. Rothenberg (eds), *Žižek Now: Current Perspectives in Žižek Studies*, 103–201. Cambridge, MA: Polity.

Johnston, A. (2018). *A New German Idealism: Hegel, Žižek, and Dialectical Materialism*. New York: Columbia University Press.

Johnston, A. (2023). 'Cake or Doughnut? Žižek and German Idealist Emergentisms'. In D. Finkelde and T. McGowan (eds), *Žižek Responds*, 27–51. London: Bloomsbury.

Johnston, A. (2024). *Infinite Greed: The Inhuman Selfishness of Capital*. New York: Columbia University Press.

Joyce, J. ([1922] 1984). *Ulysses*. London: Bodley Head.

Kant, I. (2004). *Prolegomena to Any Future Metaphysics: That Will be Able to Come Forward as Science with Selections from the Critique of Pure Reason*, ed. and trans. G. Hatfield. Cambridge: Cambridge University Press.

Kant, I. (2007). *Critique of Pure Reason*, trans. N. Kemp Smith. London: Palgrave Macmillan.

Kant, I. (2015). *Critique of Practical Reason*, ed. and trans. M. Gregor. Cambridge: Cambridge University Press.

Kaufman, E. (2012). *Deleuze, The Dark Precursor: Dilaectic, Structure, Being*. Baltimore, MD: Johns Hopkins University Press.

Kay, S. ([2003] 2005). *Žižek: A Critical Introduction*. Cambridge, MA: Polity Press.

Kaye, B. (2023). *Žižek and Freedom: Utopia and the Parallax View*. London: Palgrave Macmillan.

Kierkegaard, S. (1971). *Either/Or, Vol. I*, trans. D. F. and L. M. Swenson. Princeton, NJ: Princeton University Press.

Koltaj, B. (2019). *Žižek Reading Banhoeffer: Towards a Radical Critical Theology*. London: Palgrave Macmillan.

Kornbluh, A. (2023). *Immediacy or, The Style of Too Late Capitalism*. London: Verso.

Kotsko, A. (2008). *Žižek and Theology*. London: Continuum.

Kotsko, A. (2015). 'Politics and Perversion: Situating Žižek's Paul'. In L. De Sutter (ed.), *Žižek and Law*, 31–41. London: Routledge.

Kouvelakis, S. (2007). 'Lenin as Reader of Hegel: Hypotheses for a Reading of Lenin's Notebooks on Hegel's *Science of Logic*'. In S. Budgen, S. Kouvelakis and S. Žižek (eds), *Lenin Reloaded: Towards a Politics of Truth*, 164–204. Durham, NC: Duke University Press.

Lacan, J. (1992). *The Ethics of Psychoanalysis 1959–60: The Seminar of Jacques Lacan Book V11*, trans. D. Porter, ed. J.-A. Miller. London: Routledge.

Lacan, J. (1993). *The Psychoses: The Seminar of Jacques Lacan Book 111, 1955–1956*, ed. R. Grigg and J.-A. Miller. London: Routledge.

Lacan, J. (1997). '"Television": Lacan on the Unconscious'. www.youtube.com/watch?v=URsYj-TVFjc (accessed 19 October 2025).

Lacan, J. (1999). *On Feminine Sexuality, The Limits of Love and Knowledge, 1972–3: Encore, the Seminar of Jacques Lacan, Book XX*, trans. B. Fink, ed. J.-A. Miller. New York: Norton.

Lacan, J. (2001). *Écrits: A Selection*, trans. A. Sheridan. London: Routledge.

Lacan, J. (2004). *The Four Fundamental Concepts of Psycho-Analysis*, trans. A. Sheridan, ed. J.-A. Miller. London: Karnac.

Lacan, J. (2007). *The Other Side of Psychoanalysis*: *The Seminar of Jacques Lacan, Book XVII*, trans. R. Grigg, ed. J.-A. Miller. New York: Norton.

Lacan, J. (2014). *Anxiety, The Seminar of Jacques Lacan, Book X*, trans. A. R. Price, ed. J.-A. Miller. Cambridge, MA: Polity.

Lacan, J. (2022). *… or Worse: The Seminar of Jacques Lacan, Book XIX*, trans. A. R. Price, ed. J.-A. Miller. Cambridge, MA: Polity.

Lacan, J. (2024). *On a Discourse that Might Not Be a Semblance: The Seminar of Jacques Lacan, Book XVIII*, trans. B. Fink. Cambridge, MA: Polity.

Laclau, E. and Mouffe, C. (2001). *Hegemony and Socialist Strategy: Towards a Radical Democratic Politics*. London: Verso.

Leader, D. and Groves, J. (2005). *Introducing Lacan*. Cambridge: Icon Books.

Lenin, V. I. (2008a). *Collected Works, Vol. 38: Philosophical Notebooks*, 208. www.marxists.org/archive/lenin/works/cw/pdf/lenin-cw-vol-38.pdf (accessed 19 October 2025).

Lenin, V. I. (2008b). *Collected Works, Vol. 33: 'Our Revolution'*. www.marxists.org/archive/lenin/works/cw/pdf/lenin-cw-vol-33.pdf (accessed 19 October 2025).

Løland, O. J. (2018). *The Reception of Paul the Apostle in the Works of Slavoj Žižek*. London: Palgrave Macmillan.

Longuenesse, B. ([1981] 2007). *Hegel's Critique of Metaphysics*, trans. N. J. Simek. Cambridge: Cambridge University Press.

Malabou, C. ([1996] 2005). *The Future of Hegel: Plasticity, Temporality and Dialectic*. London: Routledge.

Marder, M. (2017). *Energy Dreams: Of Actuality*. New York: Columbia University Press.

Marx, K. (1844). *Economic and Philosophic Manuscripts of 1844.* www.marxists.org/archive/marx/works/download/pdf/Economic-Philosophic-Manuscripts-1844.pdf (accessed 19 October 2025).

Marx, K. (1973). *Grundrisse*, trans. D. McLellan. London: Granada.

Marx, K. (2024). *Capital: A Critique of Political Economy, Vol.* 1, trans. P. Reitter, ed. P. North and P. Reitter. Princeton, NJ: Princeton University Press.

Masarrat, P. (2025). 'Society of the Materialist Friends of Plato'. *Crisis & Critique* 12, 1: 149–83. www.crisiscritique.org/storage/app/media/2025-08-25/payam-masarrat. pdf (accessed 19 October 2025).

McGowan, T. (2013). 'Hegel as Marxist'. In J. Khader and M. A. Rothenberg (eds), *Žižek Now*, 32–53. London: Polity.

McGowan, T. (2016a). *Capitalism and Desire: The Psychic Cost of Free Markets*. New York: Columbia University Press.

McGowan, T. (2016b). 'The Necessity of an Absolute Misunderstanding: Why Hegel Has So Many Misreaders'. In A. Hamza and F. Ruda (eds), *Slavoj Žižek and Dialectical Materialism*, 43–55. London: Palgrave Macmillan.

McGowan, T. (2019). *Emancipation after Hegel: Achieving a Contradictory Revolution*. New York: Columbia University Press.

McGowan, T. (2024). *Lacan's Gaze*. www.youtube.com/watch?v=M1hWlOBHfll (accessed 19 October 2025).

McGowan, T. (2025). *The Cambridge Introduction to Jacques Lacan*. Cambridge: Cambridge University Press.

Meillassoux, Q. (2008). *After Finitude: An Essay on the Necessity of Contingency*. London: Continuum.

Mitralexis, S. and Skliris, D. (2019). 'The Slovenian and the Cross: Transcending Christianity's Perverse Core with Slavoj Žižek'. In S. Mitralexis and D. Skliris (eds), *Slavoj Žižek and Christianity*, 1–45. London: Routledge.

Mossman, K. (2024). 'Slavoj Žižek's War with the Left'. *New Statesman*, 27 July. www.newstatesman.com/long-reads/kate-mossman-interview/2024/07/sla voj-zizek-the-court-jester-of-late-capitalism (accessed 19 october 2025).

Nancy, J.-L. (2002). *Hegel: The Restlessness of the Negative*. Minneapolis: University of Minneapolis Press.

Neill, C., ed. (2020). *Lacanian Perspectives on Blade Runner 2049*. London: Palgrave Macmillan.

Neill, C. (2023). *Jacques Lacan: The Basics*. London: Routledge.

Ng, K. (2020). *Hegel's Concept of Life*. Oxford: Oxford University Press.

Noys, B. (2015). 'Žižek's Reading Machine'. In A. Hamza (ed.), *Repeating Žižek*, 72–83. Durham, NC: Duke University Press.

Osborne, P. (2013). 'More Than Everything: Žižek's Badiouian Hegel'. *Radical Philosophy*, 1977. www.radicalphilosophy.com/article/more-than-everything (accessed 19 October 2025).

Penny, J. (2023). 'Being Sexed: Žižek's Modern Ontology'. In J. Di Leo and Z. Zalloua (eds), *Understanding Žižek, Understanding 2016h*, 61–76. London: Bloomsbury.

Pérez, B. M. (2025). 'Žižek and Hegel: The Courage to Hold on to Paradox'. *Crisis & Critique* 12, 1: 235–48. www.crisiscritique.org/storage/app/media/2025-08-25/ berta-m-perez.pdf (accessed 19 October 2025).

Pfaller, R. (2016). 'The Althusserian Battlegrounds'. In *Slavoj Žižek and Dialectical Materialism*, 23–42. London: Palgrave Macmillan.

Pfaller, R. (2017). *Interpassivity: The Aesthetics of Delegated Enjoyment*. Edinburgh: Edinburgh University Press.

Pippin, R. B. (2015). 'Slavoj Žižek's Hegel'. In *Interanimations: Receiving Modern German Philosophy*, 91–115. Chicago: University of Chicago Press.

Plato. (1997). *Complete Works*, ed. J. M. Cooper. Indianapolis, IN: Hackett.

Pluth, E. (2016). 'Natural Worlds, Historical Worlds, and Dialectical Materialism'. In A. Hamza and F. Ruda (eds), *Slavoj Žižek and Dialectical Materialism*, 101–12. London: Palgrave Macmillan.

Rancière, J. (1997). 'Democracy Means Equality'. *Radical Philosophy*, 82. www.radicalphilosophy.com/interview/jacques-ranciere-democracy-means-equality (accessed 19 October 2025).

Rancière, J. (1999). *Disagreement: Politics and Philosophy*, trans. J. Rose. Minneapolis: University of Minnesota Press.

Ravetto-Biagioli, K. (2010). 'Everything You Always Wanted to Know about David Lynch, but Should Be Afraid to Ask Slavoj Žižek'. In S. Gourgouris (ed.), *Freud and Fundamentalism*, 105–24. New York: Fordham University Press.

Restuccia, F. (2025). 'Sublating Christianity or Christ and "Sex"'. *Crisis & Critique* 12, 1: 270–93. www.crisiscritique.org/storage/app/media/2025-08-25/frances-restuccia.pdf (accessed 19 October 2025).

Robinson, K. S. (2015). Aurora. London: Orbit.

Rose, J. ([1986] 2005). 'Feminine Sexuality: Jacques Lacan and the *école freudienne*'. In *Sexuality in the Field of Vision*, 49–81. London: Verso.

Rosen, S. (2014). *The Idea of Hegel's Science of Logic*. Chicago: University of Chicago Press.

Ruda, F. (2015a). 'How to Repeat Plato? For a Platonism of the Non-All'. In A. Hamza (ed.), *Repeating Žižek*, 43–57. Durham, NC: Duke University Press.

Ruda, F. (2015b). 'What Is to Be Judged? On Infinitely Infinite Judgements and Their Consequences'. In L. De Sutter (ed.), *Žižek and Law*, 153–73. London: Routledge.

Ruda, F. (2016a). *Abolishing Freedom: A Plea for a Contemporary Use of Fatalism*. Lincoln: University of Nebraska Press.

Ruda, F. (2016b). 'Dialectical Materialism and the Dangers of Aristotelianism'. In A. Hamza and F. Ruda (eds), *Slavoj Žižek and Dialectical Materialism*, 147–61. London: Palgrave Macmillan.

Ruda, F. (2018). 'Hegel, Resistance and Method'. In R. Comay and B. Zantvoort (eds), *Hegel and Resistance: History, Politics and Dialectics*, 22–33. London: Bloomsbury.

Sbriglia, R. and Žižek, S. (2020). 'Introduction'. In *Subject Lessons: Hegel, Lacan, and the Future of Materialism*, 3–28. Evanston, IL: Northwestern University Press.

Schelling, F. W. J. (2000). *The Ages of the World: (Fragment) from the Handwritten Remains, Third Version (c.1815)*, trans. J. M. Wirth. New York: SUNY Press.

Scott, R. L. (2025). *Reading Hegel: Irony, Recollection, Critique*. Chicago: University of Chicago Press.

Sempron, J. ([1963] 2005). *The Long Voyage*. New York: Overlook Press.

Shaul, D. (2022). 'Hegel and Hitchcock's *Vertigo*: On Reconciliation'. www.euppublishing.com/doi/epub/10.3366/film.2022.0195 (accessed 19 October 2025).

Simoniti, J. (2026). The Contingent Universality: A New Ontology. London: Bloomsbury.

Soler, C. (1995). 'The Subject and the Other (II)'. In R. Feldstein, B. Fink and M. Jaanus (eds), *Reading Seminar XI: Lacan's Four Fundamental Concepts of Psychoanalysis*, 39–53. New York: SUNY Press.

Sophocles. (1998). *Antigone, Women of Trachis, Philoctetes, Oedipus at Colonus*, trans. H. Lloyd Jones. Cambridge, MA: Harvard University Press.

Taheri, A. (2021). *Hegelian-Lacanian Variations on Late Modernity: Spectres of Madness*. London: Routledge.

Taheri, A., Vanderwees, C. and Naderi, R., eds (2024). *Philosophy after Lacan: Politics, Science, and Art*. London: Routledge.

Taylor, A. (2005). *Žižek!* https://archive.org/details/zizek_202307 (accessed 30 July 2013).

Thompson, L. (2016). 'Slavoj Žižek on His Favourite Plays' (interview). https://fivebooks.com/best-books/slavoj-zizek-favourite-plays/ (accessed 19 October 2025).

Tupinambá, G. (2019). 'Concrete Universality: Only that Which Is Non-all Is for All'. In S. Mitralexis and D. Skliris (eds), *Slavoj Žižek and Christianity*, 104–16. London: Routledge.

Tutt, D. (2016). 'Love, Psychoanalysis, and Leftist Political Ontology'. In A. Cerda-Rueda (ed.), *Sex and Nothing: Bridges from Psychoanalysis to Philosophy*, 193–210. London: Karnac.

Van Woezik, C. (2010). *God – Beyond Me: From the I's Absolute Ground in Hölderlin and Schelling to a Contemporary Model of a Personal God*. Leiden: Brill.

Varoufakis, Y. (2024). *Technofeudalism: What Killed Capitalism*. London: Bodley Head.

Wilderson, F. R. III. (2020). *Afropessimism*. New York: Liverright.

Winkler, R. (2024). *Žižek's The Sublime Object of Ideology*. London: Bloomsbury.

Wolfe, T. (2016). *Look Homeward, Angel*. London: Penguin.

Yousfi, L. ([2022] 2025). *In Defence of Barbarism: Non-Whites against the Empire*. London: Verso.

Zalloua, Z. (2020). *Žižek on Race: Towards an Anti-Racist Future*. London: Bloomsbury.

Zalloua, Z. (2025a). *Fanon, Žižek, and the Violence* of Resistance. London: Bloomsbury.

Zalloua, Z. (2025b). 'Anatomy of the Human: Fanon and Žižek'. *Crisis & Critique* 12, 1: 270–93. www.crisiscritique.org/storage/app/media/2025-08-25/zahi-zalloua.pdf (accessed 19 October 2025).

Zantvoort, B. (2025). Inertia, Resistance, Revolution: Hegel and the Logic of History. Leiden: Brill.

Zupančič, A. (2017). *What Is Sex?* Cambridge, MA: MIT Press.

Zupančič, A. (2023). *Let Them Rot*. London: Divided.

Zupančič, A. (2024). 'Lacan as Speculative Thinker'. *Rivista di Estitica*, 86. https://journals.openedition.org/estetica/17624 (accessed 19 October 2025).